# DEAF LIT EXTRAVAGANZA

Deaf American Poetry: An Anthology

Suddenly Slow: Poems

# DEAF LIT EXTRAVAGANZA

## JOHN LEE CLARK
### Editor

Handtype Press
Minneapolis, Minnesota

## ACKNOWLEDGMENTS

The publisher wishes to thank David Cummer for his assistance with this book.

# NONFICTION

# CLAYTON VALLI

## A Dandelion

Their yellows dotted the field,
their petals waving with the breezes.

An irritated man stared at them, snarling,
"Dandelions!" His hands pulled
some apart, and mowed the rest down
until the field was smoothed out
in green. The rain soon came
and went away; the sun sneaked in,
warming a seed in the soil.
The seed rose, enjoying all nature.

It waved, watching a bee
coming by with a greeting and
going away. Nights it closed
its petals, opening up again
in the morning. One day it turned
into white puffs, their whiskers
a halo, but it still moved with the breeze.
Its seedlings flew off in every direction.

Spotting its whiteness, the man,
enraged, spit out, "There!"
The brave white puff still waved,
still sending off its seedlings.
The man grabbed its stem and pulled out.
The white puff exploded, its seedlings
scattering everywhere on its own.

# JOHN LEE CLARK

## Foreword

We have much cause for celebration where the literature of the signing community is concerned. It isn't just that we have more Deaf writers and other signers writing than ever before. It's *what* they're writing.

Until recently, most everything that was put down on paper supposedly about Deaf people—whether in newspaper articles or in bestselling novels—showed only one lonely "deaf" person, either isolated or surrounded by hearing people. Only rarely was there any glimpse of the one abiding fact of the Deaf experience, that Deaf people gravitate toward other Deaf people. The few times there was a second Deaf person, hearing authors took pains to isolate the pair, as did Carson McCullers in her novel *The Heart Is a Lonely Hunter*.

It's dizzying to think of how many books have been written about deaf persons—going all the way back to Daniel Defoe—and to find that the signing community isn't in any of them. For all intents and purposes, the reading public has yet to read of multiple Deaf people in action, interacting with each other as they do in real life. This surely is one of the biggest omissions in the history of literature.

The audist canon's long insistence on isolating Deaf individuals, fictional and real alike, has made it challenging even for Deaf writers themselves to write about their lives in their own community. It wasn't until 1986, with the publication of Douglass Bullard's novel *Islay*, that we saw the community in action through the eyes of a Deaf writer. Since then, more and more realistic portrayals have appeared in print. It has been and continues to be a slow process.

Aside from *Islay* and Raymond Luczak's *Men with Their Hands*—the second novel by a Deaf writer that captures community life—this anthology has more Deaf and signing people between two covers than in any other book I know of. Even so, this collection is missing many parts of the life members of the community know. We don't have enough writing yet about Deaf people of color, Deaf people in most parts of the world, the DeafBlind community, and the lives of Deaf people who are from families with multiple generations of Deaf people. And we have a gap in translations of sign storytelling and poetry.

Still, this book represents the latest blow to the audist vision of deafness as a calamity, as something that must be fixed at any cost. It is a collective testimony against hearing writers who continue to make merchandise of us by means of false, melodramatic portrayals. It is a call to journalists and the media community to see the signing community in a completely different way and to report more accurately and effectively on the injustice and oppression we experience. It is an invitation to uninitiated readers to enter our realities momentarily and come away with a revised vision of the world we share. Finally, this book asks Deaf writers and signing writers to write more, to dig deeper with their beautiful hands.

Now on to *Deaf Lit Extravaganza*!

# FICTION

# WILLY CONLEY

## Sifting Dirt

Roger Folter leaned against the park's thick iron fence and crossed his right foot over his left. He was a few yards from the water's edge. In the middle of the Rancho La Brea pit was a gray mastodon stuck in tar; its massive trunk and tusks stabbed the sky in a frozen snarl. A squat pigeon rested on the mammoth's back, and down the sculpted shaggy sides were dried white dribbles of dung. As tar bubbles rose passively to the surface near the statue's legs, Roger envisioned his dirt-filled kitchen sink. The living room scene replayed in his head.

"You preach, still," said his wife Rhondee, standing in front of the anchorwoman on the eleven o'clock TV news.

"Move please, she's talking about Bosnia now," said Roger.

"You preach, still," said Rhondee with stronger hand movements.

Roger leaned forward on the sofa to push her out of the way but she slapped his hand off her hip.

"Hey—can't you wait till this is over?" he asked.

"No, me saw you—you correct-correct him. Must stop now."

Roger sank back on the sofa.

"Correcting what?" he asked. He craned his neck to catch the newsclip that flashed on the screen.

"You preach-preach English to him," she said.

Roger felt his gut tighten a little but he let it go.

The bubbles that bobbed up against the mastodon's leg released an oily film in the water. The pigeon fluttered its wings then settled down again on its haunches. Roger closed his eyes, trying to remember what happened next. He had been watching a closed-captioned newscast, reading fast-scrolling lines of text at the bottom of the television screen, when Rhondee stepped in. It was a chore to read the news at a frantic pace, especially when the captions were fraught with misspellings, but he kept at it knowing that it would pay off in the long run.

Roger looked around the pit to check on his son. On the other side Cody skimmed rocks across the water. The pigeon flew away. Roger crossed his left foot over his right and went back to the bubbles.

"I'm teaching English to Cody," said Roger. He emphasized "teach" with his hands, retrieving invisible information from his head and pushing it to an imaginary young boy next to him. "Now move—please?"

"You preach-preach!" The veins on Rhondee's neck and face began to surface.

Roger was proud of the way he preserved his emotions. He was a professional who sold his feelings; that's how actors work. Big emotional outbursts were all right for the stage, but the way Rhondee wasted her anger in their warm, serene living room was beyond him.

"Next year we're enrolling Cody in kindergarten, right?" Roger asked his wife.

"Right," she said. The interrupted lines of captions scrolled behind her.

"With deaf or hearing children?" he asked.

"Hearing children," she said with a bitter expression.

"Correct," said Roger. "Cody is hearing—we can't help that—he should be around other hearing children, right?"

Rhondee stared at the little scar on Roger's lower lip.

"And what language will these hearing kids be using?"

"English," said Rhondee. "What's the point?"

"Sign that again," Roger said.

Like a bored sign language student, she clasped one hand weakly over her wrist in a classic British pose.

"English."

"Right! And does Cody know English?"

"He knows enough," she said.

"Bathroom, me finish touch," Roger mimicked. "Me-know, me-know, me-want, me-want. You call that English?"

Her eyes narrowed and her nostrils pinched. The unbuttoned pocket flaps on her blouse seemed to open and close as she took big breaths.

"What's—what's wrong—that?" her hands trembled. "Before never bother-bother you, me not sit here watch-watch captions, improve my English."

"Nothing's wrong, if Cody's signing with us or other deaf people. But if he talks like that to his teachers and classmates, they're going to make fun of him."

"Give him time." Her index finger repeatedly jabbed her wristwatch. "Cody develop natural deaf language now. Dump two languages on little boy, age-four, can't. Later, English."

"I want to start now before it's too late," he said.

"Not now! First, what? he understand us, must!—you, me—our language—before too late."

"Do you want him to look stupid?"

She hit the palm of her hand with a firm karate chop in front of Roger's face. Roger flinched and thought she was going to slice his nose off.

"Stop!" she said.


The bubbles in the pit burst slowly, one after another. Roger felt something tug on his pants. Cody stretched his little french-fry fingers apart and pressed his thumb against his forehead.

"Daddy!"

"What's up?" Roger grimaced as he rubbed a stiffness in the back of his neck.

"Me hear bird. Talk funny."

"I hear a bird. It talks funny," Roger corrected.

"Can't. Hard," said Cody.

"Try it. You're a smart guy."

"Don't wanna."

"Do you want to go home now?" Roger asked. "I don't need to stay here."

"No, no, don't. Me want stay," cried Cody.

"Then you try harder."

"I hear bird. It talk funny," said Cody.

"That's better. Was that so hard?"

"Yeah."

"OK. Where do you see this bird?"

"Not see bird but me can hear—says 'Hel-lo!'" said Cody. He fingerspelled the last word leaving the *o* formed in his hand.

"Oh, c'mon Code, you know birds can't talk."

"Come look-for," said Cody.

Roger hitched Cody up onto his shoulders; he smelled his light buttery scent which came from Rhondee, only hers was sharper. As he walked around the tar pit to a nearby construction site Cody gave him the signal, with a tap of his boot heel, to let him down. Cody ran up to a mound of excavated dirt and climbed up to the top. He had the look of a miniature cowboy scanning a prairie. Roger sat down at the bottom of the mound and scooped up a handful of moist dirt, slowly letting the finer pieces fall between his fingers. He looked over at the tar pit and studied the expression of rage on the mastodon's face.


In the living room, Rhondee still wouldn't budge from her position in front of the television set.

"Face it," said Roger. "We're living in a hearing world."

"Spittie," she said.

"What did you call me?"

"Spittie—pftht, pftht!"

"I don't need to watch that deaf bullshit," said Roger. "Get out of the way. I'm getting behind on world news, you mind?"

Rhondee stepped back and used the anchorwoman for a demonstration.

"You want act like hearing people, talk-talk-talk, spit fly out your mouth."

"Are you making fun of my work?" asked Roger.

"My life, you mock?" asked Rhondee.

There was a moment of stillness in the room except for the flickering images from the television.

"Me show what you look like on stage with other hearing actors." She stood erect, expressionless, one hand over her chest and the other behind her back. She imitated a bad actor's monologue, moving only her mouth in grotesque shapes: "Blah-blah-blah."

Roger took a minute to think while the anchorwoman signed off for a commercial break.

"I thought you supported the idea of me integrating with hearing people?"

"Too much," Rhondee said.

"What's that supposed to mean?"

"You leave behind sign language, deaf culture."

"I'm including it . . . expanding it. To see how far we can go with our potential."

"Uncle Tom," she said.

"You can't deny we live in a hearing world," said Roger, overlapping her remark.

"Uncle T-O-M." Rhondee fingerspelled slow to catch his attention.

"Uncle Tom?"

"No, no, no; mistake me," she said. "Uncle Tom for blacks. Me mean Uncle R-O-G."

"What's wrong with you, Rhondee?"

"Everything! Thought me married <u>D</u>eaf man."

She stared at him, breathing hard. When he couldn't hold the glare, she backed up and left the room. The anchorwoman returned and continued her cool delivery. He went back to the news and absently read the captions. He couldn't translate their meanings.

A few minutes later Rhondee returned with her arms full of potted aloes from around the house. Dirt spilled on the floor behind her, some stuck to the sweat on her arms. She dumped the pots upside down and filled the sink with black soil. Roger watched from the corners of his eyes, keeping his head in the direction of the television. She grabbed a bunch of aloes and plucked apart the fleshy, finger-like leaves one by one. The leaves were piled up on top of the butcher block next to the toaster. For an absurd second Roger imagined her making a salad. She took a fork from the drawer and methodically mashed the juices out of the leaves. When she was finished, the clear liquid oozed over the block and onto the counter.

From the far end of the sofa Roger sat with his mouth open. He thought of what he should be feeling, but nothing appropriate registered. Her actions surprised him. There was no cue for her next move. She's going to sneer at him, he anticipated, and sign, "Now you know how me feel!" Instead, his wife walked over to the television, unplugged the wires from the closed-captioning device, and wrapped them around the machine. The television image shrank to a dot where the anchorwoman's lips were and disappeared. Rhondee snatched her keys off the top of the microwave oven and left by the front door with her captioning device under her arm. Roger waited for the vibrations to rock across the hardwood floor when the door slammed, but nothing happened. She left the door open.

Roger looked back at the television and saw that his wife left behind her muddy handprints all over the screen. He slowly got up to look in the sink. It smelled like a freshly-turned garden. He wondered which two of the leaves were the original ones that Rhondee gave him at the start of their relationship, before it had grown wild and out of proportion. Roger padded down the hall to peek into his son's room. Cody had slept through another silent argument.

Roger was still looking at the mastodon when Cody jumped on his back and knocked the remaining dirt out of his hands.

"Daddy! Me saw balloon man. He make-make balloon, like this . . ." Cody showed his father how the man blew a long, narrow balloon and twisted it into different shapes.

"Well, let's go buy a balloon. You know what kind of animal you want?"

"Yep!"

"Good. And let's buy one for your mother. You know what kind of animal she wants?" Roger was thinking that Rhondee probably drove over to her mother's to cool off from the fight.

"Don't-know," said Cody. "Have idea—we tell balloon man make-make talking bird."

Roger raised his right hand to correct him, but restrained himself. He lifted his left hand and signed, "Okay, and then we'll go over to your grandmother's."

# T. K. DALTON

## Explode-a-Moment

My name is Dewey Flynn and I do things very slowly. I will explain my thinking. With boys—with brothers—there's this list. As with any one-two-three, any first-next-last, this list has a top and a bottom. Facts are facts. I occupy the bottom of any list on planet earth. I don't like this fact, but not for the reason they think. Nope: my parents, my teachers, most kids at school who know I even exist, they're all wrong about my opinion. I used to think that moving up meant someone else moving down. Someone like my brother Grant. Then one Sunday, a few months ago, I changed my mind for good.

Earlier today, Mom and Dad made me stay here and think about what I've done. So I am. So I will. But I will also think about what I did not do. And I will also think about what they have done, and when I am done with that, I will think about what they did not do. As I was talking just now, the word "they" changed. Now "they" means my family, Mom and Dad and also Grant. "They" means my friends and enemies (some people are both) and the deaf friends I know through Grant. They go to The Learning Center for Deaf Children, TLC for short, and they used to be his friends. Now they are mine, maybe. This is a hypothesis. This is not a fact.

I don't think I know much anymore, because that Sunday, everything changed for good.

It started when Mom tapped the table for our attention. "Boys. I'm expecting a phone call. Tell me if the light rings?"

I repeated her instructions to Grant. They were easy to translate, and my brother understood.

*Sure thing,* he signed.

*You're so dependable,* Mom signed. I didn't know if she meant "you-two," or just Grant. She never means me. I remember thinking: "I'll show you who's dependable."

To show her, I trained my eyes on the wall-mounted telephone. I sharpened my eyes and made my ears as useless as Grant's. A minute passed. I got distracted. I wondered when the flashing light's bulb had last been changed. I noticed the Braille numbers on the oversized buttons were worn from seven years of use. I thought: "Good thing my brother's deaf, not blind." Interruptions like this popcorned in my mind. Distractions, even now, are my biggest bully. "Worn from years of use:" I searched my brain's files and found the word—"erosion." I learned it for a unit test.

(I take Science 7 with the mainstream kids!)

*Phone!* Grant signed to Mom. The light stopped flashing when she answered, "Hi, Nadia." The Rocket's mother, I thought, but I did not tell Grant. *You lose again,* he signed.

My brother typed madly on his Sidekick. He had to be writing a SEND-ALL broadcasting the news—"I beat Dewey in a telephone showdown"—to our mutual friends, the deaf ones and the one or two hearies with cell phones. We went to different schools, but because Grant lived at home, not in TLC's dorms, Grant was friendly with all the hearing kids in the neighborhood. Sometimes, even then, Grant seemed to know all of Kennedy Middle School. I signed well enough to have friends at TLC. But around this time, Grant's deaf friends had teased me just as badly as every other seventh-grader in Natick. I remember how bad I felt that day about the teasing that happened the Friday before. I'd left school that Friday feeling low. Standing in a room with two people on two phones and me with no connection to anyone was worse. But then I thought what I've thought a few times since: "Help yourself." I adapted.

I rearranged my fantasy baseball team, a set of magnets Grandpa gave me at Christmas. The magnets had accompanied my ticket to Opening Day 2003—which, if you're counting, starts in one hour and forty-three minutes and fifteen, fourteen, thirteen seconds. The magnets featured players from last year's Red Sox in game poses cut from photographs in the Boston *Globe*'s sports section. Grandpa had given Grant a foam hand reading RED SOX across the front. The hand made the shape of both the number one and the letter D in the ASL alphabet. Inside he'd put a true-life baseball story, "Hub Bids Kid a Dew."

"Something to keep up your sleeve," Grandpa told Grant. My brother learned all the words by New Year's Day.

Rearranging the players helped me feel less lonely, less slow. That Sunday, I think I was being slow on purpose. I didn't want to go to the arcade. At the arcade, my name was not on the good list kept by boys who were not my brother. It was on another list: the list of boys to bother, to bully, to pester, to tease. The boys who kept this list seemed their own kind of special family.

Worse, I thought then, Dean Mulligan is going to be there. I'm not friends with him anymore. He lives behind me, so we used to be friends. He's known me forever. He actually stopped the teasing on Friday. But ever since seventh grade started, he's been teasing me all the time. No, I remember thinking, I'll stay right here, thank you very much.

I should have stayed. Maybe none of this would have changed. I hate change.

I remember that Grant waved for my attention. *What are you doing?*

*Making a new line-up.* I spelled this out. Our sign for LINE-UP (BASEBALL) was the same as for LIST. Even just to myself, I wanted the ideas separated. I formed my letters clearly.

*For someone who hates change, you sure move those players around a lot.*

*I like to imagine. I like to be creative.*

*You daydream,* Grant signed.

*Change is hard for me,* I signed. *But good changes, fixes? Those are easy to accept.*

I won't go, I thought, and prepared an explanation.

At the arcade, I knew, I'd look up at a gang of boys above me on the list. That view was familiar, but I didn't still like it. I didn't want to see things from the bottom of the list. The bottom was the place where I'd always belonged, until this year, when I'd entered seventh-grade Science in a mainstream classroom. Being autistic makes most changes harder, but the transition to Mainstream Science 7—the move up that list—was smooth. Everyone said so: my teacher, Mr. Maloney; my aide, Amy Mulligan; Dad, who had said "Great idea!" last spring; and even Mom, who was "concerned" until the first report card, when she became "relieved." The next report card, which I had just brought home that Friday, made her "happy" and "proud." By next year, February 9, 2004, I thought, everything in my life will be different. What I thought then: I'm making such progress that, soon, I'll have to protect the new name beneath mine: Grant Flynn.

When I follow the directions and think about what I've done, I discover a fact: I was wrong about everything. I can't protect anyone.

I was nearly finished rearranging the baseball players when my brother waved then stomped then whooped for my attention. Ignoring a whoop isn't respectful in Deaf culture, so I turned.

*You can't put Pedro at shortstop,* Grant signed. *He's a pitcher.*

*I can if I want,* I signed. *He's my favorite player. Short's the best position.*

*You still can't do it. Pedro can't field groundballs any better than you can.*

*It's fantasy baseball. Fantasy means, "Make-up yourself." Fantasy means, "Use your imagination."*

*You mentioned that,* Grant signed. *But there are still rules.*

*It's fan-tas-y baseball,* I signed. *It's not chess.*

*Lucky for you it's not.*

Grant used his crappy voice to emphasize simple words with single syllables or slam-dunk vowels: "rule," "not," "luck." Since becoming deaf in the car accident—which was no one's fault and especially not the driver's—Grant's vocabulary had soared as high as his voice had sunk low. He knows English better than I do, I thought, but only I can speak it. But I also noticed how quickly the sound of Grant's voice drew Mom's attention. My voice never does that, I thought. What good is a clear voice when nobody listens to it?

"Boys, I'm on the phone with Mrs. Clemens," she said. *Enough,* she signed. *STOP, please.*

I understood her signs and her voice. The PLEASE was directed at my brother. I never found the difference in her manners fair. Maybe that will be better now that Grant—no, wait.

I will tell this story in the right order.

Back then, Mom was rude in speech, but not in sign. Even then, that made me angry. After all, I was the one we learned sign for first. Me—not him.

*What are they talking about?* Grant asked.

Reluctantly, I explained. *Dean Mulligan, I think.*

*What about him?*

*His behavior,* I signed, embarrassed.

*You mean how adults keep finding him around other people's penises?*

Like they did Friday. *I guess so,* I signed.

Grant's face stilled. It was the facial expression that meant, a-big-plan-is-cooking.

*What?* I asked.

*I suppose The Rocket's penis was another one of the penises Dean had been caught around lately—*

*Right,* I signed. *New subject.*

*Fine,* Grant signed. *His and then yours.*

*Enough!*

*Hey, you told me about it,* signed Grant. *Ask Mrs. Clemens "Is The Rocket feeling better?"*

The Rocket—this was what we called Raja Clemens, who was adopted from India even though everyone in the seventh grade pretended he wasn't—had played sick to skip church. Grant was a good liar because he always remembered the whole lie, all the little parts that made the machine work. Even I knew The Rocket went skateboarding in the Shoppers World parking lot with Dean Mulligan and his new friends. Now that group was 100% terrible liars, dumb smokers, bullies. I had seen them earlier, when we—Grant and I—went sledding in the woods between the Mall and the neighborhood.

*Did you ask her?* Grant signed. *Well?*

*I will right now.* I voiced Grant's question. Mom repeated it to Mrs. Clemens, adding "I know the boys want to see him." I label videotapes and weather patterns as well as the behavior of people, places, and things: DETAIL, HABIT, FACT, LIE. The information Mom added was a lie. Neither of us said it, but it wasn't true either. *He's feeling better.*

*I bet.* Grant signed. Does he know something I don't?

So I turned away from the phone, from the magnets, toward the desk in my basement room where my English homework waited. I heard Grant shuffle an incomplete deck of cards. His arched wrists mixed clubs and hearts, jacks and deuces. I imagined Opening Day—today, except with me there—and Nomar Garciaparra on the mound. What was wrong, I wonder, with imagining a different world?

Turning back to the fridge, I moved Nomar back to shortstop. My wrong answer was gone and with it went the fun of playing around with the homemade magnets, the gift as thoughtful as the tough-to-get tickets. The magnets formed a diamond, and even this shape dragged my mind away from baseball and back to cards, to Grant's destructive and futile and beautiful shuffling. I thought, What can't my brother do with his hands?

Then two words appeared and I labelled them ANSWER: *Push me.* With his hands, my brother can't push me downhill on a sled. I would add that to my English homework, to the brainstorming worksheet. At the top, I had already made a change, crossing out personal narrative and writing "Explode-a-Moment." Later, when the teacher asked why I'd done that, I just shrugged. "Personal narrative means the story belongs to you," Mrs. Phillips said. "It's the more common way to say it."

"I'm not common," I said. "I'm not like other kids."

Mrs. Phillips sighed. "'Explode-a-Moment' it is, then. Don't forget the dashes."

I didn't forget them, and that Sunday, after adding them to every item on the shopping list, I left Mom to talk to Mrs. Clemens, whose son was not disabled. There was nothing wrong with his body. Yet people thought there was something wrong with *him*. Why did parents make up problems that weren't problems, when there were so many real problems already? Stop, I thought. No distractions. I searched for a strategy to help me focus. Follow Dad's directions: worry about what you can control. I went to my room, in the basement, to finish my homework. With footsteps about as light as Godzilla, Grant crept behind me.

*Oh, hi. I didn't notice you,* I signed, once we both arrived downstairs. This was not a lie; I labelled it "a joke with myself," and then I changed the label to "manners."

*What are you writing about for your homework,* Grant asked.

*I don't know.*

*You should write about Friday.*

*No way.*

*Why not? It was an exciting moment. It happened to you.*

*No,* I repeated, fingerspelling it for emphasis. But when I think about what I've done, I realize something. That Sunday, I refused to explode certain moments, ones I did not like. Now, things have changed, and I can do that. I can look at things I don't like and not blink. I guess that's a good change. But then, I had a list of moments I refused to explode. At the top of that list was Friday.

*Review the story with me.*

*You know it already.*

*Come on,* Grant signed. *Tell it. What did I tell you last time?*

*I'm the story's hero.*

*Right. You're the story's hero. So go ahead.*

I liked telling stories in ASL with my brother. It was fun, and easier than English. Things made more sense, and everyone had access, everyone felt included. But as much as I liked signing stories in general, I disliked signing this story. But Grant could not be argued with.

*Fine. I'm in the bathroom. Jim Standard saw me and said, "Yo, Dewey, wanna smoke?" I said "No." Dean heard it all from his stall. Over the door, he said, "Dewey, man, I thought you loved nature. Now I hear you don't like Camels?" I said "I just want to pee. Buzz off." Then Harry Lynwood and Jeff Cincotta and Brian Grady stand in front of the tall stand-up toilet and the two stalls for regular people. That left the small stand-up toilet for kids, and the wheelchair stall.*

*"Gotta piss?" Standard said. "Gotta choose."*

*"Yeah," said Cincotta. "Are you a baby, or are you a retard?"*

*I thought about Dad's directions. Sometimes he will say: To fight without violence sometimes means turning your back on the situation. What did I do? Exactly that. I turned my back and watched them in the mirror while I took out my penis and peed in the sink near the door. "There," I said, "I chose." In the mirror I saw Dean smile, cover his face.*

*"Fuckin' Flynn," Dean said. "He's priceless."*

*"You mean 'He's a princess,'" said Cincotta.*

*"No," said Dean. "I said 'priceless'."*

*Then what,* signed Grant.

*Then the teacher came in.*

*It's a good story. But I can see why you don't want to tell it. He used to be your BFF.*

*No! Only girls have those.*

*I can't believe he made you do that.*

*He didn't! Everybody thinks that because of Mrs. Phillips. She gossips. She spreads lies.*

*You could fix that with the story.* I glared at my brother. *Or not. Doesn't matter to me. Anything can get fixed.*

*That's not true. Our disabilities, for example, are facts we are stuck with.*

*Maybe for you,* my brother signed. I am trying to remember exactly what my brother's face looked like when he told me the news. There must have been something there that made it seem like a joke: maybe a thin eyebrow raised, maybe his mouth curled up in a smirk. Maybe his ears pulled back, threatening to loosen the molding from its cradle. His ears, it seemed, had grown as fast as the rest of him in the past six months. Even his hearing aid didn't fit anymore. *I'm getting a cochlear implant. I'm not stuck with anything.*

I couldn't find the words to react to him then, but if I had another chance, if I had double time for this particular test, what I might have said was this: You're NEVER stuck with anything.

He signed, *Just don't take forever down here, okay, peabrain?*

I ignored the word "peabrain." I remember thinking how Grant had different versions of himself, like the Mr. Smith characters in *The Matrix*. One of the new Grants was calling me a peabrain, I thought, the Grant who wants things his way or no way at all.

*Little brother,* I signed, *I can manage my time. Go read your story once. Then we'll go.*

Peabrain-Grant was glued on top of another Grant, the one who hated being late because of the long-ago car accident that made him deaf. The accident happened when Dad drove too fast, to make up for killed time. Since then, whenever I dawdled, Car-Crash-Grant got angry, mean.

*What a special education you've gotten,* Grant signed. "You are really some-uh-ting suh-peh-see-all," he added with his voice, as if daring Mom to be the hero. She did not interrupt. Grant's Army boots battered the stairs as he climbed. Car-Crash-Grant was glued on top of whoever he was before the accident. Maybe, like in my nature videos taped from Channel Two Boston, fear made Grant evolve.

"I'll be as fast as I can," I said, loud enough for Mom to hear.

Why hadn't she defended me from what Grant had voiced? Had she not heard it? Had she not cared? Nevermind: it doesn't matter now. That Sunday, I realized that I could defend myself. You have for years, I thought, with no help at all. As he climbed the stairs, I signed at his back, as large, as loud as I could stretch his arms and shoulders, the muscles on my face, the spread of my two feet: *I don't care if you think I'm too slow.*

# KRISTEN HARMON

## Small Machinery

Yesterday, a slow news day, our fellow Gen X'er and President of the United States announced a federal initiative against deafness, *per se*. A former deejay on radio when we still had radio masts instead of ghostly wind towers, he'd recently lost some hearing and had become concerned about national implications; surely the one stood for the many. And like fossil fuel, hearing impairment must be on its way out. Clouds can be seeded, serrated catalytic leaves can split hydrogen and oxygen, and fountains in the ocean can stir the waves and breathe in the smog. What's a hair cell in the cochlea? All that is needed, they seemed to be saying, is the reversal of a microclimate.

"This was not," he said, with a sideways chuckle as he walked to his helicopter, "to be confused with Sign Language and sign language peoples. Just plain old nerve deafness," he shouted over the slow round growling of the idling helicopter.

Television anchors broadcast stories about "Genetic Stimulus Reverses Hearing," showing snail shell charts of cochleas, robot-bug listening devices, and artful graphics with double helixes. This morning, Oprah's best friend's former lover hosted a talk show segment called "Are You Hearing Things!" The host brought a blind couple, also S&M fans, onto her artfully staged stage. True to hype, the blind man did have a mild hearing loss, and he sat lunged forward in his chair. He hadn't shaved his chest or his armpits, and gray bristles curled over and trimmed the edges of his sleeveless black leather vest.

Her capped teeth pushing back her lips into a toothy doll's grimace, the jittery host took a chair beside the blind man and tried to look into his gently roving eyes.

I waved to get Mark's attention. *You have to see this.*

He leaned out from the bathroom door, still brushing his teeth. *What's up?* Mark nodded and frowned. The fresh showered smell of his hair gel, body wash, toothpaste, and body spray wafted out on the steam rising from behind him. I smiled. This was one of my favorite moments of the day with him, with his face scraped smooth and red and his hair wet and sticking up like the fierce and delightful teenage boy I wished I'd met. What would we have thought of each other if we had met each other at seventeen instead?

Sometimes I wondered about that. Sometimes I looked at his old Deaf school football pictures and fantasized about us meeting then, when he was big-chested, big-haired, and full of sex and pranks and his own power. Now a thin and muscular marathoner, a running lawyer, he laced up his running shoes with short quick strokes, nothing wasted.

I pointed to the computer screen.

The host said, TELL ME. The live captions—misheard words and all—crawled across the bottom of the video. She swayed back and forth with the blind man's eyes. BEING DEAF AND BLING, WHAT DOES IT FEEL LIKE?

With an open hand, the doll-faced host reached for the studded vest pocket over the blind man's heart, but she lost her nerve and with a wavering finger, touched the man's arm instead.

I'll write it up, that gesture that asked an aging body's questions.

Mark shook his head and leaned back in to spit into the bathroom sink.

The next day, Ian Allyn, a media content developer from one of the regional news and urban lifestyle social sites, found me on Twitter and thought to ask me this same question, as a witness to the tension between sign language and deafness and cochlear implants.

"Isn't the cochlear implant industry winning?" he asked me in his short msgs. "I want to know. Your thoughts on this and other matters. But let's try to find a fresh story for our consumers. They want fresh news, fresh perspectives, on old issues."

"By the way," he wrote at the end of his email, "loved your blog about the old lady and her white clover and the video of the dog sitting in the front seat and holding hands with his owner. I laughed out loud. Literally."

The next morning, outside our tastefully-painted, well-appointed rowhouse in the historical part of the city, Ian Allyn pressed the doorbell and stumbled back when the lights flashed inside the foyer. Mark and I looked at each other: *Here we go again.* As a locally well-known lawyer-blogger couple, we used to get a lot more of these kinds of requests when he was filing lawsuits against school districts, but more recently, the features had been focused on my blogging.

Allyn smiled and shoved his iPad in our faces, open to his company's app. He pointed to himself. "That's me."

Mark gestured, and stepped backward into the foyer.

Ian Allyn shook his head, and with exaggerated lip movements, mouthed, I don't know sign language. He pointed at us. Again, he mouthed, I don't—

"Oh, just come in," I said. "Please."

"Oh, perfect," Ian Allyn said. "I can talk to you." He launched into a monologue directed solely at me. "I'm so relieved because I was worried that [mumble] it must be hard to have to [mutter mutter awkward laugh] with deaf people."

I could feel Mark shrinking backwards.

I held up my hand. "You can hear me, but I still can't hear you."

"Cool!" Ian Allyn grinned. "Neat. That's a cool trick."

*What's he saying?* Mark asked.

*Same old, same old. Shock and awkwardness.*

"What's he saying?" Ian Allyn asked.

We sat down on the sofas in our formal sitting room. I sat Allyn down across from me, within hearing-aid range, in the cross hairs of my sightlines.

He pointed from himself to Mark. "So . . . how?"

"I'll try to interpret," I told him. "But you'll have to work with me."

Allyn looked from me to Mark, one guy sizing up another guy and then making some small internal sassy, nasty boy comment to himself before looking back at me and agreeing. I'm the guy's interpreter slash wife slash deaf lady slash somebody-he-should-be-nice-to slash . . . whatever. He'll work with me.

Allyn wanted us to close our eyes and describe the "emotional landscape" of our "hearing-impaired lives." Eyes wide open, I relayed this to Mark.

Oh, and Ian Allyn wanted to maybe someday write a bestseller about the hearing-impaired, spirituality, and urban living. Because people are tired of heavy political discussions about language, you know? They want to know what this—he gestured toward us—feels like. They want to stretch their minds.

"What **do** you hear?" he asked us. "I mean," he said, "if you don't mind me asking. Because that's what most people are interested in reading about, you know? But I don't want to be offensive or anything?" He laughed and pressed his hands together in a way that was supposed to be slightly fey and winning. "Aren't there dogs involved, too?"

Suppressing an ironic smile, Mark looked at me. This question is my territory: what do we hear?

*On hearing: you're expert*, Mark signed to me. But he made a sharp-edged pun on signs, implying that my talent was hearing people, rather than being an expert on audition.

*Funny, you*, I signed back to him. I flashed my teeth at him in my "Let's just do this, ok?" smile.

*You worship Alexander Graham Bell*, he told me. *Your fantasy man.* He showed me his teeth, his beautiful green eyes on full power, giving me his maximum attention like lovers are supposed to do. The map of his hairline seemed further away on his forehead than it had been last Christmas.

Allyn looked back and forth between us, clearly feeling left out. This, I knew, was what Mark wanted. He wanted the journalist thrown off balance and shaken out of *his* story of us.

Sometimes, I looked at Mark when he slid like this, bottom down and legs straight out in front, knife held between his teeth, down and off the top of a wooded cliff only he could see, down into this hot dry valley, the grass cut low with scythes, and it surprised me that I felt nothing for him. He'd always been the kind of man you'd want beside you in a dystopian scenario. I used to admire that in him.

*So answer the poor man's question,* Mark gestured toward Allyn in a way that suggested that Mark thought the journalist might be gay. *What do you really hear?* He flattened his palms on the sofa chair arms and looked at me, his face flat.

"I've never understood that question," I told Allyn. "I mean, what is it that you"—meaning hearing, sighted, white guys—"really see?"

Allyn made a "whoa, sassy!" face, and then thought better of it. "That's a fair point," he said, clearly humoring me. "I've heard that deaf people see better. Sure, I can write about that. Kind of like you all get super X-ray vision because your brain is compensating for your hearing impairment. Cool."

*I'm not blind, you know,* Mark told me, with a hard look.

*I don't know what you mean.* I made my face cold. I'm not the one who has women texting and video-calling his travel laptop.

*Don't play dumb. You know what I mean.*

Nodding as if he understood *something* had happened but he didn't quite know what, the reporter looked from Mark to me.

"Okay. Um. So . . . tell me. The President's new program, H.E.A.R.N. What do you think? Of it? A good idea, or a waste of time, scary stuff, playing God, the future of deafness, or what?"

H.E.A.R.N.: Hearing Education And Regeneration Now. Every time I saw that, I felt the need to marshal my resources somehow, pretend to sing along to a rousing song, participate in the good fight against this indefinable, immoral force that robbed one of one's audition. Let's go out and buy into this!

That was my response, anyway: what do you expect from an aging youngish President with LASIK, a chin implant, scrubbed tattoos, and rumors?

The whole thing was like Rush Limbaugh overdosing on drugs that destroyed his hearing and then getting cochlear implants and a new wife; it was one of those ridiculous things that make you realize even more just how ridiculous it was to begin with. It made for a great blog. I'd actually gotten re-blogged on *The Huffington Post* yesterday; that was how Ian Allyn thought to contact me.

Mark had accused me of not taking it as seriously as I should. *R E G E N E R A T I O N,* he spelled. *That L I T E R A L means gene growth, gene therapy.*

When I made a funny face, one that I used as a visual shorthand for *crazy stupid fuckers,* he thwacked my upper arm. *Not funny.*

So what do we think about the President's new program?

When he nodded at me, I voiced for Mark. "Understand that deaf people are not simply 'broken' hearing people. We have our own visual culture and language," I said, for Mark. "But we share the same physical world and government you do. We do not and should not live as lepers in your hospitals. We have a full, natural language made of signs, not just"—he made a choked face with gaping lips—"imitations at strangled, unheard, pieces of sound. We have a community. We are not alone or lonely. Not broken people who need to be fixed."

Ian nodded impatiently. "Yes, I know, but what's—"

"Not blank pieces of flesh that need to be injected with manipulated viruses, redesigned."

Whenever he's not being arch, his head tilted or his shoulders hunched to the side with whatever snide comment he's making, Mark is beautiful.

When he believes what he says, and when he feels what he says, he is breathtaking. His strong face, his eyes, his Roman mouth, his hands, his long, artistic fingers, even his arms and shoulders—light and shadow shift and shine from around him. In those moments, he looks like a statue caught mid-philosophy, pensive, then passionate, with strong nose, full lips, and a message for the people from some greater good.

Allyn held up his finger and looked at me as if I was going to call on him. "Right, I understand all that. But this is gene therapy we're talking about here. This is a completely different realm."

*You have my answer.* That's what I thought when I first saw Mark years ago, in front of the crowd and the cameras.

"Our consumers want to know what this means, not for you, but for *them,*" Ian hit the emphasis on the last word. "What if they find themselves at seventy with hearing loss? Or their baby is born deaf?"

Yesterday, after the President's news conference announcing H.E.A.R.N., Mark threw his hands back and pounded his fists on the back of the La-Z-Boy. The chair tilted and he almost fell backwards. I happened to be standing behind him watching him and the screen, so I caught the back of the chair. I stood there for a moment, holding him in balance.

*What are hearing people so afraid of?* he asked me after he'd jerked forward and found my hands holding up the back of the chair. *Becoming us?*

To distract him, I threw my head back like a wild Patty Duke as a black and white Helen Keller in *The Miracle Worker* and grabbed Mark's hand. Head thrown back in a mock ecstasy, I finger-spelled, *W A T E R,* into his hand, the letters spilling like light.

*But that's what happens,* he told me. *Exactly that. She finally understood something, right? She finally made a real connection. She became R E A L.*

He reached for the running shoes on the floor and almost jerked the laces out. He stabbed his foot in the shoe.

But, I told him. We're not like *that.* I gestured toward the press conference, the podium, the interactive, eye-popping graphics behind the President, the theatrical blue curtains in the background. I couldn't explain what I meant.

With surprisingly sure taps with piano fingers on the flat blank glass of his iPad, Allyn typed, "Now that hearing aids, implants, and sound-aid apps are becoming daily tech, the core issue is whether or not to choose deafness. In short, why be deaf if you can download a good app for sound control? To choose whether or not to be deaf is a lifestyle choice much like choosing your mate or your career. Review this in re: notes at home." Allyn pursed his lips as he re-read his notes. He seemed pleased with himself.

Mark paused and frowned at me. *He's not listening.*

I shook my head.

Mark laughed, not in a kind way, and tapped his palms on the arms of the leather chair, as if he were mock-playing the bongos, his fingers on the vibrating pulse of the dried skin stretched tight.

Then Allyn added to his notes, "But what justifies difference if the means to even partially repair sensory deficits exists? Couldn't we all agree that some hearing is better than none?"

He showed this iPad, open to an app that looked like legal paper, to me and pointed out the question to both of us.

Mark had told the story of our first meeting so often that I had begun to see it as mythic, as if it happened again and again to some other people we'd never met. His version read like a hero story, starring Mark. My private version felt more like snapshots stapled together in a daisy chain.

On the day I met Mark, I wore my behind-the-ear hearing aid carefully, my hair artfully arranged.

I didn't want to stand out in a crowd. I was different, that was all, and my progressive deafness was simply something life had given me.

"I was just trying to get by the best I knew how," I signed and spoke.

I'd interrupted Mark's story, and an exasperated look crossed his face. He signed with more force than he normally would.

I'd touched him in the place where we both lived, miserably, together.

Until I met Mark, the only deaf adult I'd ever known was myself.

We had met some Bizarro World city council meeting. The mayor had suggested that to cut down on the complaints about noise pollution from the nearby airport, all the deaf people should be moved to the neighborhoods near the airport.

Mark stated this last part again, for the journalist's benefit. Allyn looked skeptical. He looked at me, and I nodded, confirming.

I knew that judging from my audiology charts, measuring the ever-increasing amounts of hearing I didn't have, I could be requested to move if this bat-shit crazy proposal actually happened. I slid into the crowded city council chambers and found a seat in front of a conference table where a wiry man in his late twenties—Mark, as it turned out—sat with the rest of the city council.

*Please let this be a good seat for me to see to lipread,* I thought. *Please don't let the microphone block out the speakers' lips.*

I ended up sitting next to the interpreter, and I tried not to watch him signing to Mark while they waited for the hearing to start. Of course, at the time, I didn't know any sign language.

After a while, my skin prickled with the feeling that Mark watched me watching the interpreter. At a pause in the deliberations, Mark held up his index finger to the interpreter, pausing the stream of information. He looked at me: Why was I staring at them? Didn't I know that it was rude to stare? Especially at a deaf person?

Mark's eyes are heavy-lidded and he has long lashes that look almost girly, so at first, I didn't notice that they weren't actually brown, but a muddied green, like a roiled lake.

I dug around in my messenger bag, pretending I searched for a pen, found one, and nodded to myself, relieved that there actually was one in there. The name of my new media communications and consultations company, Traffic Circle, was printed in neat block letters along the side of the pen, and I rolled it between my fingers, taking assurance from the embossed lettering, like facts. Even though I stored nearly everything in my tablet computer, I still didn't feel complete without a good pen with a strong line and a small notebook. I still look at the notebook sometimes when I'm looking for an idea.

A woman introduced Mark, and her hand shook when she gestured to where he stood. "We're pleased [a photographer crouched in front of me; I couldn't see through his head to read lips] Mark Amos, a consultant with the state legislature," she said. "Mr. Amos now travels [a cameraman positioned himself right in my sightline, and so I leaned to one side, craning my neck] advocate for the hearing-impaired across the state."

She clasped her hands before her to still the nervous shaking in her fingers; in the section beside me, a cameraman zoomed in for close-ups on a few people signing, people with wheelchairs, or with dark sunglasses.

"We have a big meeting ahead of us, and we'll hear from the mayor, from the various committees connected to the building of the proposed airport, and also we'll hear from Concerned Citizens Against Noise Pollution, from the United City Citizens with Disabilities Association, and then, we'll, um, hear, from Mr. Amos."

Mark paused and with a wry look on his face, asked Allyn, *Do you see the problem yet?*

Allyn hesitated, as if Mark had asked a trick question that he really should know the answer to. Then he gave up and nodded, hesitantly.

Then, Mark said, as if the mayor's spokesperson had decided to charge ahead, politically correct or not, she nodded in his direction.

"I, for one," she said, in a louder voice, "feel inspired by the example we have before us of the kind of courage it takes to overcome obstacles in life, and I feel certain that we will end with a workable compromise over the Mayor's proposal."

She took a breath, and in that pause, I remember, the interpreter's hands made a small clapping noise when he shaped a sign. Mark crossed his arms, and the interpreter rested his hands on his lap. Distracted by the small sound and the echo it made in my hearing aid, I remember feeling amazed by the solid, unquestionable, unapologetic fact of the interpreter.

Several hands waved in the back, and the spokesperson seemed to panic, swinging up one hand before her face as though she directed traffic and an oncoming car threatened to run her down. A car with handicapped plates and a driver with dark glasses.

"Now," she said, "the mayor has asked me to clarify that when he said that the concerns over noise from the proposed airport could be simply and effectively dealt with by having all the deaf people in the city relocated to the neighborhoods surrounding the airport, this does not, in any way, shape, or form, entail a forced relocation."

The microphone picked up the extra emphasis on **not**, and feedback squealed. I winced and turned down my hearing aid. The spokeswoman gestured for Mark to come forward.

Mark stood, and the interpreter stepped up on the platform with him. A security officer handed the interpreter a microphone.

Mark stepped forward and nodded. He saluted hello. With a conductor's expansive and composed expression, Mark lifted his face and with a dramatic upswing, started signing.

"Thank you for the introduction," the interpreter said.

Mark's signing seemed coiled, unspooling as he went along. "It's good to be here, and I'm glad to see so many people here today."

Mark smiled and nodded at all of us, then raised two fingers, and tapped the first one.

"There's two things I need to tell you, in response to what the mayor's spokesperson said. First, thank you for the compliment—but—if you want to support us, don't just admire us." He swept his gaze over the crowd. "I know we're pretty, but we have other things to do besides inspiring you."

I shifted in my seat, uncomfortable with the fact that he was treating the whole thing as a serious proposal. I had hoped the Mayor's crazy idea would be treated like a joke. Surely! I thought. After all that effort to mainstream handicapped people.

His signs sped up, and the interpreter caught only quick breaths between phrases. "Second, everyone put your fingers in your ears."

I saw people all around me coughing and chuckling, uneasy at this request.

"Please place your fingers in your ears." The interpreter said this with a theatrical kind of importance, then smiled, enjoying the shifting and coughing in the audience.

I covered my ears with my hands, along with everyone else, but carefully, so that I wouldn't set off a disrupting squeal, feedback from my hearing aid.

Mark pointed to someone in the back corner. A heavy man walked forward with a huge bass drum strapped to his belly. He nodded and began striking the drum with strong strokes.

Mark accompanied him. He drummed his palms on the podium before him.

The lamp on the podium quivered light on his fists. The noise rumbled through the metal chairs we sat upon.

He stopped and smiled.

"Did you feel that?" the interpreter said. "The planes would bother us just as much as they do you."

The interpreter clapped his fist to his forehead, and finger-spelled D U H for our benefit.

Then he said, for Mark, "You might as well propose that all deaf people direct the planes so that you can save money on ear plugs."

I laughed.

Around me, deaf people lifted and waved their hands.

Oops. Should I not have laughed?

Instead of looking at his friends, Mark looked at me, with an intense and focused expression that I thought at the time was him marking me as his. I'd never been claimed like that by a man before, in public, and I found it sexy and exciting. Later, I realized it was his "So you wanna fight? Bring it on, baby" expression. He had simply recognized me for what he thought I was.

I settled my face so that Mark couldn't see how I felt, with him. Without him?

"You should have seen her the way she was when I first saw her," I said, for Mark, about me.

Mark mimed the stiff body language of a lip-reader, leaning forward, hands gripped together in his lap, and eyes staring wide open. He glanced around, paranoid, signing, with one hand, *What I miss?*

I winced, feeling all over again all the embarrassment and anger I felt constantly during those years.

Mark reached for my hand, but then turned away from me.

He looked surprised to be unhappy, the same expression he wore when we first started seeing each other, and I felt awkward with him out in public. And yet we did this sort of thing long enough to get married. I started learning sign language for him. I loved sign language. I loved him.

*And here we are now*, he said. He gestured toward me, his eyebrows arched. *She's S E M I- famous for writing funny stories about nothing, about crazy old ladies* (he grimaced) *and I'm still suing the same people over and over.*

Mark lowered his hands, resting them in a prayer clasp in his lap.

I'd been driving down a side street last spring when I passed a small, tired house. In the front yard, a thin, older woman with iron-gray hair hanging to her shoulders passed her vacuum cleaner back and forth over clover flowers. With an expert twitch and pull of the electric cord behind her, she maneuvered the vacuum over a spot of clover that seemed to trouble her.

He looked over at me, and with an arched eyebrow, Mark challenged, *You still happy?*

*I'm trying to remember*, I told him and put on an "I'm thinking" face.

He laughed. He'd always liked that part of me though I'd begun to wonder if this meant we didn't really like each other.

When I'd told Mark, over a take-out dinner of spicy curry that night, when I'd told him about the old woman vacuuming her front yard, I hadn't told it as a joke. We marveled at the story together. He paused, wondering what could have happened and who was supposed to be looking out for her. He seemed shaken out of his normal confidence. He looked thoughtful, then worried.


The reporter smoothed his fingers over the ridged cover of his iPad. He sat back, tapped his jaw, and said, "Wow, man. That's intense."

He leaned forward and squeezed my arm. I pulled back from him.

"Why don't you talk with your hands all the time, too?" Allyn asked.

In the beginning, we took turns with speaking and writing for public goods. When it was my turn, I voiced our orders to waiters, asked for stamps, whatever. Whichever method we used, people stared at us. With me, they looked up at me and listened carefully to the difference in my voice. When him, they surreptitiously tried to read the notes he passed back and forth with the waiter, their heads bowed together over the paper.

One time, in a steak restaurant, a woman in her fifties leaned her chair back and said, to me, "God bless your compassion." At those times, I always pointed to my ears and shook my head, sorry-no-hear-you-shrug.

Every now and then, women of a certain age told me, with hushed voices, that they had started sign language classes.

"I'm deaf, too," I told one such woman. She shrank back, shocked.

"But you talk," she said, in a louder voice, and with a sudden cheerful elasticity, pressing out each word like an elementary school teacher. "Sweetie, You. Would. Never. Know."

She paused, and just in case I didn't understand, she tapped her head and made an outward gesture from the wrists, as if she turned garden dirt with her hands. She looked at me as though she had said something very private and long-held in that one made-up sign, and waited for my affirmation.

"I wasn't born with sign language," I'd told her. "I just hear differently than you do."

"But I want to learn how to use my hands too," she had said.

We'd looked at each other, hamstrung.

"I'm so sorry," she'd said.

"Don't be," I'd said, with a sharper tone than I'd intended. "I'm absolutely fine."


"So what's the story you're here to get?" I asked Allyn.

At our wedding ten years ago, much to the shock of my hearing relatives, Mark and his parents had danced. My family had been afraid that Mark and his family might ruin the wedding somehow, but they ended up stealing the show with their all-hearts-and-elbows-into-it Electric Slide. They had way more fun than anybody else on the floor.

I reached for Mark. He leaned forward and fixed Allyn in his gaze. A warm patch rested on the back of the couch, where he had just been.

"There's a wall she runs into again and again. This holds her back." His signs became crisper and slower, almost exaggerated in clarity. "Last week, she was gone one whole afternoon. I paged, SMS'd, emailed, and VP'd her: no answer, no one knew where she was. Where?"

His face questioning, Mark looked at Allyn. I felt a crack in my voice.

"Where? No answer. Nothing: nobody knew. She came home, refused to tell me where."

I jerked Mark's sleeve. *This is not important. It's nothing.*

He tilted his head at me, in warning, his hands stilled in mid-air.

I sat on my hands.

When I first met him, I thought that constantly disappointed side of him meant he had answers I didn't have. I had always felt vague, like a run-on sentence trailing off into worried questions.

"*I worried.*" He told the story as though I was not sitting beside him.

"Wait, what was it that you said?" Ian said, to me. "Sorry, I didn't catch it."

I held up a finger and relayed what Allyn had said. Mark gestured an annoyed *so go ahead* toward me.

"OK, so I have this idea," I sim-commed. "What if everything boils down to one thing, and what if that one thing is your socks?"

Ian nodded slowly, humoring me. Mark crossed his arms and sighed.

"So you have all these socks that end up loose after the wash. There's gray ones with thin stripes" (I pursed my lips and made my face thin and gray), "socks with diamonds!" (I drew cheery pointy shapes on my body), "socks with crazy colors" (I winced and put up hands in front of me), "socks that slide down into your shoes," (I slid down my chair, and Mark smiled in spite of himself, and I smiled back to him), "and socks that don't make sense."

*There's only you.* I looked at Mark. Understand what I'm telling you. But what about me for you?

"But at the end of the wash, there's always only two socks. And they never match."

They both looked at me, blank.

"So it doesn't matter what . . ." I trailed off.

But things change.

"What's the big secret?" Mark looked back at Allyn. I voiced. "She went to the audiologist."

"This isn't relevant to our discussion," I said, directly to the reporter. "I don't want to talk about it."

I waved my hand at Mark. *Please.*

Ian nodded, enthralled with us. He rolled a corner of the iPad cover between his finger and thumb.

"She wants more power. The strongest hearing aid in the world." Mark swept his hand across the room, implying seas and continents just on the other side of the wall.

"So what's the problem, then?" Ian asked, with the confusion and fascination of an eavesdropper. He crossed his leg over his knee and rubbed a finger over the dull white toe of his retro sneakers. He looked from Mark to me.

Mark sighed. "Ask her."

*No, no, no, this isn't about me,* I told Mark. *With you, there's no room for* me. *There's your clients, there's your team, there's your Deaf golf C L U B, there's your weekend basketball, there's always other people, others.*

I populated the space before me with the repetition of the sign, shrinking back to show how squeezed out I felt by the sheer number of people in his life. *The other women* . . . I didn't add.

*When you married me, you just added one more person to your schedule.*

Mark shifted in his seat, and rubbed his thumbs over his calf, massaging the muscle in quick rolls of his fingers.

This hadn't bothered me at first. I'd been busy trying to figure myself out, learning sign language, and meeting his friends. I'd been busy with my surprise career in writing on the Internet. But at holidays, I'd seen my friends and his friends add children and animals and new hobbies and houses. Other than plan renovations to our circa 1915 rowhouse, we didn't have anything that we did together. I'm sure he had more in common with the women he met at his work, long-haired, divorced, bottle blonde women who were comfortable in their language and in their bodies. In fact, I could think of one, a woman who always brightened when she saw him coming in to a restaurant or back yard of a house where everyone was gathered. He always seemed to make himself bigger and brasher around her, joking near lines that should not be crossed.

*You eat, run, work. You do your thing. You leave for your conferences. You sleep. That's all.*

Mark thumped his foot on the floor, the vibration twanging through the floor and chairs. *And you'll escape to be with a hearing man with that fancy new hearing aid? That won't change anything.*

*That's NOT what I'm doing. No.*

Mark sighed. I sighed.

I turned up my hearing aid, and leaned back, listening for the click and the purring breath of the air conditioner coming on.

I had married him because I wanted one relationship, one place, one body, where I didn't have to wear a hearing aid. Mark lived in the hum of his mind, pooling out around him. He always seemed protected and vital, destined, somehow. Next to him, I felt like a fluke.

*I'm tired,* I told Mark. *I'm just vacuuming the Y A R D here.* I pointed between us.

*Don't be silly,* he told me. *This is normal.* He again made the between-us motion that I had made.

I shook my head. This surprised him.

*If we'd met before all of this*—I gestured toward the house, toward Allyn sitting and shifting in his chair—*if we'd met at some stupid high school dance, what would have happened?*

We would never have escaped together out into the night, cooler than the muggy gym, out through the parking lot, holding hands for the first time stepping together over a pothole, and then out into the soft dark summer grass of a football field.

*That's not a fair question*, Mark told me. *I had a perm.* He scrunched his hair in an imaginary jock's mullet.

I laughed but my throat tightened anyway.

*If you leave, who will make me clover necklaces in the summer?* He smiled. *No, I mean it.*

Mark looked at me in a way that I felt on my skin, the drifting memory of a touch, a word, at night.

Allyn shifted in his seat and coughed in that polite way that hearing people use to assert their presence.

"I hope you got what you wanted," I told him, and stood. Mark nodded and stood as well. Allyn packed his things, paused at the door, and with a broad grin, thrust out his hand, *No hard feelings*. Mark grinned back at him, and I opened the door.

Green dust covered the door and bees zipped from one end to another. We sent him off.

# CHRISTOPHER JON HEUER

## Trauma

There are two police officers in our dining room. They've come to take my father away.

He's standing by the table in his underwear, hands cuffed behind his back. My mother is trying to hang her burgundy housecoat over his shoulders so he won't be naked when they take him outside. The housecoat has floral patterns and looks ridiculous on him. She looks ridiculous too, being all concerned for his appearance when she's the one who called the police in the first place.

Dad is completely out of it—if he knew what was going on he would be shouting and bitching. Instead he's in a stupor. I can't hear what he's mumbling.

The police officers take him by the elbows and lead him out the door. Mom's burgundy housecoat falls from his shoulders when he stumbles on the porch. Nobody stops to pick it up.

The clock reads eleven-thirty p.m. Mom closes the front door behind them and sees me standing in the stairwell.

"Go up to your bedroom," she says, pointing up behind me. Her eyes are puffy and dark with exhaustion. Behind her I can see red flashing lights on the wall. She shuts the door, leaving me standing in nearly complete darkness. I run up the stairs to the hallway window so that I'll be able to see where the cops are going.

There's an ambulance and two police cruisers in the driveway. The ambulance pulls out first—after a few minutes my mother gets in her car and follows it up the road. Then the cruisers leave. I watch them until the line of taillights disappears over the hill.

Mom still isn't home in the morning. She used to have to wake me up when I stopped being able to hear the alarm clock. But now waking is internal and I usually leave for school without seeing her.

Everyone is watching me when I get on the bus. After a few minutes this senior girl I know, Jill, sits down beside me. She already has something written on a notepad.

*What happened at your house last night?*

Note-writing is a delicate system of avoidance that I've worked out with the hearing population of Juneau, Wisconsin. We've been using it ever since I transferred back here from the Wisconsin School for the Deaf. On the very first day of school I made the mistake of asking one of the senior guys to repeat something. We just happened to be right in front of some girls, so the location was very strategic for him. He put his hands on my shoulders and very slowly said: "Suck . . . my . . . dick."

After that I've always tried my best to make lip-reading as much of a pain in the ass for them as they make it for me. Hearing people will do just about anything to avoid writing things out—they'll puff in and out like suffocating goldfish for fifteen minutes, they'll repeat something fifty times. Anything but write. If you refuse to lip-read them they'd rather pretend you don't exist. Thus you're spared any further *suck my dick* adventures. The only downside is that if they actually hand you a note, it means that they have something important to say, and you're stuck.

I read Jill's note, and all I can think to do in reply is shrug.

*Didn't your mom leave you a note or something?* she writes.

I say "No" and Jill does a little double take, shocked that my mother didn't tell me anything. She doesn't understand—that's the beauty of the system. No note, no hassle.

"I didn't really look for one," I tell her.


People are still looking at me all through Homeroom and at the start of gym, but by fourth period World History things have died down a little. I keep to myself so it stays that way. In Juneau more people own police scanners than televisions. The local paper even publishes a weekly list of everyone who gets a speeding ticket. People eat it up out here. It's either that or *Dukes of Hazard* re-runs.

Instead of eating in the cafeteria, at fifth period I go get a sandwich at the gas station/deli on the corner. Brad is down there smoking a cigarette by the dumpster.

"Heard about your dad," he says, making a little drinking motion with his hand. The only kind of thing Brad ever bothers to sign is the one word that will sum up the last fifteen minutes of conversation. The rest I have to fill in on my own. But with him it's not hard. Lip-reading is a question of making educated guesses from a limited selection of things the other person is allowed to say. The McDonald's guy isn't supposed to ask you if you like Sumo wrestling when you're waiting for your Happy Meal. He's got to say, "Would you like Coke with that?" or "Thank you! Have a nice day!" So long as they stay in character, you're set.

"Hello?" Brad says, waving in my face.

"I don't know what to tell you."

"Well, how many cops were there?" He knows the sign for "cops" and uses it.

"Two. And an ambulance."

He hands me a cigarette. We stand there smoking in silence while he rubs his collarbone. His real dad threw him down the stairs when he was four and broke it. Twelve years later there's a big knot in the bone. He says it never hurts. But he never stops rubbing it.

Finally he finishes his cigarette and tosses it down, crushing it out under his shoe. He says something I don't catch, and then repeats it. "What you doing tonight?" he asks, signing "do."

"I don't know. Nothing."

"Come out with me later. We'll go to Hartford."

Juneau hasn't got shit. Hartford is where everyone goes—to cruise Main Street, to park in the lots by McDonald's and Burger King and hang out, to drive out to the parks and get drunk.

"I don't know." I glance at my watch. Sixth period starts in ten minutes.

"C'mon."

"My mom's going to be home."

"This is a problem?"

My mother basically lives her life from one holiday to the next. One day after Labor Day, she's getting ready for Halloween. She's taking down the black cats while putting up the Thanksgiving turkeys. All of this done, year after year, around and sometimes over my father. His body passed out on the couch is practically the only permanent showpiece in the room. For her to go calling the cops on the guy after all this time is not in character. It's the McDonald's guy asking you if you like Sumo wrestling. There's no limited selection of responses to choose from.

"Listen," Brad sighs. "Go home, get a sleeping bag, and just . . . come over tonight. Okay? Just come over." He signs "home" and "sleeping bag."

He said the same thing three years ago, the summer before I left for WSD. He was outside the bowling alley trying to pick the lock on the soda machine. I had just biked into town and couldn't remember why, couldn't remember leaving my house. He pointed at my forehead and said: *"You got something up there, man."*

Sweat trickled down my nose. I wiped it off and my fingers came away sticky with blood.

*"Did you wipe out or something?"*

Weird how I understood him perfectly. Weird to be so hyper-aware of everything. I began to shake as if it were winter instead of mid-July.

*"Hey."*

I couldn't respond. Brad slowly reached out and pulled a jagged piece of glass the size of a dime out of my forehead.

I couldn't move.

Brad said, *"Come over to my place. Come on."* In the end he had to park my bike by the soda machine and guide me by the elbow.

Sure enough, Mom is sitting at the kitchen table, wearing a gray sweatshirt and black polyester pants—not the regular white of her nursing home uniform—which means she hasn't been to work today. She has a note ready, too, and holds it out. It reads: *Your father is in the detoxification clinic in Hartford.*

Well, no shit, hey? Let's do the difficult math of adding two and two and subtracting one from five.

When she's sure I've had enough time to read it, she takes the notepad back and writes: *He's staying for four weeks.*

"Good for him."

"I needed to do it," she says. This is exactly what I mean—the limited selection of things people can say.

"Good for you."

She slams her fist on the table in real frustration, startling me. She almost never acts out. She puts a hand to her temple and fights to control her breathing, then picks up the pen again. I read over her shoulder: *Don't you blame me!* "Me" is underlined.

"I don't blame you." But I've answered too quickly. Sometimes you know a person is lying based on how fast they answer. Too fast, it's a lie—too slow, it's a lie. You've got to nail it right in the middle.

"Then why are you so angry with me?"

Again I miss my window. Nothing I can say at this point will be the truth. I tell her that I'm going to Brad's for a while, and go upstairs to get my stuff.

Brad and I wind up at some house party in Hartford. It's nothing big, just a couple of people sitting around finishing off a few cases of beer. I don't know anybody and focus on getting as drunk as I can as fast as I can. It's too hard to lip-read groups and nobody is talking to me anyway.

Here's something about hearing people's parties—they all stop being real and instead become animated mannequins running on battery power. Their mouths open and shut and their arms go flapping around, but that's it. Nothing comes out. I told this to Brad once. He looked at me like I was nuts.

I get a buzz going and lean back to rest my head on the couch. Sometime later Brad slaps my knee and I jerk awake. He hands me a can of beer. In the background the mannequins are reeling back and forth in a mocking parody of laughter.

Brad goes away and I drain the can in a few swallows. A mannequin notices me and shambles forward with a fresh can. I take it and drain that one too. The mannequin reels back laughing. During the five-second pause it takes for his battery to stand him upright again, I ask it where the detox clinic is in Hartford.

Now I am wavering against the side of Brad's car. He's talking to one of the guys from the party. Everyone seems angry. Brad comes up and gives me a look: *"You puke, you die."* Then he motions for me to get in the car. I lean my head back against the seat and close my eyes.

Five minutes later Brad slaps my shoulder and wakes me up again. We're parked in a hospital parking lot.

"It's up there," Brad says, pointing.

"What?"

"The detox clinic."

He's pointing over at a lit blue and white sign that says "Mental Health" in bold print. The sign below it says "Emergency Room." I stare at the letters until they blur out. Brad asks if I want to go up.

I shake my head no.

He says something about my shirt that I don't catch.

"What?"

He flips on the dome light and points at my hand. Something about keeping it wrapped.

My hand is wrapped in a tee-shirt. There's blood soaking through at the knuckles.

"If it's broken," Brad says, "tell me now while we're here."

I'm not wearing a shirt. I'm wearing my jacket but no shirt. Where's my shirt?

"Is it broken?" Brad asks again.

I don't understand. "How'd it get broken?"

Brad grips the steering wheel and breathes deeply—a flashback comes of my mother massaging her temples. He snarls something about how I'd *"better not get blood all over the fucking car"* and angrily reaches up to flip off the dome light. The tires squeal as we tear out of the parking lot. I know because nurses in white pants and multi-colored tops come running to the big hospital windows to see what's causing all the commotion.

Brad is already gone when I awaken on his bedroom floor, feeling sick. It's nearly ten in the morning. Third period is half over. I'll make it in by lunch if I get a move on. I can forge a note from my mom—I've done it before.

When I think about writing my right hand starts itching. It's still wrapped in my shirt.

Brad's room is in the basement—he's completely self-contained down there with his own bathroom and even a refrigerator. He's probably not sophisticated enough to have Peroxide but I'm hoping for at least soap and a better bandage. Wonder of wonders, though, he has both Peroxide and an old roll of football tape.

The first three knuckles of my hand are scabbed over and bruised purple-black. The swelling is bad. Miniature geyser spouts of acid are shooting through my stomach. It doesn't help to watch the Peroxide bubble in the scabs as I dump it on. All I can clearly remember is getting into Brad's car. Did I slam the door on my hand? The face staring back at me in the mirror is strung-out; pasty skin and long, greasy-wet strands of hair clumped together.

Standing behind me in the mirror is my mother.

She's younger and thinner, kneeling next to me as I stand in front of the toilet. I'm five years old and sick with the flu. I'm wearing my dark red pajamas with the blue collar and cuffs. One of my mother's hands is on my stomach; the other is massaging my neck, gently pushing downward so I'll bend over and throw up.

*"Let it come,"* she says. *"Don't be afraid. Just let it come."*

But I am afraid. I won't let it come.


My hand is almost too swollen to write the note, but it passes muster. Then again the secretary gives me a wary look, so who knows? As I walk through the hallways, guys laugh and clap me on the back. Apparently I'm cool now and have some sort of party-animal reputation from being drunk last night. I wonder how they all found out so fast.

I don't even know if Brad will be in the cafeteria, but I don't feel like walking the extra block to the deli. My stomach isn't doing too hot. Hopefully some milk will take the edge off, along with a bottle of aspirin I found in Brad's medicine cabinet. As it turns out I can barely force down even that, and when Brad claps me suddenly and sadistically on the shoulder as he sits down across from me—*"How ya doing!"*—I nearly choke.

"Fucking hand hurts, man," I tell him.

Brad says something with the gesture *"fight"* in it, but I don't catch the whole thing.

"What?"

*"You,"* Brad signs. *"Fight."* Then something more I still don't catch. Then he points at my backpack.

"What?"

He points again with a *"Wait a minute and I'll tell you"* expression. When I still don't understand he impatiently leans over and grabs my backpack, rummaging around. He pulls out a notebook and a pen just as I finally realize what it is he wants.

*At the party,* he writes.

"What about it?"

Brad signs *"drunk"* and points at me.

"Well no shit, Sherlock!"

He writes again: *You hit that guy.*

"What?"

He holds up his hands defensively, mistaking my irritation for denial. "You did!"

I can't focus. "I have no fucking idea what you're talking about!"

He busily scribbles on the notepad: *You asked where the detox clinic was in Hartford. You were completely fucked up. Some guy laughed and you hit him.*

I close my eyes and see blood spurt from my knuckles. The other mannequins in the room scramble away from me, shouting. The guy I just hit is huddled up on the floor holding his nose. Blood is spraying out between his fingers.

Brad is watching me. "Do you remember now?"

"No." No, no, no.

He shakes his head and writes: *You dragged him outside and kicked the shit out of him.*

Now that I don't remember at all. So he's bullshitting me. Fucking playing me. "Please stop, man," I whisper. I'm going to puke if he doesn't leave.

He points down. "Look at your shoe."

There's blood smears all along the toe of my right sneaker; and something else. At first I think it's grass but it's hair.


How does anybody really get around? I wonder about this all the time. How does your brain get you from one place to the next on autopilot, remembering some things and blocking out the rest? The stop signs ... every turn and shortcut? Suddenly you're home with no idea how you got there, no sense of passing time. People say this happens all the time when they drive. But I think it can be a whole way of life. Nobody says anything about it because it doesn't occur to them until they do remember something, and then they're too freaked out.

Like now. I'm home. In front of me is our kitchen table. I'm fourteen years old. We moved in a little over a year ago, leaving behind our farm in Hustisford. I'm drawing pictures of X-Wings and TIE Fighters. My father comes in drunk and asks what I'm drawing.

Maybe it's because I don't look up at him immediately, or because my family no longer has the farm—if we did I would be out picking off stones or bailing hay instead of sitting at the table drawing. I would be working toward something meaningful and worthwhile. I'm pretty sure this is what my father wants me to understand.

He overturns the table with one hand and grabs me by the throat with the other, shoving me into the wall. I can't get free and I can't breathe. He moves in close, breath reeking of beer, and pins my legs with his knee. Then he rips a framed sketch of an old barn from the wall above my head—a drawing of one of those rotting wooden sheds and half collapsed silos that you see all over Wisconsin. People sketch and frame them and sell the drawings at craft shows. They bring in good money.

*"Why can't you draw something people want!"* my father screams, and pushes the picture into my face until the glass shatters.

Sometime later the light flashes. It's nighttime outside. My mother has come home from work. She says, "Daniel, when did you come home?"

I'm seated at the dining room table. The last thing I immediately remember is sitting in the cafeteria. I reach up to pull the glass from my forehead but there's nothing stuck in my forehead and there's no broken picture on the floor. I feel stupid.

"Daniel, what's wrong with you?"

My mother is talking in slow-motion, her hand frozen on the doorknob. She'll cry soon. "Please tell me what you're so frightened of," she says.

I look away slightly. Brad is picking bloody glass out of my forehead.

"Daniel, please!" I'm in the dining room again. My mother is shaking my shoulder.

Brad wrote: *You dragged him outside and kicked the shit out of him.*

"What did I do?" I ask.

*"Look at your shoe,"* Brad says.

The barest pause. Then my mother says, "You didn't do anything, baby."

I can feel my heart beating. So very badly do I want that to be true.

"I was the one who sent him away," she says. "I called the police. Me."

For a second I'm confused. She called the police on me? What did she call the police about?

"Your father did it to himself, Daniel. It's not your fault."

She doesn't know what I'm talking about. Even I barely know what we're talking about. I'm going to be sick. How long is it going to take to not be sick anymore?

"We can fix this, honey," Mother is saying. "We can pull ourselves together . . ."

How can we do that when we're not even talking about the same thing?

She says something more that I don't follow. I've stopped trying to lip-read, to predict; make educated guesses. There's no more limited selection of things she's allowed to say. Then is here and now is nowhere. The character of everyone and everything—completely shot to hell.


Brad and I skip school on Friday and spend the day in his room, drinking beer and watching *First Blood* on his VCR. During the part where Rambo stitches his side back together with fishing-string, Brad says that the guy I hit is going to be looking for me. We watch television in silence for a while.

"I was talking about my dad," I say, suddenly.

"What?"

"That night, at the party."

Brad makes a gesture—*"I don't understand."*

"When I asked where the detox clinic was. They all laughed. That guy especially. They thought I wanted to go get my own stomach pumped or something."

Brad watches, silent.

"But I was talking about my dad," I say.

"Well, how the fuck could they know?" he asks.

"Yeah."

Brad starts rubbing his collarbone.

"Do you ever think about him?" I ask after while.

"About who?"

"Your dad."

It was a mistake to ask. Brad stands up suddenly, and tosses me the roll of football tape. "No," he says, and walks past me toward the bathroom.


I feel sick all the way to Hartford. If Brad notices he's not saying anything. But halfway through *Hotel California* he gives my shoulder a good-natured thump and starts slapping the wheel in time with the beat, trying to lighten the mood. It kind of works. The stereo is cranked up all the way and the enclosure of his car is the best hearing aid in existence.

We go to Burger King for some food. Brad goes in to get us a couple of cheeseburgers. I stay in the car, draining one can of beer after another from the case in the back seat. Part of me wonders if this is how my dad got started, drinking for the nerves.

Eventually Brad comes back with cheeseburgers, fries, and Cokes. He sets the food on the hood and makes a *"come out"* gesture.

"I want to sit in here."

He shakes his head *"no."* He wants me to come and sit on the hood. That's how we wait guys out around here—you don't go driving all over town looking for a fight. You sit out in the open and sooner or later one will come to you.

Once I'm sitting on the hood he pours Southern Comfort into the Cokes from a flask in his jacket pocket. He gives me one and we sit in silence for a while, watching the sun go down and the cars go by.

"I don't want to do this." I have no idea I'm going to say it until I say it.

Brad looks away, because what is he supposed to do about it? It's not like I can call the guy up and apologize. Nobody's going to say: *"Hello this is Dan's mommy! Can I please speak to your mommy?"* No: *"Look my father is in a detox clinic and these are my feelings and what should I do about my feelings?"* What would the guy say to something like that? And even if he said something, how would I ever follow it? Lip-reading is a question of prediction.

Eventually some Hartford guys pull in and talk to Brad. He comes walking back and tells me "It's on. We're going to the park. Get in the car."

It's violently cold on the way there. I can't stop my hands from shaking—my arms and shoulders. "Turn off the air conditioner," I try to say, but my teeth are chattering and my cheeks are numb.

Brad shrugs and makes a dismissive gesture with his free hand—*"It is off."*

We reach the long gravel road that leads to the park and I tell him I have to puke. He slams on the brakes and I barely make it, already vomiting up beer and Southern Comfort as I push open the door and stumble away from the car. Finally it turns to dry heaving and I steady myself against the trunk. I stare at my bad hand then look up. My mother is sitting on one of the front wheels of the John Deere tractor we used to have back at the farm. She just took the stitches out of my forehead. I tell her I want to go swimming. She says *"No."*

*"Why not?"*

*"Just . . . no!"*

No, because the pool hasn't been cleaned and she doesn't want me to get an infection, or because we'll be having lunch in fifteen minutes. There are a dozen potential explanations, but it's not them I react to—it's the fact that she doesn't explain at all. She treats me like I'm six, crying when she takes the stitches out and it's not even her with her head that was cut open. It's the expression on her face now, the impatience, the exasperation, like it's my fault.

*"I hate you!"* I scream at her suddenly. She's steps back, blinking from

the fury in it, but the swimming pool is right there! Everything I want is right there, and I can't have it. I can't have pictures of TIE Fighters. A father. A family that can talk to me. Friends that can talk to me. Everything right in front of my face, and for some reason that nobody will explain, that everyone is too exhausted and irritated to explain, I can't have any of it.

I kick her knee. She lies about it later to her friends, but that's really how it got broken.

Brad's hand slaps my shoulder. "Fucking get it together, man!" he shouts. I look at him and try but can't.

It's dark. The headlights are on. I'm sitting in Brad's car dry heaving into my hand, and he's out by the picnic tables fighting two guys at once. One guy's nose is in a splint. The other guy gets a good hard kick in the nuts, and then it's one-on-one. But the guy with the nose splint turns and runs up the road. Brad walks up and gets in the car.

"Just shut up," he says, and signs "shut up." He rips the gearshift backward into drive and sprays gravel all the way out of the park.

We take back roads on the way out of town and head for Juneau in a completely roundabout way. At first I think Brad is trying to avoid the cops—and he probably is—but eventually I realize that we're heading toward the highway that leads to my house. Right before we get to my driveway Brad shuts off his headlights and we cruise slowly past it. He stops behind one of the trees that border my front lawn.

When I fumble drunkenly with the door handle, he reaches past me and opens it. His expression is stony. I can't read him at all. Once I'm out he pulls the door shut and drives away, heading toward Highway 60. Either he's going back to Juneau the long way or he's just going out cruising. I get the feeling I'm not welcome to know which.

I go into my house through the back door because it's quieter, but my mom still wakes up. When I look up from the refrigerator she's standing next to the living room table—the exact same place my father had been standing when the cops cuffed him only a week earlier. Then is now, there is here.

"Are you drunk?" she asks. She looks tired.

I set my glass of milk down on the counter.

"What would your fath—" she begins to say, but stops herself.

No matter. *"What would your father say if he were here,"* is what she would have said. The day after Dad broke the picture over my forehead I biked home from Brad's house and walked through the front door. My father was standing in the dining room with the phone in his hand. I found out later he had been about to dial the cops. When he saw me he hung up and put his fingers over his eyes, then walked quickly into the bedroom.

My mother came out of the kitchen, her mixing bowl tucked in one arm. She said, *"Daniel, if you're going to stay out at a friend's house, make sure you tell us first."* No question on why I left, about the bandage on my forehead. Nothing. *"Your father doesn't like it when he doesn't know where you are,"* she added. She didn't even put the bowl down.

"I don't know what Dad would say," I tell her. It's now again. I know because my hand is still taped up. If not for that, I wouldn't.

My mother says, "I'm *trying*," as if apologizing. How to respond to that? I don't know. She doesn't know. Even Brad probably wouldn't know.

All of us trying, yet nobody knows.

# RAYMOND LUCZAK

## XPT556

On this overcast day in early March, a young woman with her long hair dyed a limp orange gets out of her car in the parking lot. She zips up her lime-green parka jacket and pulls on black gloves. Her boots have spiky heels that stab the crumbly slush on her path into a nondescript building with its dull brown metal siding punctuated with equally brown one-way windows. It's going to be another day at the Moore Relay Service.

In the cocoon of her cubicle, she is known as XPT556. She has been working as a video relay interpreter for six years straight out of college.

When she was younger, she loved the idea of a secret language where only she and her best friend Pammie Shelton knew. They learned the manual alphabet out of a library book, and they fingerspelled endlessly to each other. They were eight years old, and Pammie lived down the street. They traded books, CDs, and DVDs, and had many sleepovers at each other's house. Sometimes they borrowed each other's clothes.

Then she saw her first deaf person. He was a boy who lived with two older sisters and parents in the newly-built house across the street from her. She didn't know that the boy was different until she spotted the bulky earmolds in his ears. Up until that moment he was just another freckled boy with scruffy hair in a blue T-shirt and jeans. He seemed to be about the same age as her.

She was about to say something when her mother whispered sharply, "He's deaf. He doesn't talk at all." They were about to get into the car for the mall.

"Why not?"

The look on her mother's face made it clear that it was not a good question to ask. She wondered why. "Get in the car."

She saw his parents, but she never met them. The father, who wore expensively-tailored suits during the day and spotless polo shirts during the evening, was a corporate lawyer who moved his family around the country. The mother, who always wore a fashionable dress unlike most women her age, was a zealously cheerful PTA cheerleader. She saw how she tried to schmooze among her mother's friends at PTA-sponsored events. She was so clearly a phony that she was surprised no one had ever called her out on it.

Over the years the boy appeared infrequently like a ghost. He went to a deaf residential school so far downstate that he only came up for his winter and summer breaks. He didn't hang out with the neighborhood kids. It was always clear on his face that he preferred to be somewhere else.

His name was Robert McKinder. She loved the sound of his name.

Her first day as freshman at Linney High School was overwhelming. So many kids, and they all looked like they knew where they were going. But at least Pammie was with her. The two found their homeroom and sat next to each other. They recognized some of their classmates, but due to the consolidation of three high schools that had taken place over the summer, there were a lot of new faces.

She noticed a few people making signs in the hallways. She felt frustrated when she couldn't follow them. "Pammie, look," she said. "They know *real* sign language!"

That was how they found out their new school offered ASL as a foreign language. Those classes were offered to college-bound juniors and seniors only. She couldn't wait for her turn.

One weekend her parents had to leave her alone for a long weekend. They had legally complicated matters to resolve in the hometown where her father had grown up, and he did not get along very well with his many brothers and sisters. Of course, Pammie came over to keep her company.

That Saturday morning she had to feed the three koi fish in their backyard. She liked watching the bright orange-and-white fish dart right up to the pond's surface; she knew that many koi fish could recognize their human feeders. Some of them were willing to accept food directly from their hands; not her father's, though. It wasn't for the lack of trying, however.

When the koi zeroed on her and waited for her to toss peas and lettuce into the water, she felt a blush of pride. She was special enough to be recognized by fish! Who'd have thought of such a thing when it came to fish?

When hormones began raging through her veins, she cried at the sight of a few blackheads spreading across her forehead and giggled at the budding shape of her breasts. She dreamed about being in love with this or that guy in class.

By the time she celebrated her 16th birthday, she had her first boyfriend. She and Mike hung out with their friends in the back of McDonald's on the highway. Alone, they groped each other and tasted each other's tongue in the dark of his souped-up Corvette. Mike Clark was an okay varsity basketball player, but he was a great kisser. She loved the feel of his smooth shoulders when he took off his shirt. But she knew that no matter how much she wanted him, she wasn't ready to have sex with him. He had to wait.

They talked about getting married.

The names for their four kids. Two boys and two girls, alternating every other year.

The kind of house they'd buy.

The kind of high-paying job he would get. He wanted to be an auto mechanic. He worked on cars for his father's friends who were into collecting vintage cars.

Then six months later, Mike admitted to having fallen in love with someone else. He didn't say who.

Crushed, she sulked for days afterwards; she didn't want to talk to anyone at all. Not even Pammie. She moped when she walked the hallways between classes. Her parents had to bribe her with a used 50cc scooter that was repainted in pink just for her. She was apprehensive at first, but the minute she strapped on her matching-pink helmet and throttled her bike, she was off and running.

The barren spaciousness of countryside beyond the city appealed to her. It was nothing like the houses in her hilly neighborhood. The houses of her neighbors seemed perched together as if they were a flock of birds. Their backyards were big enough for koi ponds and gas barbecues. And there were a lot of fences.

Even though there were miles and miles of corn and wheat starting to grow, the countryside felt uncluttered. She felt as if she could scoot straight upward to the heavens and fly like the geese already flying north in their V formations for their summer breeding grounds.

Then Pammie got accidentally pregnant and had to put the baby up for adoption. That was how she learned that Pammie had been Mike's "mysterious new girlfriend" all along, and that he was the father. It was the first time in her life that she understood why people who loved each other dearly could turn against each other in a single flash. She vowed never to talk to Pammie ever again.

●

With Robert gone, she took to looking out for Pammie down the street and turning her face away whenever her ex-best friend happened to glance her way. Though she knew it was totally wrong of her to do so, she took a particular pleasure in watching Pammie's pregnancy transform her into a blimp.

Pammie had always been a slender girl, but impending motherhood seemed to add slabs of fat to her hips. A few months later, her size was startling.

She swore to herself that she'd never get pregnant. How could anyone look like that and still be attractive? Even Mike seemed to wince a bit when he leaned over to kiss her on the cheek in front of Pammie's house.

When she heard that Mike had left Pammie for someone else, she felt a huge load fall off her shoulders. By then Pammie had become an outcast who she used to know. No matter how hard Pammie tried, she couldn't seem to regain her previous figure. Pammie sat alone in the cafeteria.

It would be a few years before she ran into Pammie at the mall. "My God," Pammie said. "You look great, and I look like shit."

"Sorry. What?" She was surprised that she hadn't recognized her ex-best friend at first. She wore too much mascara, her flat hair looked stringy, and her winter coat looked like a bloated smock. Her own mind had been abuzz with the gifts she had to get for her parents. She was on her winter break from college.

"I deserved what I got after what I did to you."

They hugged and made promises to make it up to each other. But it wasn't the same. They had long discarded the ghost selves of their shared girlhood, and strangers had taken their places.

By the end of her first week of ASL classes in her junior year, she knew what she wanted to be: an ASL interpreter. She was fascinated by the style and beauty of her teacher's signing. She felt like an utter doofus when she tried to copy her smooth signing.

But she didn't know then that to learn ASL properly, one had to turn off her voice. Ms. Toni Smith, who was hearing, had managed to get hired at the high school even though she had only two years of ASL with some church interpreting experience and claimed to know a number of deaf people in the city. In class, Ms. Smith rarely admonished her students for using their voices while signing.

She wouldn't have known that a number of her students, thinking that they were fluent enough in ASL since Ms. Anderson had told them so, met with these deaf people only to find that they'd never thought well of Ms. Anderson's incorrectly-formed signs and found her presumptuous attitude deeply offensive. Eventually a few deaf people showed up at the principal's office and complained. Ms. Smith was fired, and a deaf instructor replaced her.

She didn't know then that many hearing administrators in high schools had often felt intimidated by the notion of sign language that they were too afraid to hire deaf instructors. The sound of a perfectly-modulated voice was always the song of relief after having used ASL interpreters in interviews, not to mention the unnecessary expense of having to hire them for meetings every now and then.

She didn't know then that ASL and English never mixed well, especially when using one's voice at the same time. Or that ASL didn't follow the syntax and grammar of English.

But who cared about such things at 16? She was in love with the way her hands could be so full of *meaning*.

Some days when she practiced her signing in front of the mirror, she imagined herself becoming translucent like an angel. Her wings would glitter like a mist of diamonds that fluttered majestically when she lifted herself upward. People were wrong when they said the Holy Bible was the Word of God. Right there in her hands was the truer Word of God. How could anyone *not* see that? By then she was taking her second year in ASL.

She wanted so much to be fluent enough to explain all these to Robert each time she saw him come and go. As much as she wanted to, she didn't dare cross the street to him. He had to hate hearing people. With such aloof parents, he had to!

She dreamed of appearing like a shimmering vision in his bedroom. Her hands would create perfectly sculpted signs to create a simple message of comfort and grace: "You may not believe it, but God is everywhere with you." He would smile and forgive her—and every hearing person—for everything.

The phone rings. She leans forward in her chair and press the ACCEPT button. Each time she does this is always a test. The stranger on the videophone will observe how she signs and fingerspells her interpreter ID number, and in a few seconds just how fluent she and whether the rhythms of her signing have been tainted by using Signing Exact English before learning ASL. She knows enough to wear solid colored tops for better contrast with her hands, and she always removes jangly earrings and flashy necklaces before she starts work.

She waits for the screen to reveal her first client of the day. She can see herself in the upper right corner of the screen. She looks good. Nearby are other interpreters in their own cubicles, talking with hearing callers into their headsets and signing to their deaf clients on the videophone. Sometimes, when a call is put on interminable hold, she puts up a privacy screen. She tends to do this when she doesn't want to have an off-the-record chat with the deaf client while waiting for the hearing caller to return to the phone. She hates it when a man wants to ask her out for dinner even though he has no idea which city she lives in. It's a huge no-no to share personal contact information.

Right before her appears a slender man in a white T-shirt and knee-worn jeans. He is sitting on one end of a low-slung sofa that looks like a cast-off artifact from the 1960s. Behind him is a hallway. His long hair is pulled back into a ponytail, and his sideburns are bushy. The floor lamp next to him emphasizes the paleness of his forearms. Tattoos on his biceps look like shadows that keep reappearing.

Right below the screen is his name and city: ROBERT MCKINDER from Marquette, MI.


After learning the rudimentary basics of ASL in high school, she couldn't wait for Robert McKinder to come home so she could practice her new skills. Every day she looked out the front windows of her house for a sign of him.

Then her father slipped on a patch of ice on the first day of her Christmas vacation. He had to be put in a body cast. His spinal cord was that out of whack. She had to get up early every morning after snowfall and operate the snowblower to clear the driveway.

One morning she caught sight of him snowblowing his parents's driveway. She walked across the street, took her gloves off, and signed with her voice, "Hi! I'm learning ASL. I think sign language is so cool! Can you understand me?"

He gave her a look that said, *You think you know ASL? Oh, please.*

She felt as if her knees would collapse. She hadn't expected such a rude response. She'd thought that all deaf people would be very happy to see a hearing person so interested in their language. After all, not enough people know ASL, right?

She didn't know then that deaf people were just like hearing people. They were like a big family filled with histories of feuds come and forgiven. That they still looked out for each other regardless was testimony to the tribal power of language inherent in their hands.

She blinked her eyes, not knowing what to do. Her tears began to trickle and freeze.

He took off his gloves and signed, "Sorry."

She lit up. "I know that one!" She didn't sign.

He mouthed along with his signs. "You same-same hearing people who want-want learn A-S-L. You think nothing fun signing cute-cute. Stop. D-o-n-t *don't* learn A-S-L with attitude a-t-t-i-t-u-d-e attitude. R-e-s-p-e-c-t where?"

She nodded meekly and didn't use her voice. "Sorry."

The rest of her Christmas break felt long and dreary with overcast skies. She still looked out the front windows but it wasn't with the same intensity as before.

She began borrowing books from the public library and reading up on the history of deaf people and their education. It was then she'd understood his anger. Hearing educators had literally tried to banish ASL because it wasn't a spoken language. She read horror stories of how they tied hands behind deaf children's backs in the mistaken belief that if they couldn't communicate with their hands, they'd learn to speak instead. Sometimes they struck their signing hands in the classroom with a sharp ruler, not realizing how much hatred they would inspire among those who felt liberated from the clarity of communication.

She felt worse than before and resolved to change her attitude when she returned to school a few days later.


In the safety of her cubicle, she searches the man's face to see if it was indeed the same boy she once knew. Nonetheless, she knows she has to stay cool, professional. She had worked very hard to earn her RID certification, but she knows she isn't skilled enough to interpret spoken poetry and stage play productions, the toughest of all to translate. She feels utterly hopeless when it comes to translating a poetic line like, "Stars are burning in the velvet blanket of my heart," into ASL. Should she sign "heart" first, then "same" "blanket black v-e-l-v-e-t" when the poet seems to mean the blanket as the same thing as a night sky? And how should she say "burning" when stars twinkled? But if she signed "burning," wouldn't the blanket burn as well? She liked the sound of that line, but she knew her limitations as an interpreter. She needed to study ASL interpreters far more skilled than her.

She signs, "Me number XPT556. Call who please?"

He signs, "E-v-e-l-y-n Evelyn."

"Call now." She presses the dial button and adjusts her headset.

As she waits for the mysterious Evelyn to pick up the receiver, she looks at him again. She wants to ask, "You before live where B-e-l-k-i-n Street around ten years ago?"

The phone rings. She counts the number of rings with her hand.

He nods in understanding.

She keeps trying not to stare at him. Is it truly him? Or was Robert

McKinder a name common enough? She had thought that her name was unique enough until she googled herself one day and found to her dismay that there were four other women with her name living in the same city.

The phone picks up on the fifth ring. "Hello." A woman's voice. She can't quite place her age.

"Is this Evelyn?"

"Yes. Who's this?"

"Hi. This is XPT556 calling from Moore Relay Service. Have you used video relay service before?"

"Yes. Is this Bob?"

She looks at him and voices his signs as he gives a hesitant smile. "Yes. That's me, the one and only."

"Oh, good. I was starting to worry when you didn't call me back yesterday." She translates Evelyn into: "Good. Me worry you-call-me not yesterday." She know it's not ASL enough, but he seems to be following her.

"A lot's been going on in my life. Okay?" She knows her proper English translation pales to his rangy ASL, which is so full of emotion, colored with apology and rage.


After high school she moved to Monmouth, Oregon for a collegiate four-year program in ASL interpreting.

She learned how to remember what she'd just heard so she could repeat in signs. It wasn't easy at first. She froze the first few times. The fear of being judged critically had paralyzed her, but when she saw how others still fingerspelled clumsily when she kept her fingerspelling hand in the same spot, she knew she had an advantage.

She thought of dating a deaf man. There weren't any deaf students at her college, which was odd given that there were so many ASL interpreting students. Most deaf people lived an hour's drive away in Portland, and they rarely came down to Monmouth.

Every Friday night she joined some of her classmates at a coffeehouse in Portland where deaf people socialized. She sat quietly on the sidelines and watched. She wanted to tell her friends to *stop* using their voices with their hands, but she didn't want to be a spoilsport.

She lit on a man who looked to be in his mid-20s. He looked like a former football coach, and his hands were full of vigor. He wore a baseball cap and a light jacket. He looked like he was talking about bowling with an older buddy of his, but she wasn't sure.

Then he caught sight of her gawking. His face said, *What are you looking at?*

She blushed and turned away. When she finally gathered up enough nerve to look his way, he'd shifted his shoulders away to block her view of his signing.

"Bob? Bob? Hello?"

Evelyn's voice snaps her out of her reverie. "Sorry," she says. "Can you repeat that, please?"

"Bob, you're not the only one with problems. Everybody's got problems." She translates that to: "You think you only-one problem-problem? Everyone-out-there same you."

"You're calling about Dad, right?"

"He's back in the hospital again. The doctor says he doesn't have long to live. Your father wants to see you."

In that moment she realizes that Evelyn is Robert's mother. She wonders if Ms. McKinder is still wearing stylish dresses at her age, or if she looks something like Barbara Bush, all jowly with pearls.

"Never. And you want to know why? You never learned my language. You expect me to come home immediately whenever Dad gets sick, but do you come here when I get sick? No. You just don't want to use your hands because it's too much work. Have you ever thought about how much work it takes me to make my speech clear enough for you?"

"Bob. I'm too old to learn sign language. I've got arthritis in my hands."

"You're so good with your excuses I'm surprised you haven't won an Oscar."

"Please. Your father has a few days left to live, so please come down here and say goodbye to him."

He stares at the interpreter a moment. "So? I'm not coming."

"Why the hell not?"

"Why should I come home if you never listened to me in the first place?"

She is relieved when Evelyn doesn't respond right away. She catches the sound of tears welling up in her throat.

In the summer between her junior and senior years the McKinders put their house up for sale. The red-and-white sign with its phone number and house ID number gleamed in the sun. It was a matter of weeks before the sign was plasted with the word SOLD. She didn't see him or his parents again.

She wondered for a long time where he'd gone. She compared every deaf person she met against Robert, and saw how different and unique each deaf person was. They didn't sign nor speak the same way. It took her a long time to differentiate the many regional dialects used among ASL users, and that's where being a video relay interpreter helped. Callers from all over the country used signs she'd never seen before. She had to learn them quickly.

After graduating from college and returning home, she dreamed of accidentally bumping into Robert, now a full-grown man, and showing him how fluent she was in his language. She wouldn't hold herself high and mighty like some of her friends in college had. She wouldn't be flashy with her signs so he'd know that she was respectful of his language. She'd be accepted into the deaf community.

The sound of Evelyn's blowing her nose in a tissue awakens her from her daydream. "Sorry. I needed to clear up my nose. You still there, Bob?"

"Yes." He looks warily at the interpreter.

"What I want to know is why you moved to Marquette. There are no jobs up there. Why do you have to make it so hard on yourself by moving *so* far away from us?"

He rolls his eyes. "You still don't get it?" He inhales. "You know what? I'm *still* not coming to the hospital or his funeral. You two are not my real family. You never learned ASL, therefore that means you never wanted me, period. Stop wasting my time. Goodbye." He makes the sign for "phone hang-up finish."

"Wait—"

"Want phone hang-up anyway?" She asks him.

"Yes."

"I'm sorry, but he's hung up already." She speaks to Evelyn and signs to him.

"Can't you call him back? Right now?"

"You'll need to dial from your own phone. I'm sorry."

She hangs up and looks at him. "True-biz sorry you-two parents problem. Hope situation dissolve soon."

He shook his head. "Doubt-doubt. Thank-you interpret-interpret."

"Welcome." She glances back through the gap of her cubicle to see if her supervisor is monitoring her. "Quick question. You before live B-e-l-k-i-n Street?"

"Yes. Why? Who you?"

"Me before live across street your house."

His face lights up. "Wow-wow. You same girl who mangled-mouth signs?"

She smiles. "Yes. Me think improve some."

"Wow." He applauds. "Me proud you. Deaf people nitpick you signing, but you suffer-suffer pah. Me proud you."

"Thank-you." She hears a peculiar warning sound. Interpreters are not supposed to chat long after each call. "Sorry, but hang-up must. Supervisor watch will. Bye."

"Wait!—"

The screen turns black and opens up again, this time to an overweight woman with a squalling baby on her lap. The glare of a fluorescent light glares at her from the left. Not ideal lighting, but she's seen worse. She signs, "Me number XPT556. Call who please?"

Later that night she dreams of shimmering like a fiery koi fish pushing upstream inside the telephone lines from her home to his place in Marquette, Michigan. Her hands would be full of sparkling electricity, and he would tell her stories he'd never tell another hearing person. And she'd tell him how he had saved her at a time of dark reckoning. No longer XPT556, she would become a real human being with a first, middle, and last name, and with a history worth learning, and he would remember her as much as she had remembered him.

# ROBERT SIEBERT

## Chocolate Chip

Johnny lay sprawled on the couch, his eyes fixated on the television screen. It was blank, lifeless, but he still stared. Empty beer bottles littered the coffee table. It was late and his roommates had long retired.

He was in the living room of his dorm room. He lived with his friends in a suite; there were two separate bedrooms with two beds each, a bathroom, and the living room. Johnny and his suitemates arranged it so more friends lived next door as well. Throughout the year, the two adjacent suites' doors were propped open by football-sized stones with smiley faces painted on them. "Keep your door open!" the stones said, the two o's of the word "door" doubling as the wide, happy eyes of the smiley face. Johnny and his friends roamed in and out of the two suites, and it felt to Johnny as if he had seven roommates instead of three.

He usually had the television turned to SportsCenter or a late-night sitcom, but tonight he wanted to think. It was the first week of April, and in a month he would be graduating. Graduating meant that he'd have to leave the familiarity of his dorm room. It meant he'd no longer have seven roommates, and no more coffee tables topped off with empty alcoholic-beverage containers. It meant the real world loomed. As Johnny stared at the pitch-black television screen, he couldn't shake his feelings of apprehension.

Beer was like Nyquil to Johnny. The soft buzz it induced in his head led to the swoon of sleep. The dip had helped him stay awake long enough to dwell upon his lack of post-graduation plans, but the effects had started to subside.

When Johnny was little, you could always find him hanging around the family kitchen. His mother, who had a full-time job teaching at a college, was never a culinary whiz. That hardly mattered to Johnny, as long as his mom let him do some stuff around the kitchen. He especially liked it when his mom made chocolate chip cookies. The recipe was nothing special (his mom used the one on the bag); his main responsibility was to mix in the flour and sugar. He didn't care much for licking the spoon clean. What he really liked about the chocolate chip creation process was when they were in the oven. He would flick the oven light on, despite his mother's weak protests, and stare at each batch until they turned golden brown. His absolute favorite part, the very reason he liked making chocolate chip cookies, was the melting of the semi-sweet morsels into the cookie dough. The chips came into the oven hard, sticking out of the dough like they didn't belong. Then they warmed up, shimmering as they liquefied, and fused with the rest of the cookie.

As Johnny lay on the couch, he could feel the boundary that separated his body and the worn-down cushions of the couch melting away. Exhaustion and sleep overcame his mind, his consciousness lost focus, and he felt like a chocolate chip sinking into the dough of the aged couch.

Just when he was about to wrest his last fingers from the grip of reality, the door crashed open and Dan burst into the room. Dan, one of Johnny's friends living next door, was holding an empty bottle of Moscato Barefoot wine.

Johnny struggled to remember if it was just fifteen minutes before that he'd seen Dan uncork a bottle of Barefoot. Was it a couple hours ago? Or was it the other day?

It didn't matter. But now that Dan was here, Johnny's body was split from the couch.

Dan set the empty bottle down among the various beer bottles on the coffee table and plopped on the chair opposite Johnny. Johnny stared straight at the ceiling, his hair in his eyes.

Dan broke the silence, as he was apt to do. Silence seemed to unnerve him. He had grown up as the only deaf child in a hearing family. American Sign Language was his primary language, and he was incredibly fluent. Although his parents and siblings made remarkable efforts in acquiring ASL, they could only offer Dan minimal stimulation. So Dan grabbed it elsewhere: his friends at the deaf school, social media websites, his school's sports teams. He stuffed the air around him with conversation, endlessly trying to fill in the gaps left from his childhood.

"Kodiak again?" Dan said. The hockey puck-sized container lay next to the empty Barefoot. "Dude, you know that stuff's gonna give you gum cancer. Remember the pictures I showed you last week?"

Johnny did remember the pictures. Nasty stuff, people with teeth sticking out of skull-like grins, people with entire lips cleaved off. But he couldn't help it. A couple Sierra Nevada Torpedoes and a good 15-minute dip, and his mind spun like a top as his body dissolved into whatever structure it was on.

"But dude, isn't beer enough? Those Torpedos, they've got 7, 8 percent. Three or four, and you're set!" Dan glanced at his empty Barefoot. "I think I'm an alcoholic."

"Ya think? Man, you *know* you're an alcoholic. You finished that bottle in fifteen minutes! A whole bottle of wine! Who does that?"

"Whatever. I'm going to my room to finish off the cookie. You want a piece?"

"Sure."

The cookie, infused with tetrahydrocannabinol, worked marvelously. Dan bought it some time ago from an off-campus dealer, a deaf Gallaudet dropout-turned-street-dealer. The dealer had a special for edibles, and the news spread through the grapevine. At first, Dan and Johnny planned to split a cookie, taking half each for one night.

But then they heard firsthand from a friend who'd eaten half of the same kind of cookie. Within fifteen minutes, the friend went ghostly pale. He could barely keep his thoughts in order. He sat there slack-jawed, staring into space, his hands scratching his knees nonstop. His friends escorted him back to his bedroom, where he stared at the ceiling and imagined entire battles being fought in the air by enemy dust motes that floated in the lamplight.

So Dan and Johnny each took a thumb-sized piece, and headed into bliss with just the right amount of trippiness. One by one, they took bits and pieces from the cookie, and it dwindled down to the last pieces. Enough for three remained in the plastic bag. They took one portion each, chewed it thoroughly, and licked their teeth clean to make sure every last crumb went down their gullets.

"So who gets the last piece?" Dan asked.

"I don't know. You can have it."

"It wouldn't be fair."

"I don't care, I don't want to talk about it now."

"All right. Later then."

Johnny flicked off the fluorescent ceiling light and Dan clicked on the IKEA floor lamp. The floor lamp had five lights, and Johnny had put in five different-colored bulbs. Red, blue, green, orange, and purple lights shadowed the ceiling in a murky rainbow. The lamp started slowly, but built and built until it reached maximum flow. The multitude of lights flooding the ceiling evoked Johnny's childhood memories of kaleidoscopes. Dan and Johnny sank into their seats, in chocolate chip manner, and waited for their digestive systems to kick-start the sensation.

And the sensation did come, growing as the lamplight grew.

"Something's been bothering me," Dan said. Johnny grunted in response.

"We're men," Dan said. Johnny took his eyes off the orange-green fragment of light, which reminded him of the Fruit by the Foot snacks his mother always packed in his lunch box as a kid, to stare at Dan.

"Are we, now?"

"Yes. But that's not the point. As men, we'll never get to experience the act of giving birth."

"That bothers you?"

"Yes! Think about it! We'll never know what it feels like, to house the creation of a human being in our tummies. The pain and joy of pushing a baby out of our very bodies."

It was a good point, Johnny begrudgingly admitted to himself.

Johnny was an explorer at heart. He wished to pack into his traveling backpack every sensation, view, and flavor the world offered. He had taken his backpack to Eastern Europe, Egypt, Morocco, Central America, and ten countries in southeast Asia. But Dan brought another type of exploration to his attention. A type of exploration that required neither planes nor backpacks, but the organs of a female human being. Something that both Dan and Johnny lacked. The act of giving birth equated a venture into the sacred origin of human life. A venture denied to each and every male.

The subject of exploration pulled Johnny back to the topic of his graduating. Graduation also brought forth the expectation of a full-time job, and that meant no more summers of travel to look forward to. Johnny's brain filled with melancholy.

"Dammit. You're ruining the flow," Johnny said.

"Feeling it, huh?" Dan chuckled. "Hey, what about that last piece?"

"Don't care." Johnny floated, his line of sight diving into the purple blotch on the ceiling and resurfacing on a beach. He swayed as the ebb and flow of the ocean took him farther and farther into the horizon. His body melted, once again, into the couch.

Just then, a short, barrel-chested dude strolled into the room.

Dan sprang out of his seat. "Joe!" he said, walking right past him and out of the room.

"Well. Nice way of welcoming an old friend, eh?" Joe said.

"Don't mind him. Dan's just being Dan. How ya been? Didn't know you were coming into town." Johnny picked himself off the couch to embrace Joe.

"Ah, figured I'd surprise the boys."

Joe was quite the character. When he was born, he was thought to be retarded. He didn't sign his first word until his fifth year of life. He fought through bullies in his childhood, and grew up to be an intelligent individual, however odd he was. He now had an extensive vocabulary, and a unique style of articulation. He fingerspelled rather excessively and rarely utilized non-manual markers, but made up for it in the intensity of his expression. Some called it an accent, but Johnny and his friends called it Weberism, after Joe's surname.

Joe compensated for his lack of athleticism and for his social awkwardness by investing heavily into his passion for the cinema. He had a 2,000-movie collection at home, and added to it with the new releases each week. He dreamed of becoming a screenwriter, and eventually directing his own movies. But at the moment, Joe worked as a teacher aide at the deaf school in Minnesota.

Dan burst back in the room, grabbed Joe, and lowered him into a recliner.

"Open your mouth," Dan said. Joe obliged, and Dan stuffed the final piece of the cookie in his mouth. "There! Now we won't have to argue over who gets the last piece."

"I said I didn't care," Johnny said.

"I suppose that was no ordinary cookie," Joe said.

"Obviously not."

"That wasn't a very big piece."

"Big enough to set me and Johnny off," Dan said.

A smug smile crossed Joe's face. "I hit the bong daily. Sometimes two or three bowls a night. What you gave me won't last me but fifteen minutes."

Joe Weber had a far higher opinion of himself than his peers thought of him. He was an underdog, indeed, but a rare one: he was a rather unlikable underdog. Johnny and Dan liked him, if only because of his unpredictable personality, and also because Joe reciprocated their affection.

"So how's life outta college?" Dan said.

"Aw man, you're gonna ask about the real world already?" Johnny asked.

"That's okay, I don't mind. You're aware that I've been working at the Minnesota State Academy for the Deaf, as a teacher aide? Now, before you groan and make fun of my job, it has its benefits. Ohho, it certainly does."

"You sure you're not saying that to make yourself feel better?" Johnny said.

"Yes. I'm a babe magnet now! You know how many girls I've fucked in my life? Seven. Five of them in the last two months. All of them since I started the job. The women at school love me. This job is the ultimate confidence booster."

"But you're working as a teacher aide! You're banging other teacher aides! How old are they, forty, fifty?" Johnny said, harking back to his elementary school days.

"No!" Joe was indignant. "The ladies I work with have the three V's."

"The three V's?" Dan asked.

"Say what?" Johnny piped in.

"Vivid, vivacious, voluptuous!"

Johnny knew better than to ask, but he asked anyway. "Where'd you come up with that?"

Joe smiled his smug smile and tapped his head with his index finger. *In here, my boy*, he seemed to be saying.

Joe went on that he'd arrived a couple days ago, and had spent all his time on campus catching up with his old buddies. "Sure miss the Clerc 807 bathroom. Find me a better vent anywhere on campus, and I'll supply ya with a nice full bowl." He also met up with his old chemistry professor, who said that Joe was wasting his time as a teacher aide after getting his Bachelors in Chemistry. "I would have told him about all the ladies and their three V's, but he's at least sixty. Figured I'd save him his innocence and a couple years of his life." He talked about heading up to New York City to meet up with a woman he met a month ago. "You couldn't exactly call us 'something,' but I'm gonna be staying in her apartment, and it'll be just us, you know?"

As he talked, Dan sank into his seat opposite the recliner, his head dipping below the head of the love seat cushion. Johnny was spread out on the couch, lying on his side, head propped up on the pillow, taking in Joe's story from a couple feet away. There was nothing like listening to a good talker while your mind was melting, submitting to the effects of the cookie.

"And then yesterday, when at the Clerc 807 hotbox, Jenny came in." Johnny and Dan shifted in their seats. Jenny was an old obsession of Joe's. Or maybe it was the other way around. Either way, they had a little fling that never really took off. It turned into a nasty situation, with the two taking turns leading the other on. It didn't end well, and Johnny and Dan hesitated, reluctant to listen to another Joe and Jenny story.

"Yeah? What happened?" Johnny forced himself to ask.

"She just came in and took a seat a couple feet from me. She was right in my face. She didn't acknowledge me, but kept stealing glances in my direction. What, did she think I wouldn't notice? She was right in front of me!"

"Sheesh." Johnny shook his head on the cushion.

"And then she said 'Wow, Joe Weber is here' to some other girl. Two feet away from my face!"

"Damn. What's her problem?" Dan asked, joining Johnny in the headshaking.

"I have no idea. But you know what?"

"What?" Johnny asked with feigned interest. Dan stared at the poster just above Joe's head, then got up to leave. Joe took no notice.

"I'm a changed man. No more. I'm not going to take that kind of shit anymore. People like Jenny, Trey, and all the others—they're gonna eat crow someday when they see what kind of man I've become."

"Trey? Didn't he graduate a couple years ago?"

"He was a year above me in grade school. He rubbed my face in dirt, kicked my shins, and made fun of me every time I stuttered. Called me Porky Pig."

"That's all, folks!" Johnny mused. "Why do you care so much about what they think anyway? Just let it go, go on your own way, and you'll have your vindication that way."

"Let's face it. I'm a walking idiosyncrasy. I never have, and never will fit people's vision of an ideal man. But I'm succeeding now, and I'm full of confidence. I'm a changed man. I want nothing more than just being able to take all those people and make them feel like shit for what they've done to me."

Johnny lay there for a while pondering. He hadn't yet set foot in the real world. The challenges it posed, the transformative process reality bestowed upon the individual, he wasn't familiar with. He knew for sure, though, that Joe needed to rid himself of the anger he held.

Dan came back into the room, his lips clamped shut.

"Dan, Joe here is bent on vengeance. He wants revenge on every person who'd wronged him since grade school. Tell him that's no way to live."

"It's not," Dan confirmed without a thought.

"Guys, I appreciate your input. But my mind is set on this subject. It's final. I am superior to the people that have wronged me in the past, and I am ready to rub my success in their faces."

Johnny's sideways view of Joe was a bit funny. Joe had lost lots of weight—he said he'd lost thirty. His body used to be shaped like a beer barrel with four stubby limbs and a chubby head sticking out. Now his chest had some 'v' in it. It was rather impressive, the transformation Joe had gone through. He slimmed down, gained confidence, and now was (or so he said) a regular womanizer. But, and Johnny had worked through his hazy mind to gain this clear conclusion, Joe had to go on living for his own sake, not to show up others.

Johnny, stretched out on the couch like a dog enjoying a thorough rubbing on it belly, his head still on the cushion, told Joe what he thought.

"Okay. Still not changing my mind. In fact, I think I am superior to you and Dan. So there." He said with an expression that was more a sneer than a smile.

"I don't have a problem with that," Johnny replied.

"Me neither." Dan still seemed to be staring at the poster behind Joe.

Johnny gave up trying to focus after that, figuring Joe'd used up the last of his goodwill with that last comment. He retreated into his consciousness, and imagined the familiar heat of his childhood oven as he sank into the couch, a chocolate chip once again.

After a few more anecdotes about the women he'd seduced, Joe said goodbye and left.

Johnny lay on the couch as Dan continued to stare at the poster.

"What's with you and that poster?"

"I can't figure out if that thing in the upper left corner is a lion or a nine-tailed snake."

Johnny sighed. "Joe sure looks good."

"That's what the real world does to you."

"Got a lot of confidence too."

"The real world."

"And five women in the last year? Who would have thought old Joe could be such a player?"

"Strange things happen in the real world."

"Dammit, Dan. Is that all you've got to say? Man, Joe was hellbent on revenge, and that ain't healthy. Why didn't you speak up?"

"It wouldn't have mattered what I said. Didn't you listen to him? Joe's in the real world. It ain't pretty out there. Ya think he loves being a teacher aide? Come on, five women in a couple months? And you think he exercised to lose all that weight? Could've easily been something else. You and I, we're just college students. We aren't qualified to comment. All we can do is be there and listen."

"Is that what you were thinking all that time? That's deep."

"Yeah, while I was looking at the lion-slash-snake. I really think it's a snake." Dan talked weird now, his mouth stiff, as if filled to the brim with liquid. Johnny lifted his right eyebrow.

"Dan, is that tobacco in your mouth?"

"I couldn't resist," Dan said, chuckling and spilling tobacco juice over his bottom lip. He drew out the tin of tobacco and dropped it among the disorderly ranks of glass bottles on the coffee table, then covered his mouth as he stumbled out of the room, knocking the smiley-face stone from under the door. The door swung shut, leaving Johnny all alone in the living room.

Johnny sat up on the couch. Acute clarity replaced the hazy sensation that filled his mind. In less than a month, he would be *graduating*. He could relax, roll with the punches, and settle for a job as a teacher aide at a deaf school like Joe. Melt into the cookie like a chocolate chip in the oven and become just like another everyday person. Melt into the cookie, like he'd been doing practically every day since he enrolled into college—a chocolate chip warmed by beer, tobacco, or whatever substance was at hand.

But he thought of Joe. Joe, who had melted into his own cookie and wallowed within its sugary confines. He never mentioned his passion for the cinema in their conversation, had not even discussed his opinion on a single movie. In such a short time, he turned bitter and angry. All he had to show for his effort in the real world was a vengeful streak.

Johnny looked back to his childhood days spent in front of the oven. He'd always thought that the process was mutual, that the chips and dough combined willingly. But he saw it differently now. The dough, making up the vast majority of the cookie, absorbed the chips as they melted. The chips had no choice but to submit to the heat of the oven and fuse with the dough. It was an act of submission.

Johnny stared at the blank television screen until it seemed to stare back at him. His future was as blank as the screen in front of him. And then Johnny looked down at the coffee table. He could barely see the light yellow of the wood laminate under the thick forest of bottles.

His hand wandered out to the table, weaving in and out among the bottles. Finally Johnny found what he was looking for: The tobacco tin. He picked it up and looked at it for a while. With a flick of his wrist, the tin was off, flying, headed for the bare bottom of the wastebasket at the foot of the five-colored lamp.

# MICHAEL UNIACKE

## This Incontestable Superiority

Liverpool, Great Britain, November 1880

"Mr Archer. Sir! Boss wants yer!" These words from young Joey, the copy boy with permanently inky fingers, were my summons from Mr Harry Cruikshank, and immediately aroused in me interest and apprehension. Mr Cruikshank was the editor of the respected London newspaper, *The Globe*, and normally he would have little reason for dealings with a junior journalist such as I. He preferred the company of senior writers such as McKenzie or Smithers. However by nature I am confident, and I strongly believed I had given the paper cause for complaint about neither my work nor my conduct. Indeed, surely the very opposite was justified! Had I not recently succeeded, where many others had failed, in uncovering the real story of the collapse of the Seven Seas Shipping Company, which occasioned much consternation among the City financiers? So, with a jaunty air I made my way to Mr Cruikshank's office, and outside his door paused for some moments. I straightened my tie, brushed the shoulders of my suit-coat, and rapped smartly on his office door. Thus began the stirring tale of my first trip to the Continent, which alas led to my fall from grace and consequent banishment to this seaport of Liverpool. But of this I of course knew nothing as I heard Mr Cruikshank's muffled "come in," and entered.

I spotted Mr Cruikshank immediately at his desk, amid piles of newspapers and clouds of blue tobacco smoke. To my considerable surprise I recognised another gentleman, a portly, imposing figure standing beside Mr Cruikshank's desk. It was Sir Henry Rashmore, the famous shipping magnate! A wealthy philanthropist, he was a man of great influence and was well-known in London's financial and industrial circles, and was a part-owner of this very newspaper. Such exalted company was usually denied me, but following the most cordial of introductions, as I settled in the leather visitor's chair at the urgings of both, I fancy I felt my confidence justified, for Mr Cruikshank's bewhiskered visage beamed at me. He sucked on his pipe, expelled a great volume of blue smoke, and cleared his throat.

"Mr Archer," he said, "am I mistaken in my belief you are conversant with the Italian language?" I kept my wits about me, because Sir Henry, with arms folded, peered at me intently.

"*Si signore, certamente conosco qualche Italiano,*" I replied jauntily. "I do know a little Italian, sir. My grandmother hails from Naples, where she lived until she met my grandfather, an English sailor."

Mr Cruikshank and Sir Henry exchanged glances. "He will do, Cruikshank," said the latter, and with that mysterious remark, took his leave. I stared after him, and my face must have registered bewilderment, for Mr Cruikshank explained.

"Sir Henry was impressed with your Seven Seas story, and he does not hand out compliments lightly. Anyway, I'm sending you to Italy. To Milan."

"*Milano,*" I exclaimed. What a delight this was! What was the story? Whom would I interview? Mr Cruikshank's next question to me was completely unexpected. "Do you know any deaf-mutes?" For a brief moment all was confusion as I digested the thoughts of a sojourn to the Continent amid deaf-mutes. Was I to interview a deaf-mute? How was I to communicate with him? However I quickly recovered my senses.

"No sir," I replied. "The grandmother I mentioned occasionally makes use of an ear trumpet, but of course she speaks. In fact she speaks only too well."

Mr Cruikshank grinned. He sucked on his pipe, but kept his eyes on me. "There's a chance we'll soon be hearing a lot more from the deaf-mutes themselves. The deaf can be taught to speak. Some new method of instruction. I'm sending you to Milan to cover a conference of educators of deaf-mutes. You'll write a story about the conference. Describe the method and get a few interviews."

There was indeed a rush of thoughts to my head as I absorbed this good news. I was going to Milan! And because of this new method of instruction, the deaf could speak! This was another exciting development of our age, and how doubly glad I was that I chose journalism as a profession, rather than law, with its fusty volumes, or medicine, with its cold, grey cadavers and interminable beakers and test tubes. As a journalist I would be the first on the scene in this golden age of discovery and development, reporting to all the world in my solid, concise yet fluent prose. Why, I fancied I could see the opening lines of my splendid report:

NEW INSTRUCTION METHOD TO ENABLE DEAF-MUTES TO SPEAK
By David Archer

MILAN, ITALY, TUESDAY. A conference of educators of deaf-mutes in Milan today resolved to speedily implement a new method of instruction ...

Such was the keenness of my mind that it has taken me several minutes to inscribe these words telling of my very thoughts, yet these perchance took mere half-seconds, and Mr Cruikshank broke in on them just as I was pondering the split infinitive in the first sentence of my report.

"There's apparently some opposition," he said.

I was aghast. From whom? Surely not Blakely, that odious *poseur* who once thought a Proper Noun was a village in Warwickshire? Or was it to sending me to foreign shores? The paper had been losing staff, and I was indeed surprised that a foreign assignment could still be afforded. But of the paper's parlous finances, much was rumoured and little was said, and I could hardly expect Mr Cruikshank to reveal the intimate workings of the company to a junior such as I.

It was then that I realised my editor was referring to this conference. "To the new instruction method? But how could there be?"

"Some advocates of the deaf say instruction should be in the manner of the language of signs."

"But our world demands speech," I cried. "Speech is essential for ordinary commerce. Why, sir, the idea is so obvious. And if this new method ensures the deaf can speak, then surely the advocates support it fully."

"They don't, apparently. Be sure to find out why."

"Oh yes, that I must," I assured Mr Cruikshank. A journalist must report all sides of a debate, without fear or favour. I would certainly report the views of these advocates, but even so, looking at it with such fairness and objectiveness as I could muster, how could anyone oppose a way to bring the deaf into communion with their hearing fellows? At least it added an interesting piquancy to this journey of mine, my first beyond the shores of Britain.

Mr Cruikshank informed me of the practical details of the assignment. *The Globe* has a writer on European affairs, a Mr Romano, who would be travelling north from Rome on another assignment. Mr Cruikshank said he would delay Mr Romano's assignment so he could spare a day or two to assist me in Milan.

"I said assist you, not nurse you," he said, but the bushy thickets of his eyebrows rose, and there was a twinkle in his eye. He leaned back in his chair. "Mr Romano is of course familiar with European ways, and he shall be instructed to keep an eye on you and to help where necessary. But you are a fast learner and I should be surprised if you keep him busy. And we can only spare him for a couple of days." He shuffled some papers on his desk, put them in a folder, and checked his pipe. I watched as he inserted a metal probe into the bowl, before he looked to me again. He tilted back in his chair, and I wondered if the day would come when he tipped the chair too far, creating an unexpected vacancy in the editorial department, thus entertaining for me the possibility of a promotion.

"Any questions, young man?"

"About Sir Henry," I enquired, "does he have an interest in this?"

"He does have a deaf daughter. She's a sweet young thing. So to that extent, yes, he has an interest. And a very natural interest, if I may say so." He straightened his chair, shuffled more papers, and I realised the interview was concluding. "Wilson in Accounts will see to your bookings and itinerary. We don't have a lot to spare, so watch the pennies. We expect a good story from you."

"That you may, and that you will get, sir," I grinned, and took my leave.


Soon I was aboard a train speeding south through France enroute to the city of Milan, in Italy! When one is a young man, one's hopes are new and fresh, and weighed down by neither domestic cares nor financial encumbrances, one sallies forth into the world, eager to make one's mark. Certainly I took this assignment seriously, but there was a small voice in my mind that suggested I could be excused for thinking it a pleasant working holiday. Mr Cruikshank granted me five days leave of absence after I filed my report, and I determined I should see a little of the Continent, but not much, alas! I dearly wanted to visit the seaport of Naples, my grandmother's home town, for my story on the Seven Seas Shipping Company perhaps stirred some maritime longing in my blood. Of money matters I was thrifty, but my grandmother was needy and depended on my support. I had little to spare, and my expenditures had risen considerably with the neccessity of engaging a nurse for her during my absence. My grandmother cared for me when I was a child, but was left impecunious by my wastrel of a grandfather who cared more for rum and gambling. At the very least, I planned to secure some cheap lodgings near Milan, and by careful enquiry, indulge in a walking tour of a suitable local district, perhaps some vineyards, perhaps one of the northern lakes, such as Como or Maggiore, or even, if finances permitted, a quick trip south to Genoa. This would be my reward, and was one of the things that gave me much to contemplate as my train sped southwards.

Of course, I did not neglect my professional duties! I reviewed the debate on the issues of the education of the deaf-mutes, for the first duty of the interviewer is to acquaint himself intimately with the subject under discourse. I managed to tear my eyes from the sights of the green French meadows and the charming *petites villages* at which the train would halt for a few minutes, and I bowed my head to study the pamphlets and writings of those experts in the education of the deaf who were riven by a fierce controversy. Many educators favoured speech as the prime method of instruction, and believed that with diligence and patience, the deaf could be taught to enunciate. These were called the oralists. On the other hand (Ha! Good pun that!) the deaf advocates maintained that signs were the deaf-mute's natural mode of expression, and therefore, this should be preserved and encouraged. With some vigour they argued that signs gave the deaf all they needed in order to learn about the world, and that to them, speech was artificial, and efforts expended on learning to speak would be better expended on education itself. The oralists' arguments however were many, and to my enquiring mind, the more convincing. Signs were unnatural; signs lacked connection with thought and feeling; signs could not convey abstract thought; signs lacked the precision of speech; speech was what distinguished us from the animals, and signs excluded the deaf from speech which was the common heritage of all mankind. But of course; I felt this was all so doubtlessly true that there scarce appeared cause for argument. Perhaps DEAF-MUTES WIN GIFT OF SPEECH would make a splendid headline for my report!

I believed I was adept at languages, and wondered if this was behind my selection for this assignment, which after all, was about language. I knew a good deal of Italian, I was handy at French, and my profession naturally demanded skills in language. I even went so far as to speculate that this assignment was a test to see if I would make a proficient reporter of European affairs, like Mr Romano.

With much excitement and a growing sense of purpose I disembarked at the central railway station of Milan shortly after midday. The early autumn air was most agreeable, and the open four-wheel cab that took me to my hotel, the *Pozzo*, afforded me a view of the purposeful bustle of the modern Italian city. After unpacking, I had ample time for a promenade of the city environs, for I had digested the written material of the controversy, and this was an ideal way to relax prior to meeting and talking to some of the delegates. The hotel *concierge* recommended some of the sights, and thus I passed a pleasant interlude, strolling through the market and along the bustling lanes, and gazing at the magnificent Gothic splendour of the *Duomo,* and the *Palazzo Marino.*

It was approaching darkness when, famished and not a little weary, I returned to the *Pozzo*. I was shortly due to meet my colleague, Mr Romano, and I contemplated indulging in the Italian custom of a glass of wine before the evening meal. As I passed through the lobby, the *concierge* caught my attention. He gave me some papers, a monograph, that he explained were being made available to the delegates, and said that most of them had arrived. This was ideal. Such important papers would certainly make for some useful reading over a glass while I waited for Mr Romano. I proceeded to the dining room doors, pushed them open, and was overcome with confusion.

I thought I had entered a seminary. Everywhere I looked there were gentlemen in black and dark brown robes, with clerical collars and other ecclesiastical raiment. However this mass of priests and preachers made for a jovial gathering, and I soon discerned other assorted gentlemen who sat with the clerics at tables crowded with papers, bottles and glasses. Among the hubbub of many animated and spirited debates I recognised Italian and some French, interspersed by bouts of laughter. From their bright outlook and cheerful demeanour, a bystander could be excused for assuming here was a group commencing a roistering tour of the Continent. Imagine the look of surprise on his face were he to be informed they were attending deliberations upon such important and wide-ranging matters!

I ordered a glass of red wine, and settled down at one of the few vacant tables remaining. I was gazing at the assemblage when a short, barrel-chested gentleman came and introduced himself. This was Mr Romano! I enjoyed a convivial discussion with my colleague, who took considerable interest in my assignment, and listened attentively to my story thus far. He helped me a little with the monograph. It was in French, my knowledge of which was good, but inferior to Mr Romano's. He read it for some minutes, looked at me and grinned.

"You are right—it is written by the director of a French school for the deaf, a M. Magnat," he said. He gazed at it again for some moments, and looked at me, puzzled.

"What is the purpose of this congress? You told me it is to consider a new method of instruction for the deaf-mute?" I said it was. "Well, I do not understand," he continued. "This document is, how do I say, is not of even temper. It does not inform. In Italian I can say it better. This paper, I think, is using a large hammer in order to crack a *pistachio*."

He gave me some words of advice; I had not asked for advice, but I realised it must have been perhaps a part of his brief, and his soothing and reassuring air meant I did not take offence. He told me that things are not always what they seem, and if one side in a dispute tended to be heavily favoured and spoken for, that was good reason to question it thoroughly. I wondered if Mr Romano spoke these words in the light of my earnest conviction about the merits of oralism, and I admitted some surprise at them, but there was little opportunity to question him, for there was an announcement that dinner was to be served, and soon he wished me well and left.

There were many smiles among our introductions as we gathered at tables. I may say that considerable interest was shown when I informed my companions that I was a journalist on assignment for *The Globe* in London, and I fancy this excited comment on more than a few tables. Indeed, one of the clerics, in a dark brown cassock and white collar, introduced himself to me just as I completed a most pleasant dish of *rissoto*, the consequence of which I began to feel much revived. We struck an agreeable conversation almost immediately. The Reverend Don Balestra, a tall man with watchful eyes and a vigorous countenance, was the director of a school for the deaf near Lake Como. When I revealed my plans for a walking tour in that vicinity, he immediately and with much warmth invited me to visit his establishment and inspect its facilities. He even intimated that through the offices of a friend of his I might be able to afford a visit to Naples. That was promising news! Of the controversy, the Reverend Balestra pronounced views that to my mind were deserving of much merit, and I began to ponder the heading DEAF RESTORED TO SOCIETY for my report. The Reverend Balestra urged me to seek his counsel if there were points about which I was uncertain.

During the evening I spotted a little group huddled at a table in a far corner. I could see them wave their arms, and even from a distance I could observe the grotesque expressions on their faces as they conversed in the language of signs of the deaf mutes. They appeared to take much longer to complete their meal than the rest of us, no doubt because of the energy necessitated by the signs, and I resolved to mention this as an amusing aside in my article.

After the many new sights seen, gentlemen met and conversations conducted, and knowing the morrow would bring fresh debate, I soon became pleasantly weary. I retired to my room, and slept comfortably.


If the delegates enjoyed laughter and carousing the previous evening in the dining room, then on this bright morning, as we hurried to the assembly hall, they were models of sobriety and reservation. Several heads nodded at me as we sat in tiered rows before a stage upon which was a table with papers, glasses and jugs of water. Five men sat at this table—the Reverend Balestra; the leader of the Congress, a pudgy Italian cleric named Giulio Tarra; and others whom I did not know. The Reverend Balestra even caught my eye, smiled, and said something to his colleagues, with the result I was pierced with glances from these eminent dignitaries! This made me resolve to observe and record as carefully as I could the proceedings, and when the Reverend Tarra rapped his gavel, I, with my pad and pens, was poised and ready.

*Opening address: Augusto Zucchi. Who? Where? President Royal School. Milan. (Check. Private or govt school?) Big man. Rapid speaker. Living speech is the privilege of man. Expression of the soul. Obviously favours oralism. Links with God. Then some shouting and a heated exchanged PASSION HERE!! before one of the delegates starts to read. And reads. And reads. PASSION NO LONGER. It's Magnat, Marius Magnat, who wrote the monologue that was handed out. Is reading from it. Dull speech. (Dull fellow?) Follow from paper. Very anti-sign. (What did Romano mean?) Delegates restless. (Maybe fait accompli?) Some mutter among themselves. One in front of me cleans fills lights pipe. It stinks. Little attention.—Tarra cuts him off! Ha! Ha! Some delegates nearly cheer. Support for signs?*

*Next speaker: Adolf Franck, a scholar (Check). Saying something in objection to Magnat. Who gets up again. Wants to read more of his wretched mono. Tarra puts it to the vote. Good majority against Magnat—he sits down, muttering. Ha! More shouting, calls, seems a bit anarchic. Balestra holds the floor. He has presence. Book written in 1855 (get title). Everyone quiet. Calls for vote on the question. Speech or signs? Motion not carried—passed over. Floor granted to a Mrs Ackers. (English speaker at last!) Reads from a paper, another in favour of oralism. Says speech imp for intell dev. of child. Shouldn't compare with sign schools in America where deaf pupils have a longer education than children at an oral school. ("Pure oral" what's that?)*

*Next Edward Galladay (? check sp) from America. Looks calm but determined, defensive. Age perhaps 40s. First speaker in favour of signs!! Speech is imp., but so are signs . . . have to be able to speak properly and for deaf, v. difficult—worth it? Says even if signs can be happy, educated, intelligent, etc. Balestra again. Looks agitated. V. passionate, says deaf Italians CAN speak. If deaf goes to confess. in signs, difficulty for priest (odd argument?? Is also diff for deaf if they have to speak??) Pleas for vote for speech. (Lopsided—Edward G. only voice for signs) Next Tarra. Long oratory.*

"The kingdom of speech is a realm whose queen tolerates no rivals. Speech is jealous, and wishes to be the absolute mistress." The Reverend Giulio Tarra was short, fat, and dressed entirely in black, with a white collar. I remembered his oration well because not a few things struck me as incongruous. An orator in heavy black garments does not often speak such high-blown, florid language, although I would concede an exception were he to address matters of heaven and hell, especially the fiery horrors of the latter.

"Let us have no illusions. To teach speech successfully we must have courage and with resolute blow cut cleanly between speech and sign. Who would dare say that these disconnected and crude signs that mechanically reproduce objects and actions are the elements of a language?"

*Tarra: Can follow a lot of what he says. Very anti-sign. (They all are!!!) Laboring the point? Delegates silently cheer him on. Finished? Speech repeated AGAIN—in French. Edward G and his party barely taking notice. Congress seems biased. This session: 9 speakers, only Edward G favours signs. Franck? Doubtful. Heavily slanted for the oralists. Need more direct proof.*

That afternoon, after lunch, I mingled with many of the delegates as we gathered in the hotel's reception foyer. The excited hubbub grew silent at the urgings of a little Italian man, besuited in black, with a gold chain looping to a fob watch in a breast pocket, and with the air of the professional greeter and waiter. He conferred in earnest with the Reverend Tarra, and then spoke to us, in Italian, then French, and then in precise, meticulous English to explain that we would be afforded every opportunity to see for ourselves the results of the oral method, and therefore we would witness an assembly of pupils from the Provincial School for the Poor, where Tarra was the director. The pupils at this school, previously unable to speak, would prove the oral method by a demonstration and a recital.

This was news to me, and looked as if this may provide the evidence I believed was lacking heretofore. Impassioned speeches were one thing, but where did they leave the children? Surely this would settle the argument once and for all! Perhaps the oralists were a trifle over-excited, but there was certainly no denying the claim that speech, the natural mode of expression, kept men in communion with their fellows. Thinking deeper on the subject, it became clear to me that because signs were formed by the physical expression of the arms and hands, it was not possible for the deaf-mute to express concepts in the abstract form, and this must of consequence, therefore, impede the deaf-mute when he wished to communicate the higher realms of thought such as truth, beauty, and sobriety. Indeed, I wondered if this could even limit the development of their mental faculties. What about SPEECH: THE KEY THAT FREES THE DEAF for my article?

We spent a delightful hour with a charming group of about a dozen well-groomed Italian boys and girls, all instructed under the oral method. They recited The Lord's Prayer, and answered clearly their instructors when asked questions. Some of them gave perfect and well-enunciated replies to very many questions. If these children could be so successfully instructed, then there was hope for the future of deaf-mute children everywhere. DEAFNESS IS ABOLISHED would say it all! Indeed, I contemplated retiring early to my room for the express purpose of composing a substantial outline of my report, for as those children demonstrated to me there hardly seemed many further matters for debate.

That evening, as I settled happily to supper in the dining room, I made the acquaintance of a Mr Elliott, a tall Englishman with an aquiline nose and a teacher's authoritative air. I made a friendly remark about the fluency of those Italian children whom we witnessed that afternoon, and to my very great surprise he looked up and emitted what sounded like a short groan. At first I suspected some digestive discomfort.

"Did you really think so?"

"Well, I heard for myself. True, their speech was not perfect, but without their oral instruction they could hardly have spoken at all." Mr Elliott carefully put his knife and fork down on his plate. He dabbed at his lips with a napkin, and almost slammed it on the table as he turned to me.

"Did you notice that one boy commenced his recital even before his teacher finished asking him? Did you notice just a few boys were questioned at length while others were asked but a single question? Why did only the Italian teachers examine the pupils? I am a teacher myself. I asked to observe the children while a stranger read a passage unknown to them. My request was refused." I stared at him, my mouth open in surprise.

"Are you not a journalist, Mr Archer? Did you not observe? Surely you must have seen how practised and rehearsed was the presentation? Did you notice how carefully the teachers enunciated their words? Do you think people really speak like that?" I could scarce believe my ears, but Mr Elliott did not relent. He leant close to me, keeping his voice low and firm.

"Did you not notice it was just too correct, too polished, too perfect? Did you ask anything about the star pupils? Did you think to ask the teachers such a basic question as whether their star performers could speak before they even entered their academies? Were you satisfied with the pap they served to fool us all?"

What could I reply to this barrage? I mentioned I had just started my research and was gaining first impressions . . .

"Then for God's sake don't make them your last," he snapped. He picked up his knife, and waved it in a direction across the room. "Speak to Dr Gallaudet. Dr Edward Gallaudet. He's with the Americans. The dagoes are screwing us." I was too embarrassed to admit I had not sought out the champions of the deaf-mutes. I looked in the direction Mr Elliott indicated.

I had the oddest feeling that my arrival at the signers' table was not unexpected. I approached as unobtrusively as possible, not wishing to interrupt what was obviously an animated discussion. Then it seemed I was shaking hands with everyone of these gentlemen, five in number, and in a thrice I was ushered into a chair. A glass of red wine appeared before me, a cigarette was proffered, and I was transfixed with many expectant looks. And I had not even advised my role as a journalist!

I was exceedingly apprehensive. I, who had not the foggiest notion of signs nor of the ways of the deaf-mutes, was now expected to discourse intelligibly with them! However the advocates went to great pains to put me at ease, and I shall never forget the very first sign I was taught.

Of our party, it was only Mr Denison, from Washington, who was deaf, but the others, including the aforesaid Dr Gallaudet, signed so fluently and rapidly one imagined it was their native language. With the greatest of ease they translated both for Mr Denison and myself every word that passed around our table. There was a brief exchange when Mr Denison enquired of Dr Gallaudet something obviously to do with me, and there was a roar of laughter and glances in my direction.

"Obviously you are aware the joke is about you, but don't be afraid," said Dr Gallaudet, his keen eyes twinkling as he spoke and signed simultaneously for Mr Denison. "We all have special signs for our names. You have just gotten one." I was flabbergasted. I looked at Mr Denison, who had a broad smile on his alert face. He pointed to my chest. Then he brought his hands close together, and holding them at chest height, formed them into fists. With tension he drew his right fist back towards his right shoulder, as if drawing a bow. The meaning was unmistakeable. "Ar—Archer," I cried, amidst a roar of laughter and applause.

Even now as I sit before a fire in my Liverpool flat, reflecting on my sojourn to Milan, I know that the tale I have to tell is nought but of sorrow, betrayal, and dashed hopes. Yet that instant, when first I witnessed my name in sign language, was a most singular moment.

After I learned what was called a name-sign, I am afraid I relaxed my journalistic endeavours. The professional enquirer, such as I was, ought to keep a little distance from his subjects. I had fully intended to pose a few questions, perhaps lead a short discussion, in order to ascertain the views of these advocates. However the wine was rather excellent (even to my uncultured palate), the conviviality was infectious, and the subject of our intercourse was of the greatest interest. I realised there would be time enough for questions, for this was my introduction to the world of the deaf-mutes, and much did I learn. I was shown the method of manipulating the hands and fingers to form the shapes of the letters of the alphabet, and fast learner as I am, I soon mastered it. Many other signs, too, I absorbed, simply by seeing them repeatedly, and hearing the English for them.

My new friends were vociferous in their defence of the language of signs. Articulation, they said, was important if the deaf-mute could master it, but for the majority, it required intensive effort for a great many years. "And what," asked Dr Gallaudet as he leant forward, "of their general education? Years and years of effort in getting them to pronounce a dozen words, and meantime the world has passed them by!" The basis of instruction, he said, must start with the language that is familiar to them. He pointed out the great number of teachers and other professionals who themselves were deaf, and intimated their success was due to their education in their own language. "The deaf chemists, the deaf astronomers," he said, "would they be so accomplished if instead of learning and mastering the complexities of their professions, their entire education was devoted to the enunciation of a few words? There would not be the deaf teachers and the professionals we have today!"

Mr Denison took up more cudgels on behalf of the mutes. His signs were wholly absorbing, and I could capture a broad sense of his communication, even if I did not know the fine detail. What I previously took to be the grotesque expressions of his visage was in fact a canvas that conveyed with exquisite clarity the nuances and subtleties of his discourse. With his wiry frame he seemed to create a very theatre in the air; when angry his signs became sharp, clipped, and angular, when jocular, he leaned back and his signs became larger; and when serious, he appeared to shrink a little, and his signs somehow became more vertical. Mostly his signs flowed, with an ease and grace that was indeed a pleasure to watch. Best of all, was the opportunity to put to them questions that had been forming in my mind.

"What Don Balestra pointed out to me yesterday," I said, "was that speech was necessary to restore the deaf to society. That seems not unreasonable, given that speech is the way we commune with our fellows." A rush of voices and signs followed as all of the party replied at once. After quick glances among them, Mr Denison replied.

"Mr Archer, if we are not already in society, where are we? We live and work amongst the hearing. Certainly, we gather in our schools and clubs, but so do the hearing gather in their own little communities! The oralists want to restore us? From what? And to where? And what do the oralists mean by society? Of whose society do they speak? What do the oralists know of our world? They know nothing. But they presume everything!" His arms slashed through the air, and his hands formed blades.

"This congress is all about the deaf," said Dr Gallaudet. "Why, then, are they not permitted to attend? The oralists show such concern about restoring the deaf to society, yet ban them from this very congress," he cried.

How could I reply? It seemed as if for the second time in less than an hour I was subject to a barrage of questions the answers to which I could not know. I freely admit that my interrogation by Mr Elliott had stung me, and for some moments I felt I was remiss yet again. However I collected my wits to understand that this anger was directed not to me but to the opposing side of the debate, and more glimpses did I perceive of the fiery passions behind the issues. How misguided was my earlier enthusiasm for speech! I did not even know one deaf-mute personally, yet

I presumed to know what was best for all deaf-mutes. I paused for some moments to digest this, and a congenial silence descended on our table. I sipped some wine, lit a cigarette, and thought about DEAF BANNED FROM CONGRESS. Presently I turned my attention once again to my new companions. I asked another question about the language of signs that had much engaged my curiosity. How could such a physical manifestation convey abstract thought?

Mr Denison smiled. "Ask me the signs for some of these concepts." I quoted some—truth, beauty, honour. He smartly executed the signs.

"It is a common yet erroneous belief that signs cannot convey abstract ideas," said Dr Gallaudet. "You mention the physical manifestation, but speech itself is a physical manifestation. Speech can no more present abstracts than can signs. Mr Denison's signs conveyed abstract ideals to the signer just as your very words also conveyed them to the interlocutor."

Mr Denison added some more comments about this language. "Signs take place in three dimensions, and so this language is an excellent way to convey spatial arrangements. In front of, behind, next to, near, and so on. Hearing people use gestures to do this all the time, even oralism's greatest champions! Have a look around you."

This I did, and my eyes locked immediately on the Reverend Balestra, who was seated at a nearby table and staring straight at me. He could not have failed to observe my obvious interest at the discussion at our table. I quickly looked away, and I warned myself I must not be intimidated.

"The Reverend Tarra affords me much amusement," said Mr Denison. "He is a classical Italian, and a born sign-maker. Look at his extreme mobility! His expressiveness! You may have noticed the irony, Mr Archer, of how Tarra uses signs to reject signs."

"He is certainly a dominant fellow," said I.

"Too dominant," cried Mr Denison. "This is really an In-Tarra-national convention!"

Presently our party broke up, and having completed farewells, I made my way back to my own table, as yet uncertain of what I should do next, for my head was spinning with the fascinating revelations of the past hour. GRAVE INJUSTICE AGAINST THE DEAF now seemed more appropriate. I only knew I would abandon my earlier plan of composing an outline of my report, for indeed the subject took on considerably more complexity than I had at first imagined.

My reverie was interrupted by a shouted greeting. "Mr Archer! Mr Archer! This way please!" I looked up to see a shortish man, expensively dressed, well-groomed, beckoning to me. He carried the air of a man used to giving orders and getting his way. Soon I was plied with another glass of wine and another cigarette, and was seated at the table of the gentleman who introduced himself as Benjamin St John Ackers, a barrister and member of the British Parliament. He wore a goatee, and his receding hairline revealed a high-dome forehead that glistened slightly in the light. He peered at me intently, with a penetrating gaze, steepling his hands as we made small talk.

I asked, "Was that your wife who spoke at this morning's session?"

"Yes. What did you think of her paper?"

Whatever I had thought at the time had since become submerged in the new perspective I was rapidly gaining of this congress.

"She spoke lucidly. As a mother of a deaf child she certainly gave a new perspective not evident from the previous speakers." I prayed that my quick-witted reply assumed there were in fact no other parents who spoke. St John Ackers smiled, so I guessed my assumption was correct.

"And Sir Henry Rashmore, I believe, serves on the board of your newspaper," he said. "We are acquainted." He took a sip of wine.

"What is your interest in this congress? Your child?"

"Sir Henry's daughter and mine are deaf, and naturally we wish to give them the best possible start in life. Do you have children, Mr Archer?"

"No."

"Well, perhaps you may not appreciate the gravity of this conference. I have travelled to America and throughout Europe and Britain, inspected their schools and academies for the deaf, and have spoken to many dedicated educators who have made the welfare of the deaf their lifelong vocation." He smiled, but his features did not soften. "I have carefully given the fullest consideration to the methods presently in train, and I believe, very firmly, that the gift of speech is the greatest gift we can give our daughter."

The revelations I learnt from the signers' table rose and died in my throat as an instinct told me not to contest his claim.

"Young man, you've been getting around a bit," he said. I was certain he observed my encounter with the deaf advocates.

"It's my job," I replied carefully.

"Your first time on the Continent?"

"It is."

"Do you like it?"

I realised I was being cross-examined. Perhaps this barrister knew no other way of conversation. Already I was giving clipped answers in the style of an interrogation of the witness box.

"I appreciate the European culture, the thought, and the influences that so recently led to the discoveries and colonisation of the New World. They are the subject of much personal interest."

"Yes. There were brave men who pursued with vigour an ideal. And the very best temper their zeal with kindness and compassion," he said. "The seafaring traditions of the Italians interest me. It was their ports—

Genoa, Naples—that launched many great voyages of discovery. You must try and visit them."

"I hope to."

"Make the most of this opportunity, Mr Archer. I know Rashmore. I am sure he will reward diligence and accuracy. The implications of the many new discoveries of our age are still being felt, and we rely on dedicated young men such as yourself to reveal them to the world."

"Thank you, sir. You can rely on me."

"Anything you need to know about this congress, ask me," he smiled. "I can certainly disabuse you of misapprehension."

"Thank you, sir." I took a deep breath. "Can you tell me why there are no deaf persons at this congress? The matter of course concerns them greatly." St John Ackers gazed at me for some moments before taking a sip of wine.

"The question is not unreasonable, if misguided," he said. "Does the patient query his treatment by the physician? The physician has undergone many years of rigorous training. He knows the latest treatments, the newest drugs, the current researches. He is in communion with his learned colleagues. He knows his patient and is the only one who can prescribe the best possible remedy. How can his patient possibly know, much less question, the physician's breadth of knowledge?"

"I understand your point, sir."

"Those gathered here are pre-eminent in their fields, and unquestionably are devoted to the deaf-mute and to his best interests. Even Dr Gallaudet. I sat next to him this morning, and his dedication was obvious. But I suggest, Mr Archer, that you heed the difference between fruitful progress and discredited fears. Do not linger with those who dwell in the past!" St John Ackers drained his glass, and the interview appeared ready to conclude. On impulse, I thought of something.

"I will remember that, sir. I wondered, just now. Your daughter and Sir Henry's. Are they of a similar age? Do they play together?"

"They are just a few months difference in age, but they do not play together. In their own interests they are best apart to avoid the great temptation they will revert to gestures, thus injuring their articulation lessons. That is a risk we cannot and will not take."

That night I lay in bed, but sleep had gone to the devil. On the one hand, my progress was excellent, for had I not interviewed the key persons of the controversy? But sorely troubled was I, of my own feelings on the matter. I could not deny the great difference twixt my reception at the table of the signers and at the table of Ackers, oralism's fervent champion. And was it a coincidence that Ackers mentioned Naples? I remembered the counsel of Mr Romano, that things are not always what they seem.

And thus I cudgelled my brains until at length I must have fallen into exhausted slumber.

"Oral speech," cried the Reverend Tarra, his arms flailing, "is the sole power that can rekindle the light God breathed into man when, giving him a soul in a corporeal body, he gave him also a means of understanding, of conceiving, and of expressing himself. On the one hand, mimic signs are not sufficient to express the fullness of thought, on the other they enhance and glorify fantasy and all the faculties of the sense of imagination."

One of the Reverend's arguments afforded me much amusement. The cleric made the interesting but dubious point, using the confessional as an example, that signs re-awaken sinful passions. The deaf sinner, by using signs, re-creates the the very passion that led him to sin in the first place! On the other hand, he claimed, speech allowed cool and calm reasoning. Merely by observing the Reverend himself I spotted the flaw in an instant. If signs awakened passions, then so did speech! One had only to notice the Reverend's passion and how it soared whenever he spoke the Italian word for speech! It is well-known the propensity of speech, when handled with eloquence and flair, to inflame the passions of the listeners. I resolved to put this very question to him in an interview. Yet there was no stopping Tarra.

"The fantastic language of signs exalts the senses and foments the passions, whereas speech elevates the mind much more naturally, with calm, prudence and truth, and avoids the danger of exaggerating the sentiment expressed and provoking harmful mental impressions." He certainly was not speaking with calm and prudence, even if I could not comment on the truth. If signs were so wicked, he was using them plentifully, flapping his arms with the utmost vigour, and slashing the air in angry jerks. He challenged anyone to define in signs things like the soul, faith, hope, charity, and God. He pointed to the ceiling for that, and he could merely have meant the chandelier. "No shape, no image, no design," he shouted, in high excitement, "can reproduce these ideas. Speech alone, divine itself, is the right way to speak of divine matters."

A clamour erupted in the chamber, and I heard shouting and saw the waving of arms. It was then I realised the proceedings were drawing to a close, and resolutions were being put. With my knowledge of Italian and the help of the bilingual translator, this is what I heard:

"The congress, considering the incontestable superiority of speech over signs, for restoring deaf-mutes to social life and for giving them greater facility in language, declares that the method of articulation should have preference over that of signs in the instruction and education of the deaf and dumb."

And amid the uproar there was yet another resolution: "Considering that the simultaneous use of signs and speech has the disadvantage of injuring speech, lipreading and precision of ideas, the congress declares that the pure oral method be preferred."

At once, almost every one of the delegates raised their arms amid much shouting of *si*. And the hubbub died a little, when in response to calls from those opposing the resolution, six arms arose. Five were from the Americans, and I was not surprised to see the Englishman, my interrogator, Mr Elliot, stand tall with them. But I had barely time to take in such a forlorn gesture when a cry from the podium rent the air, *"Vive la parole!"* This cry was taken up, filling the hall as every delegate seemed to be shouting these words in their languages *"Vive la parole!"* "Long live speech!"

Swiftly I gathered my papers and tucked them under my arm as I slipped down to the exit, and dashed along the curving corridor to the last entrance at the end, near where I knew where the American delegation sat. I shivered at the sudden drop in temperature. I sped up the stairs and pulled open the oak doors, and the hubbub, smoke and sweat enveloped me in a rush.

It was hard to see Mr Denison because of the press of bodies, the shouting, the brandishing of papers, the waving of arms and the pointing of fingers. I spotted him and was taken aback. His signing was all angles, harsh, sharp, and uncompromising. The grace and fluidity which on previous occasions gave me cause to remark with pleasure had vanished completely, and for some moments I was not sure if this was the man I knew before. So furious were his signs that I held my distance as I approached, lest one of his sweeping gestures should connect painfully with my person. As I was wondering how to signal my presence, he suddenly turned to me from his companions, rushed over and clasped my biceps with a fierce grip. His face was angry and red, his hair was dishevelled, and his mouth worked silently. He suddenly released me, and signed furiously, with a type of angry pleading. Dr Gallaudet, his face flushed and eyes moist, was instantly by my side, translating.

"What have we done to make them hate our language so much? What is our crime? What have we done? Why do they hate us so?"

With regret, I realise now that I did not then comprehend the import and profundity of his pleas. The intense emotions of my companions certainly aroused me, but against the Reverend Tarra. In the clamour, the uproar, and the excitement, I selfishly had only concerns for correcting the cleric on one small sign. "God," I said to Mr Denison, as clearly I could. "God. God. God." Mr Denison watched intently, not my lips but my whole face in the disconcerting way he had. His eyes seemed to widen in order to take in my whole visage. He dropped his arms as I brought my hand up.

Thumb and forefinger parallel, remaining fingers curved into palm—G. Tips of fingers resting on thumb to form a ring—O. Index finger in pointing handshape, held upright—D. I pointed down to the podium, where the Reverend Tarra gesticulated at the centre of a knot of admirers, several of whom appeared anxious to shake his hand. Mr Denison followed the direction I indicated with my finger, and then watched carefully as I imitated the sign for GOD which the Reverend Tarra had demonstrated only moments earlier.

Mr Denison's response was remarkable. He slapped my hand down, and proceeded to demonstrate the sign for GOD. It bore no resemblance to the contemptuous way in which the Reverend Tarra pointed to the ceiling. Mr Denison's sign ascended gracefully, and seemed to encompass the glories of the heavens above while also indicating its highest point. I was astounded that such a reverent sign emanated from such an angry man. Mr Denison raised his eyebrows at me. Did I understand? And then Mr Denison executed a most marvellous sign. He suddenly flashed a pointed middle finger at the Reverend Tarra below, then twisted his hand and smoothly raised it, still pointing but to the ceiling. To my mind, as yet untutored in the signs and ways of the deaf, Mr Denison made perfectly clear two things. Not only did he successfully imitate the Reverend Tarra's sign and the feeling behind it, but he also clearly showed his contempt. I still do not know how he conveyed such mischief. Perhaps it was the narrowing of his eyes or a shift in the angle of his finger, or perhaps it was some trifle unobserved by me, yet I declare he excited the very air around him with the depth of his contempt for the Reverend. I wonder if what Mr Denison actually demonstrated to me was a pun.

With heavy heart I must now write of a grievous error on my part caused by haste, a lack of judgment, and a foolish desire to use a simple right to correct a complex wrong. Wiser heads would have counselled forebearance, but my own head, so filled with the sight of so much conveyed in so simple a gesture, determined I should rush down to the Reverend Tarra and immediately confound him with all my vast knowledge of this wondrous language of signs, gained in barely two or three minutes! What a fool I was! I have a memory of rushing quickly to the exit from where I stood with Mr Denison, of the latter remonstrating as if to obstruct my passage, and of thinking as I sped down the corridor that as a journalist I was under a strict obligation to give equal reportage to all sides of a dispute. I remember too that this was my opportunity to engage the Reverend in an earnest discussion. Perhaps, flushed with excitement, he would be amenable to my questions, even to some probing questions gained from my conference yesterday with the signers. This thought surely added to my headlong haste!

The Reverend greeted me kindly, and listened respectfully as I introduced myself and gave the name of my newspaper. I thanked the Reverend for his most illuminating address, referred to his request for a demonstration of the sign for GOD, and advised that I knew the proper sign, so unlike the sign he showed in his address as to render possible an alternative view of the language of signs.

"And this sign. What is it, my child?"

My senses deserted me. I, who had just witnessed Mr Denison's eloquent gesture of the deity, could not will my body. I fancy I raised my arms and hands upwards in a confused jumble of thumbs and elbows, stopped, tried again and gave up, and I felt myself reddening in the greatest of embarrassment.

The Reverend smiled sweetly. "My child, the Lord in His wisdom has demonstrated for you the spiritual poverty of signs and the great need to bring the enlightenment of speech to His deaf children. I shall pray for His blessing on your endeavours to report to the world the good news of the bringing of the light of speech to the dark world of those cruelly deprived." I stood there aghast, and stared at his greying temples and his perspiring dome of pink scalp. Such composure! Such arrogance! Then another of his brother clerics grasped his shoulder and pumped his hand. Rapid Italian assailed my ears, and the Reverend Tarra turned his back to me.


I now feel weary, very weary, of this business. What is the point of recounting my story? Methinks I have as little influence as a straw tossed among the roiling seas. I believe—no, am certain—I have been used as a pawn.

Certainly the Spaniard Balestra accosted me soon after my scene with the Reverend Tarra, and intimated it might be possible to fulfil my wish for a holiday in Naples; he would not go so far to say it depended upon a favourable report of the proceedings of the Congress, but I soon realised it was a bare-faced bribe. I looked for Mr Denison and the Americans, but they were nowhere to be found. I rushed to the hotel reception in a vain bid to cable a message to Mr Romano, but was informed he had departed for Germany. I retired to my room in the highest indignation, and wrote a full and frank report of the congress, and again I erred because in my haste I gave vent to outrage and failed to heed the journalistic objectivity to which beforehand I had prided myself. Angry words gushed from my pen, of the extreme oralist bias, of the dubious demonstration by the children, of the banning of the deaf from the congress. I think I even described the congress as a farce. Against my better judgement I wired this report to London, and very soon there was a curt order to me to return in all haste, and my plans to tour the districts or the lakes near Milan were in tatters.

I have no energy to report the horror I experienced when back in London I read the paper's report, written by I know not whom. I have no energy to recount the dreadful scene with Mr Cruikshank, how narrowly I avoided instant dismissal, and how I was assigned—demoted—to report the shipping news at Liverpool, where I now gaze at the forests of masts at the quays even as I inscribe these words.

Many times I take a stroll along the quayside and gaze out to sea, for at least the sea is solid, substantial, and unchanging in its changefulness, unlike the turbulent ways and devious means of the affairs of men. Every now and then I put my two fists together, and draw back my right fist to my shoulder. That is my name sign, Archer, and to a handful of people it is a sign that carries the memory of an impressionable young journalist who tried and failed to convey their message to the world: do not try to make us into something we are not; accept us for who we are. It was such a simple message, but it aroused fear and loathing among so many men of substance and learning. Frequently I ponder Mr Denison's plea: *What have we done that they should hate us so much?* I do not know what, but I wonder it lies in a fear of things that are different and unknown. And I have vowed that where ever I go and whatever I do, it is this fear I shall strive to conquer.

# PAMELA WRIGHT

## Holding Up

Food stamps. It's amazing how such a simple thing could possibly become a study in human nature. The staples were miniature vises holding the booklet together. I flipped through the paper rectangles and crisply plucked each correct strip of paper out of the booklet. The fake dollar bills were in order of ones, fives, tens and twenties, but how many of each bill per booklet was unpredictable. Some booklets had been partially used, and some were fresh, but they had been stapled together according to how much the government felt I was allowed. Once I had decided to be ingenuous and save myself time by snipping out all the papers, and organizing them by value, but then I couldn't buy food. The belated but strict instruction was that the value only existed when those papers were ripped out in front of a cashier. In all, it was excruciating trying to find the right amount of money with icy sweat beading up on my hot face and neck, and running in slow rivulets down my body. Judgmental eyes stared at me from vague heads floating in my periphery, igniting my insides with humiliating fire. Breathless, I slapped down the last bill then gasped for air. Slowly, I looked up into the cashier's pinched and pious face, and peered from behind my heavy schoolgirl bangs at the people in line. Varying degrees of disgust glowered back at me.

I looked at my son fidgeting in the cart, dissatisfied with the confines the cart allowed him. He played with his toy, babbling and moving his hands jerkingly. He happily communicated something in baby-language to me and I blanked, unable to play-talk back. I quickly caught myself, "Not-his-fault . . . not-his-fault . . . not-his-fault . . ." I put a finger into his palm, and felt his tight grip become a fist. I began thinking, "Who is holding up who?" I stood in the grocery store line waiting for the cashier, who had just watched me ferret out my food stamps, to pick up each bill slowly, collecting them in a neat stack and pinching them in her fingers, then raise them to eye level and count them out slowly. I watched each bill flip backwards, and with each flip, the heat in my face went up several degrees. Each week, the same routine. Different cashiers, same drama. I took a quick look behind me and repeated my weekly thanks that I was deaf; at least I don't have to hear what the condescending eyes behind me were muttering. And I could see clearly, those people were muttering something. I was holding up the line.

•

I was nineteen when the joys of independent motherhood were bestowed upon me. Some were impressed with my moxie when I refused to call myself an unwed or single mother. I despised the term *unwed*. Not only is it so archaic, simply voicing the word is horrible, considering that the stress of the word lies in the *un* not the *wed*, therefore emphasizing the of shame of the *un*. I refused to be called a single mother for the same reason I hated the term *unwed*. Using the word *single* still had a ring of "you should be married" to it; it was like saying, "lacking a substantial, endorsed-by-society other half." The word slides off people's minds loaded with pity.

So I called myself an independent mother. I was adamant in my *choice* not to marry. My predicament was enough; why add the idiotic mistake of marrying a dead-end guy, even if he was an Adonis with a neglected IQ of 135? He had been perfect as a witty playmate boyfriend, and we toyed around with the idea of marriage, but when honesty pushed its cards, he wasn't the forever-and-ever type. So I wasn't too surprised when he turned on his heels and ran. I was devastated but not surprised. But then I said to myself, "Why, in this day and age, does marriage have to be the stamp of approval for having babies? What if it is an absolutely rotten, stupid, and illogical union? Think about it! Why should I add issues to my son's life by forcing a marriage with a disinterested playboy?" Therefore, I chose to call myself independent, choosing to raise my child without a husband, without a father, and consequently without the support of this fragile entity named Society.

Support was a strange thing. Before becoming pregnant, I took approval for granted. Of course, I went through the normal teenage push and pull for friends, clique acceptance, and teachers' and parents' attention. I didn't object to the labels given to me. I liked the oxymoronic twist of being the valedictorian, the preppie virgin, and the class flirt with the most raucous jokes! I went into college with the steely determination to be somebody, fought up the ranks, went to the right parties, and had the friends that counted, but I learned fast that my much needed break cancelled every ounce of my hard work: I was now a nobody. Outta sight, outta mind. A few months later, when that double line appeared on the stick, my self-image, everything that I meant to me started at my head, and crumbled. I had to rebuild. But all buildings require support, don't they? Will I have this support? No, not from my peers. No. Not from my so-called world. Support came from the strangest niches I never imagined existed.

And, oh yeah, the government gave support, for a price, in the form of coldly calculated food stamps.

•

So here I stood in the grocery store line waiting for the cashier to finish flipping bills. I looked back to the fog of faces that made up the line behind me. I skimmed mouths for a smile. Once in a while, a smile would catch my breath and I'd gratefully smile back. But no, this time just a glittering charm hanging on a necklace. I looked up into the face of an older woman with hollow cheeks, a long slender nose and deep-set ice-blue eyes. Her gray hair was teased into a huge bouffant, her clothing was carefully chosen for propriety. Her eyes pierced into mine, her lips pursing and flattening with punitive criticism. My eyes dropped again to her charm: "John 3:16."

Without hesitation, hostility exploded inside of me, and my eyes narrowed with hate! The most god-damned thing it was to have had a baby without a jack-wedding band in the Bible Belt! Jesus fucking saves?! My mind tumbled backwards . . . thoughts . . . emotions . . .


My fingers woodenly typed on the TTY:

POSITIVE YEAH GA
do again maybe there is a mistake ga
NO MISTAKE I DID THE TEST TWICE THERES NO QUESTION GA
are you sure qq
YES I AM SURE QQ GA
it's not mine ga
WHAT QQ YES THE BABY IS YOURS GA
we were on and off for three years how do I know theres no proof ga
YES ITS YOURS IT HAPPENED WHEN YOU WERE HERE FOR 3 WEEKS LAST JANUARY THAT WAS 2 MONTHS AGO AND IM 8 WEEKS PREG WE TALKED ABOUT GETTING MARRIED WHY WOULD I SEE ANYONE ELSE AND WE ALWAYS SAID WE WOULD BE HONEST GA
fine then have an abortion im not ready to be a father if you have abortion then we will stay together ga
WHAT QQ CANT WE TALK ABOUT WHAT TO DO QQ TALK FIRST THAT'S A BIG DECISION LETS THINK ABOUT IT FIRST GA
you keep baby q then baby your problem sk

The red light went solid.

•

Dear Melinda:

We regret to inform you that you no longer can continue employment at Byrd Hosiery. The screen-printing process uses chemicals that may be toxic during pregnancy. Due to your present condition, we cannot risk exposing you to these chemicals. Thank you for your service.

Sincerely,

Cledell P. Burns

The damn fool woman was hopping up and down, a maniac grin on her face, her big breasts jangling, and her hands clapping furiously out of rhythm with her jumping. Lynn stopped hopping, hugged herself tightly and shuffled excitedly over to her husband whose attention was diverted momentarily from his three simultaneously running televisions by the vibrations from her antics. He peered up at her from hooded lids, not wanting to move his head too far from its perfect alignment, lined up to watch three football games concurrently.

"Mel will have baby! Mel will have baby!" Lynn did a quirky little dance, her grin so wide she was giving herself double chins and her eyes had disappeared. Glen turned his head to look at me with his beard hairs around his lips twitching as he curled his lips. He nodded once, glanced quickly to my stomach, and took a chug of Bud Light and went back to his precise reclined pose. His other hand never stopped petting his wildly coiffed Bichon Frise-Shih Tzu mix.

"Mel have baby! Mel have baby!" I looked at Lynn incredulously. The first person that was thrilled, and it had to be Lynn. Lynn with her missing teeth. Lynn with her third-grade education. Lynn with her old wives' tales and superstitions. Lynn that was gonna die young because she received a blood transfusion from a 75-year-old man, believing that it numbered her days.

She stopped suddenly, finally understanding my subdued stare. "You not happy??" she asked. I shrugged.

"NO!" She flopped on the sofa, and patted an indention next to her. "Sit!" I sat. She clasped her hands together and shook her head so hard that her long dark hair swung.

"You not happy? Shame! Shame! You should happy!"

"Careless, accident pregnant, everyone look at me." I looked down to the floor.

"So! So! Give them talk! Let them give your name shine! Baby will come!" Her eyes shone with glee. "Baby will beautiful!" I gave a shrug, much slighter than the first, reluctant to catch onto her enthusiasm, yet starved for it.

"My mistake."

Lynn's face darkened. She frowned angrily and shook her head. "God give you baby! Beautiful baby. Baby come into this world! Baby never never mistake! You understand!?"

"Baby no dad. What me do?" I watched her expression soften.

"Dad not help?"

In reply, I barely shook my head.

"No dad, no matter. Shame that boy! Shame, shame! Baby will come. I will help you! You will fine, deaf friends here help you. That baby important! God give you baby." Her crazy happy expression had come back and she was back on her feet scurrying around again. "Look-at-me . . . you let God. Let."

"Now I plan for baby shower!! Baby coming! Dear sweet baby coming!"


I sat on the low wall, watching my charges, all 51 of them, splashing rhythmically. Their arms exited the water, and reentered at the point I taught them, with their hands aligned correctly: kick and pull then repeat. And repeat. Repeat. A year ago, none of them could do anything more than a proper doggy paddle. "I taught them," I squinted at the glittering pool, allowing myself a surge of pride. I breathed the chlorine air. And repeat. And repeat. Forty-five minutes passed before the important community mothers started leaving their meeting. I watched them. Mothers who had grinned broadly at me the year before. Mothers who begged me to give their child additional attention. Mothers who were thrilled that *someone* knew *something* about competitive swimming. Mothers who didn't care that I was deaf. Many eyes were averted. I looked away, furtively, at the pool in the sparkling sunshine. Denise rushed out, her long legs overtaking the gap between us quickly. She grinned, and her southern accent flowed her words out. The accent I had learned to lip-read. "It's okay. You'll be fine." "You'll coach, okay? You can coach. They give you permission. They will let you. Some don't think it is appropriate. It's not Christian, you are unwed, you know . . . But we don't worry about them, okay?"


The TV flashed in the semi-darkness. I curled my legs under my mother's latest afghan, my mind blank. Click. Click. The remote changed channels swiftly. Click. Click. BANG! BANG! Oh gee! The door frame rattled with someone's banging. Unexpected deaf visitor. I walked over and looked through the screen door to the dim porch. Roy? What in the world . . .

"Hi!" Roy threw his arms wide and grasped me in a tight hug.

"Oh, come in. Surprise. Me watching TV." I eyed Roy suspiciously. What would this 63-year-old trailer park geezer with eyebrows the size of small trees, and wrinkles deep as the Grand Canyon want from a visit with me? He had never given me a second glance before.

"No problem. I come here want chat. I know you got bad news. I cheer you up!"

"Lynn not think I have bad news. Lynn happy for me."

"Oh, that Lynn! You know Lynn, her mind strange."

"Lynn's mind, I like. She support me. Why you come here?"

"Just chat! Wrong with that?" Roy gave me a wide grin.

"Nothing. Fine, only chat. Fine." So we chatted. I kept my tired body under the blanket. We talked about people. About happenings in town. About the deaf school town and the people there. Talked about the next state over. After an hour of talking, I was ready for him to leave. I eyed the clock . . . then he said:

"You know I used-to work deaf school. I teach printing there"

"Yeah."

"You know many pretty girls there my students."

I paused, unable to decide how to answer this comment.

He continued, "Me know girls well. I know girls their personality know fast. You . . . me wrong, me surprised!" Roy laughed.

"What you mean?"

"I can tell who like sex. Now I know you go ahead sex."

". . . ???" Fear rose up inside me; I glanced over quickly to the spot where my mom sat jabbering on the phone.

Roy shrugged. "S-O you willing sex. I thought you clean girl but ha-ha you easy . . . me wrong. I want you and me sex. Come on, you me fun?"

My eyes blinked. "No. No. NOT! I not sleep-around! That boy with me we together three years! I not sex with you!"

My mother strolled in, oblivious. The old man hugged her on his way out and left laughing.


HELLO GA

hi here is luke is there mel ga

IM HERE WHATS UP QQ GA

i saw you over lynn's house you look mad you go home you not say bye to me that is ok i not mad at you lynn told me betsy talk about rumor with jim v and roy you nice girl i not believe jim v and roy they make up story i get so mad! ga

IT IS OKAY DON'T WORRY THANKS GA

i know you not sex with jim v and roy they tell everyone i know they talk because you p.g. they think you do bad thing and you are easy girl ga

THEY CAN TALK ABOUT ME I KNOW THE TRUTH I DON'T CARE I WILL BE FINE GA

Truth is right i feel bad for you stuck stay home i invite you lake you out sizzler eat good dinner feel better forget about baby daddy ok i help you ok qq ga

HOLD . . . FINE SOUNDS GOOD I WILL GO WITH YOU FOR A DINNER GA

dont worry I never ask sex with you i know jim v and roy talk but i not believe so we will go out eat dinner but i never ask sex i am christian man i know good thing respect woman ga

OKAY GOOD I KNOW YOU ARE A GOOD MAN IT WOULD BE NICE TO GET OUT FOR A WHILE YEAH OK THANKS FOR INVITING ME GA

ok i will get you friday o clock 6 okay pick you up ga

YEAH FRIDAY 6 SOUNDS GOOD THANKS GA

ok save talk later bye skga

YEAH SAVE TALK BYE SKSK

sk

My body, a large eight months pregnant, covered with home sewn clothes, toddled down the long, steep driveway to the car. The baby kicked, reminding me of his presence. I smiled. I knew he was going to be a boy. "Okay, my little baby," I thought-communicated to him. "We're getting the mail." I thought-communicated with him all the way to the post office. "We're driving down Main. We're passing the Gimbel's place. There're the railroad tracks. Thump thump! Here we are! Just a speed bump. Let's see what we got. Let the nice old lady go. Okay, which key. Umm. Bills. Bills. Ads. Another ad. Here. There's something fat for me! No return address. Aw. Go to the car, and we'll read."

I slid my tummy behind the wheel and rested the mail on my stomach-table. I eagerly ripped open the thick envelope. "Just love mail!"

"Daughter of Eve, your soul will burn with Satan for eternity!"

"The whores of Jezebel will feel the wrath of God!"

"God will cast into hellfire the evil seductresses that tempt Man from God's Path!"

"Whores repent and be saved! Hell is forever!"

"God shuns abominable filth! Adultery is filth! Unnatural fornication is filth!"

"There is no forgiveness but through Jesus!"

In utter shock, I slowly pulled out pamphlet after pamphlet. Tears blinded my drive home.

●

That grin again. Lynn was sitting in the corner clutching her purse with both arms. It was six in the morning and I had already been strapped into this bed for four hours. Water continued to trickle out of me and that was the height of my discomfort. I had no idea what to expect, but I sure did not expect Lynn to show up before the morning nurses, ready to watch me go through my labor and to "be there."

She chatted furiously, telling me that the spicy gumbo she fed me worked. The spices had heated up my insides enough to make the baby hot and uncomfortable, and start labor. Maybe it was that, but maybe, she went on, it was the walk she suggested. The bouncing from walking makes the baby want to come out. She checked, did I ever lift my arms with heavy boxes? No? Good, because that makes a noose out of the umbilical cord to hang the baby with. By now, I was charmed more than annoyed with her homilies.

Lynn left at nine to go home, make calls and came right back. By three in the afternoon, just when the labor pains crept up the contraction monitor, and failed to return to normal, but stayed within the brackets that indicated the pain was blinding to excruciating, Lynn was still there, but she informed me that the waiting room was packed with people I'd see later that night. Glen. Luke. Betsy. Denise. Sharon and Cindy. All their kids. Twenty-seven people in all waiting for my baby. She laughed and clapped with pure joy as I finally, breaking my white gripped clench on the bedrails, kicked her out, "Baby coming! Baby coming! Beautiful, beautiful baby!"


I glared at the haughty bitch with the John 3:16 necklace. Now, help me not to break the stare. The moments stretched out. Slowly, bit by bit, I began to detach. My fury unlocked, and my rage emptied. My emotions were no longer inside of my body, but replaced with a scientific and metallic curiosity. A slightly evil-feeling smirk started in my eyes.

The sunken woman's expression never changed, but . . .

I thought about it. She is obviously enough of a fundamental Christian that she wears a Bible verse on her neck. She proclaims to the world what she is, and announces that her life has been compartmentalized into a certain path. The narrow righteous pathway to the Lord, she probably calls it. Her pickled expression tells me enough. Her viewpoint is one way, a black and white view of life. Her way is right, and any other way is wrong. Her necklace, my fake dollar bills. Our badges. The roles we play. She chose her role and I couldn't control her choices. But I did have some choices, didn't I?

While looking into her eyes, I realized some things. First, it was strange that the people that needed help the most were the first to be judged and punished. I watched church-based agencies decry the deterioration of the family unit, but they were the first to feed single mothers to the vicious jowls of society. Not only the religious groups, but society expects women to nuture and make decisions that best benefit their children, yet when the decision is at its toughest, there is the least support. Most people's first reaction to a teenage mother is disgust, not sympathy. Then there's the issue of marriage. Is the responsibility solely the woman's while also having to maintain a guise of being a sexual virgin? Isn't it a wonder that women are so often depressed?!

What about the many so-called Samarians who faithfully espouse the virtue of charity, while I ran the gauntlet every week with my food stamps? Would they prefer I attend a church-run soup kitchen where they make you sit through hours long sermons on an empty stomach? Did charity always come with conditions?

And what about abortion? Ask the ones protesting in front of abortion clinics to adopt, and see if they do. Nevertheless, think about this: If I had an abortion, which, in the Christian's eyes is the most unforgivable sin of all, nobody would ever know, and I'd just be another person in line. They judge me for keeping the baby, but don't want me to have an abortion. So my thanks for keeping the baby is judgment. How puzzling! Like Lynn said, "How shameful."

It made me wonder. I kept the baby and put my so-called sins out for the world to see. A gift from God, my God, I put out into the world. My gift. Not this pinched woman staring at me. Not theirs. Not the intelligentsia that wrote me off. Not the cowards that sent the hate mail. Mine to share with people that cared about me and my baby. A baby for whom I made difficult decisions, and the most difficult ones before he even arrived. I chose to keep him, I chose to face the consequences, and I chose to be independent. The shame isn't mine.


Years later, I found myself held up in a grocery line, watching a young couple with a newborn baby floundering with miscalculated food stamps. The young girl's eyes welled up with frustration while the young man's back stiffened. I waited, because I knew it would happen. Sure enough it did and she looked furtively up at me. I offered a small nod and a smile.

# POETRY

# ALISON L. AUBRECHT

## Mrs. Meeser

Mrs. Meeser was assigned to this small closet
Of a room.
Had to sit knee-to-knee
With the deaf kids. There was no escaping
Their hoarse, flat, guttural voices.
Mrs. Meeser went home with a headache most days.

There was one kid in particular. Mrs. Meeser dreaded
Those Tuesdays. It was always the same
Long, drawn-out routine.

Mrs. Meeser would go to the classroom
And hover in the doorway, waiting.
The interpreter would tell the deaf girl,
"Meeser is here." But she would never,
Never, ever look back. The girl just sat there, doodling.

And so it began. The uncomfortable walk to the front
Of the classroom. The awkward pause in the lecture.
The shoulder tap. And again,
Just a little more forcefully. The heaving sigh.
Boy, could that deaf girl sigh. She couldn't
Breathe right when she spoke
But the room would shudder with her sighs.

And then the dragging shuffle back to the closet.
That deaf girl always walked slow, her hand grazing
Against each dangling lock, every clang
Echoing all down the hallway.

Then there was just silence.
She'd slouch in her seat, arms crossed, pouting.
That kid was a champion slouch-pouter.
Until she got around to the usual:
"I'm missing art."
Only it was "ahm messi hat."
It was easier to let her go back to class.

Worse, that deaf girl's mother.
Now that was a difficult day when that mother called
To complain about one thing or another.
That was a four-aspirin, two-martini day
And pray it didn't happen on a Tuesday.

Mrs. Meeser stopped teaching deaf kids in closets
A long time ago.
These days she's a consumer service manager
At K-Mart.
She still goes home with a headache most days.


## Unsteady Hands


i have long wanted to write of the beauty of my hands
Flowing through the air but it feels somehow insincere
And i instead write of the anger that is always present just beneath the
surface
The occasional iceberg tip playing peek-a-boo

i don't write of the beauty of my hands
Because they are not beautiful to me
In the way that fingers-in-motion are
When others execute such artful tales
With seemingly effortless precision

Bienvenu's bold strokes
Swooping through the air
Sharply plunging, like hawks hunting,
Vigorous talons seizing prey

Bahan's stubby fingers
Flirting with twinkling eyes
Fat furry caterpillar brows
Bobbing and weaving

Lentz's flower garden
Where bloom tender buds
Fragrant fumes raining down gently,
Like dust, on sturdy shoulders

Commerson's stormy clouds
Lashing down, a steady squall
Lightning flashing across land
Touching down where sand becomes glass

I am not a natural       I am a fraud

Body my land, ravaged
Soul my language, pillaged
Mind my power, ripped out

Dirt-Bloody patches of peeling skin
Hanging in limp shreds,
Teasing the blank slate that is my face

My identity forcefully manipulated
Like thrashing limbs nailed to a cross

There was never a safe haven
Nowhere to rest, to heal
In the ever helpful line of healers
Who violated us in uninterrupted cycles,
In wasteful excess

Now when I try to write of the beauty of my hands
That little girl, her placid arms
Raised raw red welts

Her head bows, shuddering
No, no, no

No, there has been no beauty
No curing and no cleansing

Only criticism and control
Demands and consequences
Shoulds and woulds
And shame, always shame

# A Letter to My Friends

*and to my family*

I found you quite by accident
You were the quirky witch,
The jesus-in-a-tutu savior
A nicotine rush, a smoke signal
That would guide me for years

*You could say our life was also an accident*
*A raging fever that changed everything*
*When I woke up unable to walk, talk,*
*No longer your perfect baby*

I think our meeting was happenstance
Wild curly irony, hot pink slurpees
Atop Harley in the ghetto
Speeding toward heartbreak
Which would melt and meld us tighter
As we traveled across state lines in search of

*I suppose your neglect was also happenstance*
*The classic frigid mother and absentee father*
*Your fire was ice and mine was heat under all that freeze*
*Your language was never mind and shame on you*
*And get out of my face and I would run far, far away*
*Only to circle back with hopes of filling the broken*

Jagged pieces of me that you picked up
Deliberately, your eyes boring holes
Through my soul, drawing out
All my poison secrets which you embraced
Without judgment over sweet coffees
Twin red lines bled into vivid images that I still carry

*Sometimes I think your verbal incisions were also deliberate*
*Smartly placed cuts designed to bring me to my knees*
*And despite how routinely you do this*
*I could never see you coming*
*And I think I am still trying to catch my breath*

You were the papyrus across the pond
Nudging at me with teasing bobs and your
Wonky Aussie lingo which would coax me out
And I would sink into a colorful riot of love and laughter
Rolling in the desert sands of all the crushed pieces of us

*I still search for you in the great beyond*
*Haunted by your stoic silence and the wall*
*Upon which I would scrape my palms*
*In hopes that I would save you*
*So you would love me*

# KAREN CHRISTIE

## Deaf Awareness

In a small operating theatre that doubles as a classroom,
I am seated for a panel discussion.
The student doctors in their lab coats practice observation.
As living clothed bodies, we are
wholes instead of parts but
the first interpreted question is:
Don't you wish a cure?
If I could I would
wish for healing hands,
my own. One touch
on each of your closed eyelids—
*Ephphatha*, "be opened"—
now you see us.
A miracle.

## Something to Fear

Know this: I am afraid.

My fear surfaced
in childhood.
I was taught to fear
unpackaged candy,
DDT,
strangers, earthquakes,
and the nuclear bomb—what were we to think of
as we did those drop and cover drills?

I learned to fear
my teacher's impatience,
my speech therapist's frown,
my classmates' mocking,
and my mother's disappointment.
My fears welled

in the dark of the dark.
I learned to drain them away
by trusting my dogs to protect me while I slept.
Regardless of who shares my bed,
dogs still guard my sleep.

But those early fears rooted deep,
grounded and fed by tears and darkness.
In that swampforest of fears
is a graveyard
of victims, who perished from
epidemics,
violent crimes (intended and random),
holocausts,
and all the world's wars.

Unmarked plots hold
political prisoners,
medical subjects,
death row inmates,
and the missing.
Despite my efforts to
neglect their graves, I often visit
and leave black stones
before sleep, before the dogs settle.

Recently, I uncovered
a mass grave.
Those who—
due to modern genetic engineering—
have perished unborn:
the dream children of the sterilized,
the aborted imperfect,
and countless others
deemed expendable.

As the dogs begin to circle into their night positions
my fear rises
like the familiar cobwebbed mist
that permeated my childhood bedroom
reminding me
I am afraid
because I am human.

## Teaching to Learn

My first teaching job
was at the Washington School for the Deaf.
I was the first
teacher they had hired in ten years.
As a high school English teacher,
my students were all
less than ten years younger,
and my colleagues were all
twenty years older.

I wanted to teach poetry.
I thought my love of poetry
could be shared
among the grammar lessons and vocabulary lists.
Speaking and using some signs, the English coordinator
smirked, "We aRe success FUL
e nough I-F We GET THeM T-O under stand
A Sen tence."
All around the faculty room,
others nodded.

Despite the veteran teachers' advice,
I decided
I was as inexperienced
in teaching writing and reading
as I was in teaching poetry.

I remember copying on the whiteboard
a poem about a high school basketball player
who had graduated but still dreamed
of the cheering in the stands
while he worked
pumping gas.
Frank, sitting against the back wall, yawned.
Julia nodded and took notes.
Jimmy stared at Tonya, who was doodling.
Robbie looked at me, puzzled.
And Josie,
a third-generation WSD student
and star athlete,
raised her hand.

I had explained
the poem taught about
unrealized potential—
that there was much more to life
beyond high school accomplishments.
BUT,
Josie signed,
HIMSELF SATISFIED.
BASKETBALL CHAMPIONSHIP WIN
HIMSELF SATSIFED FINISH FINISH.

As I studied the poem again,
her viewpoint came through the lines.
I hadn't seen it could be
the poet was saying
that living on those cheers
was enough.
He had those brief memories
of victory
forever.

And so,
during that first year,
I began to learn
how to learn
from my students.

Twenty years later, Josie
sits in the stands of the old gym
where she captained
the 1980 WSD championship team
and now works
as a houseparent.

# Daybreak in Hartford
*after Langston Hughes*

When I get to be a smooth signer
I'm gonna sign some poems about Daybreak in Hartford
And I'm gonna use some of the pure old ASD signs
Spreading across the sky
Like the branches of an oak tree
I'm gonna sign about scads and scads of dandelions
And their fluff floating on slow breezes
And show how spring smells drift
With long-reaching arms
And a calm peaceful face
And there's a field of daisy eyes
Of Deaf and Hearing Deaf Hearing Deaf people all watching
And I'm gonna grasp Hearing hands
And Deaf hands and baby hands, and CODA hands
And Clerc and Gallaudet hands, Alice hands, all joining in,
Tapping fingers on shoulders
And reaching out to each other natural as vines
In that misty dawn of poetry
When I get to be a smooth signer
And create a poem about Daybreak in Hartford

# JOHN LEE CLARK

## It Is Necessary

It is necessary for every boy to think that his mother is beautiful

Heads turned wherever my mother went

She smiled and said it was because she didn't know how to walk quiet in her high heels or because she had forgotten to hold her keys from jingling

I smiled because I knew different

One day that smile left my face

There was a beautiful deaf girl on my short yellow bus who got off at a different school

We made fun of the bus driver a big woman with a mustache always eating out of her giant lunchbox

One day the girl asked if she could meet my mother because she had never seen a deaf woman before

I smiled and said yes and I asked the bus driver to wait because I wanted to show the girl something important

We ran to my front door and I flashed the lights

My mother came smiling under hair curlers and her face in green mud and she said nice meet you to the girl

The next day the girl said your mother ugly same bus driver

I said nothing and when she got off at her school tears came

When the bus pulled up to my school I didn't move

The bus driver asked me what was the matter and patted my back and opened her lunchbox and gave me half of her big cookie

# The Politician

The Honorable Larry Nesvig strode to the podium and Linda Gallea the resident interpreter followed him and stood at a respectful distance

He opened his address to the Class of 1992 of the Minnesota State Academy for the Deaf by joking that he knew a little sign language

He gave us a thumbs up

We snorted

He said that when he was in the Air Force he learned another one

He said when we really mean it we do the double decker thumbs up

He made a thumbs up with his other hand and inserted it into the butt end of the first one

We gasped and laughed

He was delighted with himself and decided to plumb it for all it was worth

He kept the double decker thumbs up there as he spoke now and then lifting it up and shaking it

You all have done a constipation job and I am sure you will have a constipation future and don't forget to vote for me because you know I'm your constipation senator right

We were choking by the time the Honorable Larry Nesvig lifted what he didn't know high above his head smiling like he couldn't believe his luck

We couldn't either

# The Bully

We boys were marching up to Rodman Hall for supper and he stopped
and I bumped into him

He whirled around and pointed at me and touched his lips with his
middle finger and slicked it back over his head

I protested

He said yes you touch my butt

I said accident me not not see

He said not believe you

Before breakfast next morning he saw me watching Gilligan's Island

He switched the channel

Hey

He laughed

Next morning he did the same thing

I said oh that better thank you

He frowned and pressed the remote

That interesting me like

Switch switch switch

Then Gilligan's Island was back on

I said no no not that awful boring please other other

He laughed and left Gilligan's Island on

One time I was in the shower room and a rocket of water slammed into
me

Fire extinguisher

I couldn't see anything except for a baseball cap

It was his cap

I laughed and said more more feel good come on

His last year I was still learning the art of the white cane and sometimes got delayed tapping off course at night

One night I veered off between Noyes Hall and Frechette Hall and a boy offered his arm

I didn't know who until under a lamp I saw a baseball cap

Inside Frechette Hall I thanked him and he smiled

A few minutes later Gary Karow our houseparent came up to me and told me that the bully was so happy after helping me and maybe I should ask him next time I needed help

I never did

Some years later he drove down to Texas with a friend to help him pick up a pick up truck

On his way back alone it was twilight and he turned off his headlights and veered left into oncoming traffic

A car swerved in time

Another swerved

Then it was a truck that couldn't swerve and that baseball cap

# WILLY CONLEY

## The Ivoryton Inn
### *(in memory of Dorothy Miles)*

Empty bar at the Ivoryton Inn
just the bartender, me, and the TV.
The odor of stale cigarette smoke
and beer cling to everything made of wood.
This is the town where they used to ship elephant tusks
up the river and forge them into piano keys.

He's skinny with sunken cheeks, deep-set eyes.
All he wears is black. He tries to strike
a conversation but I hear nothing; only
see mumbling lips and CNN
on the tube in the background.

So I just nod.

Though no one has come in
he constantly wipes the bar.
I order a glass of wine and when it comes
I make sure the glass stays
on the coaster.

I lived upstairs in this place
two summers past to interview deaf theatre students
from the world over. They came to this bar
to eat, drink and rehearse play scenes
for drama school held in an
old renovated grist mill nearby.

Their silhouettes sit beside me and
some with drinks in their hands
lean on the baby grand piano:

Shan from Hong Kong complains
about the lack of opportunity

for deaf actors in his country.
Anu from India isn't here to learn
about acting but ways to meet American men
and get a green card.

Loretta, the redhead, from Australia—
unaware that she has no stage presence—
thinks her flashy personality will attract all
sorts of Hollywood offers.

Tom from England studies a Pinter monologue
and drinks milk; he tries out words in
two-handed British fingerspelling.

As if it was just yesterday
I see their facial expressions and
native sign languages,
each with its own signature and syntax.

At one time in the early '70s
a deaf theatre company won a Tony Award.
A sudden growing interest
in hiring deaf actors came about.
Hundreds and hundreds of eager deaf students
enrolled in the summer program
each one manufactured—
some against their will—
to the specs of well-known acting teachers
from New York City who could hear.

I finish my wine and leave a tip
at the bar's edge. The bartender
gives me a shifty glance and then
swoops in like a vulture to grab his
money and put the wine glass away.
He wipes the entire bar again even
though a small area was smudged.

On the way out I touch the baby grand
my hand trails along the curves
stopping at the keyboard.

I strike a black key, an unknown note,
thinking about fabricated deaf actors.
I tap a white key and wonder about
the elephants in Africa or India
or wherever they were caught.

What were these humble creatures
feeling when the poachers held them down
to saw off their noble tusks?

# FRANK GALLIMORE

## The Good Interpreter

I know what a good sign language interpreter is.
He does not exist. Willing a seamless dialogue,
he should make up somehow for deafness,
sign so well he's invisible as others pass through
the shapes drawn in the air.

But a girl remembers being told her brother died
and it's me that told it, the phrase frail
as a body in my hands. I want you to die,
I tell an old man, his son's hands writhing up
my throat like a ventriloquist's. When a husband
will not come home, the one waiting for his wife
to stop sobbing before giving the rest of the bad news
is me. Today, I'm hired to tell this woman
in great detail just how and when she will die.

I describe her nerves as misaligned piano wire,
explain the convulsions, the brain's erosion,
why she reels through a vertigo that had long ago tipped
the cup of her senses; and when, nearly blind,
she asks me to come close and slow it down,
then even closer until she can touch my hands
and feel each shape collapsing into the next,
the turned palm and the fingers curled like a spider
on its back, these words I choose, the curse she spells
in my palm, the quiver of understanding, are mine.

## Elegy for Miss Calico

O the year before they hauled the deaf woman
from the trash. O the fishnets that crisscrossed
her legs, the florets in her straightened hair.
Asking how to pronounce *Baby* and *How much,*
she felt my throat for the trick of it. In a window
she made a primping Blanche DuBois over Felony Flats.
And Mondays with her stolen shopping cart she'd go
dumpster jumping the lot between the fairgrounds
and the School for the Deaf. Who found the cart
up by the gabled houses and their turn-of-the-century
dream of baked alaska, amaryllis belladonna,
so many grandmas asleep in a goldenrod grave?

When they fished her out, the Eastbound roared
through necklaces of skyline, or so I remember,
or so I say. By rust-ravaged fronts, I sensed
a hustler's craft, device of handshake and for-the-best,
while there lay syringes by which to tune his happiness.
I used to watch his girls cluster like flowers on a mock-
terrazzo ledge, pressed on a barred patio. I'd watch her coo,
make mouths of inscrutable lingo for the long lash of his body.
And O the too-short calico dress, hand-me-down,
arranging itself on the breeze of his battered porch.

*How do you say my name?* she'd ask at dusk,
smooth fingers again on my throat to feel the syllables rise.
By morning her smell like a wrung rag's. *Whore,* I'd say,
the word puckering as she tossed her ratty head back
and laughed. We laughed. I wiped my cheek
with the back of my hand, the sign for her like rubbing a scar.

# PAUL HOSTOVSKY

## Deaf Culture 101

In the deaf world deaf
is good. That's the premise
that sets the deaf world apart.
So when the audiologist says
to two deaf parents,
"I'm sorry, your baby
is profoundly deaf," they do not
weep or mourn or
blame themselves or
God. They rejoice.
They embrace each other and even
the confused audiologist
who was the bearer of great
tidings. Healthy deaf babies
are good, the more the better!
Deaf brothers, deaf sisters,
deaf mothers and fathers
confer considerable status
in the deaf world.
90% of all deaf people
are born into families who hear—
poor, benighted, hearing families
who have never heard of the deaf world.
That's why deaf families
are a kind of aristocracy
where deaf is the currency.
Deaf grandmothers and grandfathers,
deaf aunts and uncles,
deaf nieces and nephews and cousins and more
deaf cousins. There are even
some who are fourth or fifth
or sixth generation deaf.
These are the deaf royalty.
Sometimes you can see them
surrounded by dilating circles
of envious, awestruck deaf eyes

just listening to the old stories
told in elegant, flowing ASL—
stories of vast family trees
hearkening all the way back to the first
deaf community on Martha's Vineyard,
or back to the first school for the deaf
in Paris, France—
to Laurent Clerc, and his teacher
Jean Massieu, and his teacher
the Abbe Sicard, who wasn't deaf himself
but who nearly lost his head
when the heads of the French aristocracy
and clergy began to roll in the streets.
But he didn't lose his head and it was only
because the deaf of Paris loved him
enough to write a letter
to the Jacobins on his behalf,
in elegant, flowing, flawless French,
calling him their Father and their Teacher,
and winning his release.

## Away Game at the School for the Deaf

Maybe we were thinking *ears*
instead of *hands*
and *eyes.* Stepping off the bus, we glimpsed
a flicker, then a flitting
from a sleeve. We felt
annoyed, then afraid,
like spotting an ant on the tablecloth, then
another and another till it hit us:
what we had on our hands was a nest,
a population:
everyone here signed
except for us, and our bus driver
was departing in our empty yellow school bus
leaving us standing there, wondering
where the gym was.

Once inside, we polished our lay-ups,
stole looks
at the deaf team polishing theirs:
we were taller,
but something in the air—tunneling, darting,
singing among them—
said *they* were quicker.
Their whoops when they scored, their groans
when the ball rolled round the rim full circle
and out,
were perfectly intelligible.
But the ref was at a loss:
he kept blowing his whistle but they kept on
dribbling to the hoop,
scoring points that didn't count.


## Dracula's Rat
### *for Paul Ducharme*


In the school play
they give the deaf boy the part
of Dracula's Rat,
because the school believes in inclusion,

and because it's a non-speaking role,
and because he more than a little
resembles a rat, with his pointy incisors
flaring out next to his impacted premolars.

The truth is, on those rare occasions
when his voice pokes out of the dark tunnel
of his throat, where it hibernates most of the school day,
he even sounds like a rat might sound,

especially a rat from Transylvania.
So he attends all of the rehearsals.
And he comes when Dracula calls. And all agree
he's got the look of obsequiousness down pat.

At his curtain call he bows deeply,
and the decibel level of applause rises
higher even than for Dracula himself—
which everyone notices, except for the Rat,

who leaves the cast party early,
his makeup smudging his temples,
and burrows into bed and falls asleep quickly,
and dreams again of that other country.


## Dear Al


Here's the church and here's the steeple.
And the deaf students have barricaded the doors,
hot-wired the school buses, moved them
in front of the gates, and let the air out of the tires.
They've shut the campus down and the police
can't do a thing about it because they don't
know sign language. And neither does the president
of the college. And neither does the chairman of the board
of trustees, and neither do the trustees themselves.
The trustees can't be trusted with this college, this
church, this school, this blessed sacrament.
                        Here's the hospital and here's
the urology unit. Open the door and see all the doctors
with their deft fingers and expensive educations.
Here is one performing a vasectomy
on a deaf patient who has elected to have it
because he doesn't want any children.
And the surgeon has a slight accent, maybe
German. And the sign language interpreter
has a professional code of ethics,
and is signing what the surgeon is saying
but not what the interpreter is thinking
about German-speaking surgeons and vasectomies,
about Aryans and eugenicists and the forced
sterilizations of deaf people all over Europe
only 40 years ago, not to mention
cochlear implants being performed today

in this very hospital on deaf children who haven't
elected to have them; not to mention
you, Al, making your speeches and lobbying Congress
to pass a law preventing deaf people
from marrying other deaf people. What were you thinking?
                    Here's the church and here's
the steeple. The deaf students are burning
their oppressors in effigy. They're saying: *Look!*
To anyone with eyes to see, they're saying: *Look!*
And the interpreter's fingers are flying,
and the surgeon's fingers are snipping, and the nurse is
adjusting the light above the deaf patient
lying on the table with his johnny hiked up, his little
deaf penis the center of attention. And the interpreter
who has been trying all this time not to look at it,
looks at it. Takes a good long look.

# RAYMOND LUCZAK

## How to Cure Deafness

1. Actual folk remedies applied or poured into the ears.

Fry peach tree seed kernels in pure hog lard.
Squeeze daisies for the juice of clarity.
Dribble earthworm oil into the soil of sound.

Stir up onion juice, ant eggs, and urine; apply.
Have someone spit into the cesspool of your calamity.
Breathe deeply into the ear and resist the fear of contagion.

Drip mercury into the pit of silence and show mercy.
Mix camphor oil with the ears of a weasel.
Fill the ailing canal with deer blood and hear the rifle's clack.

Drink holy water from the fountain of St. Aloysius Church.
Blast the trills of a trumpet at close range.
Drill in the ear with an auger while facing the sun.


2. Sometime in the mid-1970s.

Marquette, Michigan, was a three-and-half-hour trip away.
My mother said to me that I would be operated on.
I didn't quite understand what that meant,

except for one thing: I would stay overnight in a hospital,
far from home, and too close to the audiology clinic
where she and I traveled in the dark cold dawn of winter,

usually in a station wagon filled with other pilgrims
who too needed a ride to Marquette. I snuggled to her
as she murmured to voices floating like clouds above me.

The next day I lay on the gurney and looked up at her.
She smiled. "You'll be all right," she said before she looked
at Dr. Diddams, already a patron saint in her eyes.

Of course I remember nothing else of that day.
Tested later, my right ear showed no sign of improvement.
She tried not to show disappointment. "Well, we tried."


3. More remedies with commentary.

Spread the grease of a church bell's mountings like butter.
Perhaps you can respect God a little better.

Invoke the Trinity as you pour water and oats into your ear.
Sounds like a good Sunday morning meal to me.

Stuff your ear with the gall of a sandhill crane.
Perhaps you'll finally appreciate the music of them migrating.

Spread squirrel piss into your ailing ear. You'll hear
the heartwarming sound of an acorn cracking.

No one suggests the safest cure. A change of heart,
a tender understanding, a pair of hands signing.


## On Preservation
*in memory of George W. Veditz (1861 – 1937)*


In Milan, Italy, proponents of the speech-only method at the International
Congress on Education of the Deaf conference voted to ban sign language,
which quickly affected the quality of education for deaf children worldwide.
The year was 1880. The deaf community was never the same again.


I.

Mr. Veditz, you haunt me like a shadow.

In 1913, you established a program of short films
created through the National Association of the Deaf
in the name of preserving sign language.
In front of a huge drape, you stood
slightly hesitant at first, but your hands soon
imparted the understatement of eloquence:

"For the last 33 years, with eyes filled
with tears and hearts broken,
the French deaf people have watched
this beautiful language of signs
snatched away from their schools.

"For the last 33 years, they have strived and fought
for the restitution of signs in the schools
but for 33 years their teachers have cast them aside
and refused to listen to their pleas . . .

"We want to preserve the signs as others now use them,
to keep and pass on to coming generations.
Many have tried to preserve and pass on their signs.
But there is one known means of passing this on,
through the use of moving picture films . . ."

2.

I capture footage of myself on my cell phone.
I see instantly what needs to be fixed:
the lighting, the tripod, my shirt.
I perform my ASL poem. Again and again
until my signs are properly articulated.

I upload my best take to my computer and trim it.
I translate my ASL into English subtitles
for the signing-impaired. I upload the polished clip
online where millions can view it.
Then I go outside and walk my dog.

3.

You continue explaining the purpose of these films:
"We have raised a fund of $5,000 . . .
I regret that we do not have $20,000,
for we could have used it all.
If we had this amount of money,
we could have performances in sign language,
sermons in sign language, lectures in sign language . . ."

You still appear as a ghost standing behind me
and behind each person posting signed videos
online. In your eyes are tiny flickers of light
reflected from our warm computer screens,
like streetlamps illuminating a greater clarity
until the roads everywhere converge toward home
where hands aflame make shadows evaporate.


## Silences

*after Clayton Valli (1951 - 2003)*


"After I lectured about ASL poetry, using an interpreter, I answered some questions. But the man who studied music looked at me very seriously and said, 'I would like to talk about music.'

"I thought, 'Oh, come on! Give me a break. I'm not interested in music—it has no place in my life.' But then I thought, 'I'd better listen. Maybe he'll offer a different perspective.'

"He made one comment that made my jaw drop. He said that people think music is about sound and wavelengths. 'But I don't care about that,' he said. 'Music is made of silences. When there's a silence, rhythm happens.'" — Clayton Valli, from an interview translated by the author


You've been dead ten years.
It doesn't seem possible.

Gone there on the operating table.
Your body covered in a white sheet
overhanging like angel wings.

Hearing poets had sat in awe
of you onstage, sending
messages louder than theirs
without a microphone.
Each line was pure elocution:
not more, not less.
You demonstrated that a poem didn't
need paper or sound to exist.

You hated it when hearing people
not knowing your mother tongue at all
proclaimed how "beautiful" your poems were.
You could've gotten away with signing sloppily.
But you listened to the faces of deaf people
watching you: the only critics who mattered.

You knew how much they hated "Poetry,"
the ASL sign for "music" initialized with "P."
Childhoods filled with their intelligence belittled
had turned them against the Bible of English
and its acolytes who preached the superiority
of speech, the only religion that had to matter.

But you weren't a missionary to save
those poor helpless savages, just like so many
hearing people in fear of affliction.
You wanted to show them a whole new bible
where they could create their own psalms,
untranslatable yet clear as constellations
to all in worship of the mother tongue.
You promoted the new ASL sign for "poetry":
a hand holding something from the heart
opening up and outward to release at last
a feeling, a thought once kept sacred.

You'd videotaped yourself,
observed your work on a TV,
and made mental notes on what to change.
Over and over again until each line
couldn't be any more or less.
Even a subtle shift in motion could be as earth-
shattering as a perfectly-placed comma.
You never wanted to be translated
in English, the language that had
long oppressed
your people, my people.
Your hands, lit like a candle in fog,
have become a lighthouse
for all the lonely ships looking for a harbor.
Only at sea do we deaf people learn to breathe,
dreaming again a common language.
There is a reason why we love looking at

babies deep asleep. They're breathing
poems without the need to say words.


[in ASL gloss]

Valli-name-sign you dead ten years
Impossible

Operation finish you body dead
Sheet white cover-you
Table-sheet-drape look-like angel wings

You perform audience hearing
Sit watch-jaw drop
Your poems loud compare theirs
Microphone not needed
You perform lines perfect
Elaborate not, trivial not
Proof what? Poem require
Sound paper call " " p-o-e-m: no no no

You sick-of hearing people
Know-none ASL tell-you *wow beautiful*
You knew better: signing sloppy
Same reaction *wow beautiful*
You perform observe-observe deaf
Audience their facial expressions

Deaf vomit P-oetry
P-oetry same music, hearie-snobbery
Deaf people mind-scarred hearing deflate
Feel like nothing, clumsy
Deaf resistant hearing speech
Speech English only religion finish

You not same hearing heart-touched
Poor animals redemption need
Hearing think deafness affliction
Instead you show deaf
New poems, new religion, new bible
Stars clear stars litter-sky
You changed ASL sign "P-oetry"

New what? FROM-THE-HEART that
Look-like deep-inside feelings-glide-hands
Bring-out-open

You develop poems how? Videotape
Watch yourself figure-out change do-do
Again-again until sign poem perfect
Change impossible
If sign-speed change, meaning change can
Same c-o-m-m-a where line p-oem
Sometimes you-offend hearing want
Translate poems English
ASL poetry English impossible
English hearing, ASL deaf:
Here there apart!

Your hands signing bright still
Same candle f-o-g fog look-like lighthouse
Beckoning lonely deaf searching home
But deaf alone: learn what?
Breathe, dream signing all-over-same
People stare babies sleeping hours why?
Babies breath no words necessary
Poetry perfect

# KRISTEN RINGMAN

## MARC Train—Baltimore to Washington, D.C.

The train passes slowly
through growing green.
Trees broken by winter.
They lay on the ground
deaf, like me
ignoring the vibration of metal upon metal,
silver lines passing above
my smooth chariot takes me
to the past—
a city I navigated
when I was the broken one,
a city that did its work putting me
back together.
I found the most pieces in
Arlington Cemetery, then in the bright blue hues
of Adam's Morgan, in the liquid darkness
of a basement aquarium, migratory fish
moving from one tank
to another.
I spread the new pieces over my skin, like
torn stripes of newspaper, wet
with flour and water, so they stick.
I wouldn't paint them until later,
until a friend's car drove me north, away
from the political repercussions of
out-of-country abuse.

America is awkward in its healing
it wasn't supposed to get hurt, ever,
so I've often found that crossing a sea
can turn new leaves and
the deaf red roads of India
or Africa know exactly what
to give back, they know
how to heal because they know
how to suffer, each step against them,

I am closer to the rhythm of the Earth, the trees
that lay down and the trees that grow
green—every leaf
as startling as a flower.


## A Boat Carries You


A boat carries you like a bird
soaring with wings dipped
into the world below.
A world where everything is deaf,
where communication happens with
touch, breath, vibration.
Air and water move like sisters
sharing their edges
made hard or soft
depending on wind,
tides, rain, sun, ice.
Each moment is enough in itself
to shatter the next, swallow
a storm within a hush of white.

On this boat, this bird,
we glide between them,
rising with the ripples of their
exchange. Our miniature island
cannot stay level. (Since when
is the world a solid place to stand?)
The flat illusion of land drifts
away, melts into the fog with
the ghost ships, as we sail on.

At night, the water glows with green
jellied organs, churning in the dim foam
of the breaking waves. The water,
like a mother, speaks to me, carries me
in silence. I cannot voice within such quiet
moving dark, such untouchable beauty balancing
on the edges between water and air. Trembling

lights dusting the surface of a world more alive
when it is blind as well as deaf, when
the air hugs the surface tightly with her
smoky gray arms, tickling the water until
another wave breaks, rippling in green.

I am caught in the spell
of the water's surface,
the light and shadows. I cannot speak
for fear of breaking this serenity, I cannot speak
without missing one note of this song, one pulse
of the sea before me:
telling me my dreams,
telling me how it all should be,
telling me I am home.

# CURTIS ROBBINS

## Solo Dining While Growing Up

My whole family sat down at the dinner table

There was always
                a lot to eat from corner to corner

There was always conversation
                between forks and spoons

There was always conversation
                between glasses and cups

There was always conversation
                between napkins

There was always
                empty plates and empty bowls

But the knife that laid between them all—
                from mouth to ear—
                        from mouth to eye—

cut me off.

## West Point

Suddenly, in full volume,
my hearing aid picked up
a Sousa marching tune—
it was that loud, too.

Suddenly, on B&W television,
a line of men—
white sashes crossed

their gray chests
with centered buckles;
white trousers kicked
left, right,
left, right,
left, right;
high hats with dark prickly plumes
pranced on top
with shouldered, bayoneted rifles—
marched smartly
across the screen.

The vividness of
the Dress Parade
at West Point
has entered nearly
every dream
I dreamt
since.

One day,
Dad asked me,
What do you want be when you grow up?

I stood smartly,
saluted him,
and replied:
Go t'West Point,
Daddy.

He chuckled (to mask misgivings
about my deafness)
and replied:
No, Curt,
you can't hear.
Don't you understand that?

No.

## Russian Roulette

Every chamber is loaded but one.

I've written letters to a lot of employers
who have advertised
available positions
asking the interested to apply.

It was worth trying, or so I thought.
    It sounded so ideal
        so perfect
        so definitive
        so excited – in fact,
        too good to be true.

I waited
    and waited
        and waited
            and waited.
The ad said not to call.

Week after week
I waited
        and waited
            and waited.

It seems that none of bullet holes
    on my resume
        struck a chord.

Typically, my qualifying deafness
    left them with a bang.


## I Want to Sing

I want to sing the blues
    in words that no music
        could tune.

I want to sing jazz
      in words that no music
           could tune.

They're soulful but
      not like those from the streets of New Orleans
           from the cotton fields
                  around the Delta.
The heat is on me
      snapping my fingers.

No cane flute to whistle
but hurricane winds
      rains dillydally
           drip dropping on my head
                rummaging for rhythm
                    moaning jazz
                        mumbling blues.

Midnight!      Moonlight!

Thousand stars twinkle-tinkle.
      I want to sing the blues
           in words that no music
                could tune.

I want to sing jazz
      in words that no music
           could tune.

Midnight!      Moonlight!

They're soulful but
      my ears could never be set to the tunes.
           The heat is on me.
                No piano to tap but
                    the make-believe
                        twang plucks

No cane flute to whistle
but hurricane winds
      rains dillydally
           drip dropping on my head

mustering for muted meanings
moaning jazz
mumbling blues.

Midnight!     Moonlight!

# SARAH SEGAL

## Black

Crouching with you in the black
as men tear each other apart and enter tents uninvited.
But I will never really know.

Around us, so many flapping mouths—
tongues flash and flounder, bear gleaming teeth
while sounds tumble from their open pockets,
scraping floors
when there is nothing worth saying.

As I show you with my hands and point at text on the table,
I am really trying to tell you with my eyes
that I know the still tongue that envelops
and rocks you in the night,
pulls you in the hole that holds you.

I want to pack it all into a ball,
roll it toward your aching eyes,
show you that your kind of human is most beautiful.

Instead, I pack my books,
hand you a pencil and
hope you will do your homework.
You arrest me with a look that says
Why are you leaving me already?
But I cannot stay.

Every night now,
as I am lulled by the silence that used to pull me
toward the Really-Alone-in-the-Universe,
I am sitting outside a dark tent with you
breaking up the wood from our boats
and stoking our soundless stories in fire.
We are the oldest tellers out there, you and I,
out there in the black.

# EDDIE SWAYZE

## The Fable of the Fox and the Heron

A distant ornamental temple stands tall,
An eyesore, a reminder of its hidden schemes.
A fox and the heron exchanged friendly dialogues in the distant past.
Time clicked and they face each other again.
Their fiery hunger clashes for enhancements of power.
They seek a banquet to feast upon:
The frogs and an eel in the glass jar.

Frogs croak and moan in the pond,
Astounded by the sheer oppression.
A duck treads water, annoyed, and quacks in protest.
Turbulence prevails crispy clear, up front:
And it is very old - since time immemorial.

Moral decay bites their hearts.
They can't get any satisfactions.
The glass jar is almost enclosed,
Won't let them reach their meal,
And everyone knows this ultimate truth.

Open your eyes to the events today.
There are foxes and herons
Fighting for more and more.
Frightened frogs jump and jump through the war.
Ducks splash the water against decadence.
Diabolic schemes explode by the whistle blowers.
Morality twists itself into gnarled roots of an
Ancient tree next to the temple.

## Diva

Young wise woman.
Brown-cinnamon flesh.
Black braided hair.
A heart listener.
No one can exploit her.
Listen to her stories.
Honest as an open bowl.
Men don't understand.
She knows what she needs.
She is a  diva!
A deaf woman she is.
Doesn't matter.
She isn't a light-headed bird.
It won't work if men try playing tricks.
Beautiful she is.
Intelligent she is.
But she doesn't lift her tail feathers up.
She doesn't want to be a pawn.
Respect her dreams!
Respect her existence!
She carries the armor.

## Fragile Earth

As an alien in a cocoon,
I can see below.
They intermingle like discordant debris,
The thousands of emptied cotton gins.

Down below, they are playing with fire,
Abnormal with sheer insanity.
Blood and pleasures abused,
They turn grass blades into weeds.
Abandoning love,
They rip their hides
As vicious as ludicrous vampires.
They rape water lilies and water

Into rusted-brown oil.
Zeus's lightning zaps and cuts
Them into broken parts.
They turn their Earth into a shape of the heart
With fragile fractures.

# PIA TAAVILA-BORSHEIM

## Hats

Every evening we kids would gather
on the front porch steps, an assembled,
motley menagerie of stripes and polka dots,
shorts and T-shirts, torn denim,
hugging our scabby knees, waiting
for the '57 baby blue Buick to pull
into the driveway. We'd run to the door,
pulling at the handle like mad while our
tired deaf father leaned against collective weight
to barrel his way through the horde of grubby
fingers, smeared faces, our insistence that he
hand over that day's goods: newspaper hats.
Designed and folded during midday breaks as
the linotypes hummed and clattered away,
the hats held the daily comics, the editorial page,
headlines from distant lands, ads from Hudson's,
where our deaf mother sewed drapes for the rich.
No two hats were ever the same.
Mine was like Napoleon's, with wings enough
to lift me straight to my father's shoulders.
My brothers got Navy sailors' hats, or those like Robin Hood's,
or a Greek boat captain's, or the tam of Robbie Burns,
or like an officer from the French Foreign Legion.
Off we'd run to new adventures, wild conquests,
while our father sagged in the easy chair,
watching the news without sound.

## Deaf Club Christmas Bazaar

Long tables, decked in holiday holly,
staffed by the eager, line the dining room
at the deaf club. Hand-crafted items for sale
abound, everything from dolls to quilts to

white elephant knickknacks and piggy banks.
Metal folding chairs huddle near the bar
where the deaf people sit, playing gin rummy;
only the sound of cards slapping,
of chair legs scraping the floor, can be heard
as the action heats up.
The Santa waves all the girls onto his lap.
His boozy breath, laced with cigarettes,
sears the back of my neck. He bounces
me on his knee, then signs the question:
*Christmas time. You want what? Santa bring.*
I want that fireplace fan on the corner table
that my father says is too expensive. It's a cinnamon
and peach floral design and the bracket is brass.
My mother signs, *Do? Do? For? For?*
*No fireplace home. Money waste. Why?*
I know I will die without this fan.
I start to cry. Father John asks, "What's the matter? "
My mother signs, *My daughter. Finish crazy.*

That nice man, Nick, who always jokes around,
comes over. He takes my hand, as if he is going to
kiss it, like Maurice Chevalier in *Gigi.*
Last minute, he kisses his own hand; this makes me laugh.
I stop crying. He has no wife, no kids.
He signs, *Fan. How much cost? I buy.*
*Why baby make sad? For? For?*
He walks me to the fan table. My mother rolls her eyes.

## Hang Where?

Long time ago . . .
My age what?
Five.
Where?
Kindergarten.

Do? Do?
Me arrive,

walk into classroom.
Look around. Little scared.
Tall woman come.
Teacher?
I sign: *sweater hang where?*
Teacher frown.
Teacher look down at me: huh?
I look at her. What?
Try again.

Sweater. Buttons. Take off.
See? Sweater. *Hang where?*
Teacher understand? Not.

I sign: *Sweater. Put here?*
*Put there? Over here? Where?*

Teacher look down on me.
I must talk? Move mouth? Make sound?
Oh. I try. Move mouth. Make sound.

Teacher understand? Not.
Do? Do?
Me take. Where?
Speech therapy.
Candle. "P-p-p-p."
Out.
Gold star on forehead. Itchy.
Kindergarten all the way to
fourth grade.
"P-p-p . . ."
Candle?
Candle out.

# STEPHEN TENDRICH

## The Morgue

Entrance

Two silver doors
60 degrees
Footsteps
Footsteps
Footsteps
Look to the left
Pause
Look to the right
Blink
Forward and march
April
May
June 27th
3:17 a.m.

Notice on a wall
Headshot
Chilly spine
Goosebumps
Mind in awe
Turn around
Look to the left
Dark
Look to the right
Dark
Forward, center, and halt.

Footsteps
Footsteps
Halt
White sheets
Bouquet of blue roses
Toe tag
Dangling arms

Chilly spine
Goosebumps
Cause of death
Cancer
HIV
Loner
No love

Move right arm
Sheets slowly
remove from pale face
Open eyes
Mouth slightly
open
Gunshot wound
to the head
Gunshot wound
to the head

Silence fortifies
Mind in awe
Tears
Heart slowly beats
Thump thump
Heart drops as arms
cover up face with sheets
Head tilts
to the popcorn ceiling
and rectangular lights
with trapped moths,
cockroaches and

Image of lover
Flashback
Flashback
Flashback
Exit.

81 degrees
5:20 a.m.
Footsteps
Footsteps
Goodbye

Farewell
I miss
I love
you


## The Rogue Identity Which Happens to Be Lost

Crescendo

Silence

Silence

Silence

The rogue identity which happens to be lost

Silence

Silence

Baby cries
Exit wounds of the bearer, the rogue identity which happens to be lost

Crescendo disrupted
Blonde streak
Homogenous blue eyes
Pale skin
Yawn
Subtle hand movements

Crescendo

Silence

Silence

"I am sorry, Ma'am, but your baby is deaf."
Bad egg

It is now.
Now or never.

*Very special, bad egg*

Even in his youth,
rich was chocolate melted in his

*lonely hands.*

Albeit, he yearned for a neutral point;
never would he want to, but if need be,

damn it! I ordered scrambled eggs!


## Deaf Numbers

*One* is a boy with autism and a laugh that is ballistic.

*Two* is a girl from Chile with a perpetual smile, yet she is not prompt.

*Three* is the queen who drowns her own secret and personality.

*Four* is calling out for attention and permission to act like a girl.

*Five* is loquacious and refuses to alleviate.

*Six* is inane yet insane, emotional, but conceals his intelligence because
of abuse.

*Seven* contains a hyperactive ego and uncontrollable affection for
comedy.

*Eight* is normal and immature, but needs to admit his disability.

*Nine* is impaired and friendly, but depends on mother too much.

*Ten* is a mentor with a motto, "To be deaf is a miracle."

# MICHELE WESTFALL

## Speech Therapists I've Known

Can't remember one
Too many to remember
All had their hands on my throat
Saw their tongues
Too many times

One had huge boobs
With last name "Hay"
Sign name looked strange
Too much like 'roll in hay'

Another one was from Jersey
With last name Tague
Learned 'ue' was silent
Speech is so strange

All these rules
to remember
with no idea if I am even
saying them right

Didn't like any of them
automatically
Didn't matter if they were nice
Speech was not my favorite
Although it helped being in a group
Shared misery
Shared suffering
Almost all of us without any idea what we were doing

Am an adult now
Have not been in speech therapy
since after end of sophomore year
But my brain is still
littered with all these useless speech rules

Guess they win after all

# DONNA WILLIAMS

## When the Dead Are Cured

Zombies surround me:
Bodies, faces, say nothing.
Only their mouths move.

They communicate
With lips, teeth, tongue, wriggling around.
Their bodies are dead.

I am surrounded,
Outnumbered, overwhelmed.
But not defeated.

I seek out survivors.
We erect the barricades.
Keep the cold ones out.

Our bodies are alive,
Our hands, our faces, our eyes.
We are warmed by Signs.

The dead walk on outside
And tell us we are broken.
Oh, for a majority!

Or a flamethrower—of Signs
To drown the zombies in heat,
Until their bodies live.

Hands twitching, awaken,
Expressions of joy, delight.
Look! A miracle!

When the dead are cured,
And they know the warmth of Signs,
The world will be saved.

# NONFICTION

# ANDRIA ALEFHI

## Today I Am a Janitor

I'm reading Raymond Carver short stories while at work at a job. When I get here, I immediately distance myself and make it clear that I am not gonna follow the lady around while she cleans. The stupid interpreter yesterday set them up with that expectation and followed her around to every floor, trailing the cleaning cart to all the bathrooms, floors 29-41, inside this tall building. The chemical smell gets to me right away. I'm sitting here being paid to read, occasionally being called on to go up in an elevator to tell the deaf trainee she should use the scrub pad on this spot or something of that nature. Freed from the spell of her cleaning products, I have only the fluorescent lights to contend with.

My jobs are always different, always interesting.

Sometimes the most boring of boring jobs is still fascinating to me because I am there at all. I am a fly on the wall in people's lives where someone would not normally be. A commodity for the hearing who don't sign. An appendage for the deaf who don't hear, maybe don't speak, maybe don't read lips. Some degree of all these. Or sometimes they don't actually need me.

Sometimes there is no deaf person at all, but we are hired to do a platform speech in case deaf people are out there, unidentified, in the audience. I call that air guitar. Sometimes there are deaf, but we don't know whom, and we have to kind of find them, usually in the front rows. I call that a deaf check. Other times we do an on-call. It's air guitar in reverse. We are there for a deaf employee, in case they get a phone call that needs interpreting, or a co-worker swings by for a brief interchange. You never know, sometimes you work really hard, there's a lot going on. Other times, it is totally dead.

I try to be friendly. It's business, after all. This morning O, the foreman guy who started off as a janitor like the others but got promoted, gives me some of his tea. It's fantastic. Green tea with ginseng but loaded with honey, which is how I like it. I'd only had donut holes for breakfast. We talk about health food.

Sure, I would rather be in one of the offices upstairs, interpreting a real assignment. As we look on each floor for the "bathroom girl" as he calls her, we pass multitudes of federal offices, and federal office workers dressed politely. Framed pictures of W., Cheney, New York State commissioners of something. I think about how today I could be interpreting a deaf Chinese immigrant's first meeting with Social Security, explaining Medicare. I feel aware of the class difference, and I feel mixed loyalty. I know the government employees walk past us and think, "Those people pick up my trash." They are always too nice, thanking them out of guilt. I know because I've been on the other side.

But I am the other side. Here I am, talking about tea, talking about where I am from. I lower my English a notch. I grew up blue collar, so what the hell, it's mine as much as it is anyone else's. Even now, as I type this, trying to describe my feelings, O walks in and asks if I am bored. How ironic. Before I can say something which I think will sound lofty (like "I'm writing a story"), he sees my book and saves me.

"Whatcha readin'?"

"Short stories. I like short stories. I got this book for free. It was in my apartment when I moved in. Ha. So I got it for free. You like to read?"

"Yeah. I like to read."

"Yeah, I'm lucky. Sometimes, like today, I get to sit around and read—"

"Catch up on your reading, yeah." Pause. "Guess I'm gonna go on my break."

And then I stupidly reply, "Thanks for stopping by."

I can't believe I said that. But there you go. I don't know how to interclass. It's a verb I just coined. Here I am, being paid good money to read a book. Chumming with the guys whose time is accounted for, work categorized by checklists that say "needs improvement," "meets expectations," "exceeds expectations."

I have interpreted for countless employee evaluations, orientations, intern roundups, 90-day trials, and disciplinary hearings. If I had a dollar for every time a supervisor went on the topic of arriving at work on time. There's eight ways from Sunday to approach this topic. Depending on how thick or savvy the deaf person is, I vary how hard I lean on the warning stick. Yeah, I'm supposed to interpret the exact content and intent of the person talking without adding an opinion or emotion, but that's not the real world. The deal is, I know how important it is to be to work on time, even though I don't punch a clock. I resent having to interpret for The Man.

Plenty of folks work as janitors. What if I became a janitor? Wouldn't family and friends say to themselves, "What happened to her? She could do better."

Today, though, I am a janitor.

I know how to interclass, and that's the conflict. I *know* I separate myself from the interpreters who walk into jobs like this as though they don't take out their own trash at home. But how do I maintain this all day? Will I be found out?

I only have to keep this up until 4:30. I come back tomorrow. On

Thursday, I interpret for a freshman art student. I can wear my coolest yet professional clothing, and feel a twinge of regret that I'd let my nose ring hole close when I had moved to DC. Plenty of the college staff and fellow terps have nose rings.

# VERONICA BICKLE

## In the Lion's Den

Before, I thought of the agency VOICE for Hearing-Impaired Children abstractly and from a distance. Of course I didn't believe in its principles and philosophy, which oppose ASL, but it wasn't real. It wasn't in my world. Yes, maybe VOICE was the enemy, but it was a faceless one.

Laura and I were field placement students at the Ottawa Deaf Centre. She was a part-time student at Algonquin College while I was a full-time student, and we were studying for our Social Service Worker diplomas. She worked on Mondays and Fridays while I worked every day of the week except Tuesdays, when I attended school. She focused on family support issues while I was more interested in Deaf senior citizens. Laura was planning to host a Family Picnic one weekend in July as part of her placement experience.

One day Laura asked me about whether it was a good idea to go to a VOICE meeting and advertise the picnic. I shrugged good-heartedly, if a little absently, and said, "Why not? The idea is to welcome everyone, no matter who they are, to the picnic and socialize." I was referring to the age-old controversy of "to speak or not to speak," which had evolved over time to include the wider recognition of ASL as a language and the popularity of cochlear implants which had upped the stakes between the two camps. The radical passion of "Deaf Ontario Now" of 1989—inspired by the Deaf President Now movement at Gallaudet University—was next to non-existent now. While our philosophy has not changed, we have recognized that out-and-out protest—such as entering hospitals carrying anti-cochlear-implant signs—was ineffective. We learned that to be violently against cochlear implants was to make the situation worse rather than improve our cause. It also hurt the children who had cochlear implants when they were the last group of people we wanted to hurt. So the T-shirts with slogans shouting, "Against Cochlear Implants" I remembered from the early 1990s were now considered tacky, and they pretty much disappeared.

"Mary-Anne said that I may go to the VOICE meeting. Can you come with me? For support? I'll bring Justin with me, and Stefan may come too." Laura asked this after she came back from consulting with our supervisor. "I'll also go there under the guise of being an interested parent, but of course I am definitely not interested in that for him." Justin was her nearly-one-year-old son who had been diagnosed as Deaf when he was a few months old and he was a third-generation Deaf member. Stefan was Laura's boyfriend and Justin's father. As for me going with her—of course I would. It was a chance to see the other side and a chance to go over that invisible no-man's-land separating us and them to see how things worked in the enemy's camp. "Yes, I'll go with you."

A few days before the meeting, I asked Laura if she had booked interpreters yet and she realized she had forgotten. "I'll do it—I'll send in the request for interpreters to Algonquin College." In principle, if we wanted interpreters, VOICE should be the one paying for them, but with VOICE being what it is, it was impossible. It was part of our education and part of Laura's field placement experience, so it worked for Algonquin College to cover the costs.

And I didn't think about it and I was a bit late in arriving because I promised Caitlin, my roommate, that I would be picking up a bottle of wine on the way there. Anyways, there were a fair number of cars parked on the street, but again I didn't think anything of it. I saw that there was some space available right next to the building—I parked diagonally and skipped up the stairs and entered the upper part of ODC where the hall was.

Entering it, I was dumbfounded by what I saw. There was a sea of people sitting and facing the stage. I almost didn't notice the person by my side handing me a paper with a list on it. I looked first for the interpreters and then found Laura, who was sitting with her boyfriend, Stefan, and I recognized Wanda and her boyfriend—both of whom I knew from the Deaf community here in Ottawa—and Wanda's 13-years-old hard-of-hearing daughter, Rebecca Petersen. I went over to them and got a seat behind them.

"You're here now!" Laura said, turning around in her seat to talk with me—she could tell from the slight eye contact and nod of acknowledgement from the interpreter on the stage that I've arrived. "I bet you were surprised by the number of people here?!? There's so many of them, I couldn't believe it. I was shocked!" I nodded and turned my attention to the stage, where there was a child standing and speaking. But my eyes kept straying away from the stage to survey the audience.

It was the children who captivated me. There were many of them, but not all of them were involved with VOICE as some were the siblings of several Deaf children. Still, here at VOICE, it was easy to recognize the Deaf children—they stood out as they were the ones outfitted with cochlear implants or hearing aids. There was a scarcity of Deaf children in our own community and I realized now, with sudden clarity, where they had gone. They were here, with VOICE, those missing children.

My attention drifted back to Laura. With Justin wiggling in her arms, she told me to look across and behind me—tall woman with grey and black striped dress, you see her?—and I bent over in my seat to get a look at her. "Yeah?" I answered Laura after I saw the woman she was talking about. "She's the one that works at CHEO, she tried really hard to force me to 'cochlear implant' Justin." It is interesting to note that, in the Deaf world at least, the term "cochlear implant" also functions as a verb as well as a noun. (CHEO stands for Children's Hospital of Eastern Ontario.) I turned around again to study the woman. She sat straight, taut and tall, with thin shoulders pressed back and her attention straight ahead at the stage. She was formidable and she looked strong and tough. She would do very well as the Wicked Witch of the Deaf world.

"And you know what happened at the beginning with the interpreters? They told the interpreters to move over because they don't want them be in the videotaping they were taking of the children," Laura also informed me. I raised my eyebrow and looked at the interpreters. They were Fiona McDougall and Heather Mackie, and I was glad of having good interpreters for tonight's gathering. They were dressed and appeared very professional. Fiona McDougall was a seasoned interpreter but she was young and modern-looking with red-brown short hair and spiffy thick purple glasses, the style that is popular nowadays. Heather Mackie was not as seasoned—she hasn't passed the OIS screening test yet—she was still new. But she was young, blond, and she also dressed well. While she did a good job, she didn't seem at ease interpreting in what was a slightly hostile environment.

Pondering on it later, I thought it was important that the interpreters looked capable and professional and attractive. Often it is about appearances, and images are powerful--very powerful—especially when one wants to play games with the enemy. In my surveying of the people in the room—I noticed that their eyes often strayed to the interpreters signing on the stage, especially the children, but the parents did their fair share. It was almost as if the interpreters stole the show that evening. There they were, on the stage, embodiments of dissent, and a reminder that VOICE is not the only way. Agencies and organizations like VOICE have so much influence on the survival of our culture as we know it now, so was time we should cast a shadow over theirs, no matter how small—if we dared.

This whole event had been advertised as the Annual General Meeting of VOICE. I have been to quite a few Annual General Meetings and this was nothing remotely like an AGM. It was a recital I was viewing—of Deaf children standing up on the stage with a microphone to demonstrate their voice, their speech abilities. This struck me as queer because those parents and audience were not listening to the content of what the children were saying, so much as to the nuances of their voices. Later Stefan, who has full hearing in one ear, said that some of the Deaf kids' voices were obviously Deaf, it was hard to understand them. Oh some of them were good, he conceded, but the others, not so great. Can those children hear themselves talk? Do they know if they are good or bad? They are forced to talk to please others, to accommodate others.

One woman who was one of the organizers managed the transparencies on the overhead to accompany the speeches, but the transparencies were of poor quality, the overhead screen small. The transparencies were slapped on haphazardly, only as an afterthought. This was not the important part. The *miracle* of Deaf children's voices was.

Still, I could not concentrate on the program that was going on. My attention kept on straying back to those Deaf children. I stared at them, mesmerized. They sat in a row at the front, their cochlear implants prominent on the side of their heads. With them sitting that way, what I could only look at was at their heads, where a magnet stuck on their head like it does on fridges.

These cochlear implants—these machines—took away the individuality of those children. I did not look at them as they really were without first taking in the cochlear implants. Sitting in a row like that with their cochlear implants, they looked robotized. Something like a science-fiction story, indicative of a zealous, bionic future? There was something oppressive about it. Why, it was akin to an ancient Germanic, or Prussian, approach that aimed toward an idea of what is "perfect," striving to reach it at all costs.

The loss of their individuality reminded me of old pictures of my mother from when she went to the Metro Toronto School for the Deaf. In those black and white pictures, she and her classmates sat for their class portrait with big, bulky FM aids harnessed to their chests. My eyes always looked at those first before looking up to their faces, their clothes. During my own childhood, I also wore FM aids but since I was a child of the 1980s, I wore a small box buckled at my waist while wires snaked up my body to my hearing aids. We rarely wore them for pictures.

After each child was done, the master of ceremonies, that same woman who took care of the transparencies, announced a new person to come up and recite. I felt like shaking my head in disgust—she held a microphone in front of her face and any chance for lip-reading was limited. Will the children sitting in the front understand what she was saying? Was she so confident that cochlear implants worked?

There was a young, good-looking man with a 8ish-years-old son who sat beside Laura. He had his son on his lap like Laura had Justin on hers. Justin was restless and fidgeting and often reached over to get the man's son's toy. (Or perhaps it belonged to Justin—I wasn't sure.) He tried to talk with Laura but Laura turned to Stefan for assistance. Later, Laura told me that he was asking if Justin was Deaf and if so, was he going to get a cochlear implant. "We talked some more—he seems to be nice—and guess what he said? He said that his son's cochlear implant doesn't seem to work. He always had to put his mouth close to his son's cochlear implant so he could hear what he was saying." Aha—an expose, a confession of what we knew all along, was the reaction we had, me and Laura. "I gave him a flyer about the Ottawa Deaf Centre picnic and who knows, maybe they'll come."

Sitting by myself, I felt stiff and formal and uncomfortable. I had a leg crossed over the other, still having the paper I was handed when I arrived in my lap. I felt pressure to present a composed, polite front mimicking those hearing people—I felt I was being observed discreetly, my signing hands had attracted attention. But few rows up in front of me, Laura, Wanda, and Wanda's boyfriend were busy chatting, their moving hands a distraction and they showed no signs of stopping. And in this room full of hearing parents who looked at them and saw adult versions of their children—had they chose ASL—they probably saw crude, impolite, and restless Deaf people who don't know how to pay attention.

I felt embarrassed and experienced some conflict inside me. Sitting back, I could see the small cluster of Deaf people from a distance and saw they did not contribute to, but worsened, the image of Deaf people as competent individuals who were just as good as any one of them. Looking at them from the hearing-parent perspective, I could see why I would think twice about choosing ASL. But then again, why can't they be free to be themselves instead of pretending to be like them?

Is this folksy, outgoing, and chatty behaviour part of the whole Deaf culture thing? I could not help but think of Wanda's loud behaviour, which was so typical of her. When all the participants went up on stage for an ovation at the end of the program and all the children received free lunch boxes with the label "VOICE for Hearing-Impaired Children," Wanda stood up and signed to Rebecca who was standing on stage. "Lucky you get free lunch box! Get one for me!" She was simply an outgoing, proud Deaf mother being herself. But will the other hearing parents see it that way, especially when they don't know what Wanda had been saying?

Later, when discuss with Laura how I felt, I said, "It's not Deaf culture to talk while someone is presenting on stage,"

"I know," Laura replied. "We should've paid attention and not chatted too much. But it was hard to ignore Wanda. She had gone to those things before with Rebecca many times and it was boring for her. And to have other Deaf people there and having the interpreters too—she was thrilled."

"I know," I sighed. "But those parents . . . it's about images. They will remember what they saw."

Laura interceded, "I know, you don't have to tell me that again."

And speaking of Rebecca Petersen—I don't know how much hearing she had, but she had rejected the idea of going to the Belleville school and had opted for the mainstreamed experience when she was younger. Wanda had wanted her to go to the Belleville school but she respected Rebecca's wish. Rebecca also took speech lessons and can speak pretty well. Like the others, she had her turn to go up to recite a piece and it was peculiar to see her use her voice, because for the few times I had seen her before, she always signed. But I didn't mind—she had made her choice and if it was what she wanted, then why stop her?

Later, after it was over, I talked with Rebecca and the outspoken Wanda. They were also distasteful of the woman from CHEO. "She put pressure on me and told me I should not sign with Rebecca, just focus on using speech," Wanda said dramatically. "But of course I refused! How the heck am I going to communicate with my own daughter when I can't use speech?!? I am her mother and I say, Rebecca uses both languages—and what's wrong with that? Other children do that with English and French."

I turned around to look at the CHEO woman again. She was indeed the Wicked Witch, the embodiment of Milan 1880, and it was a bit chilling to put a face to the movement against ASL—the foundation of what is familiar in my life.

"She's crazy and she's weird," Rebecca said of the woman from CHEO. "Of course I want to use ASL to talk with my mom."

"Can you help me hand out the flyers?" Laura asked me when the parents were getting ready to leave.

"No," I said, startled. It was enough that I was there. Handing out flyers to potentially hostile parents was asking too much. Later, I would regret not helping Laura. But at the time, it was enough for me that I dared to be there with the interpreters who had came over to our group to chat for a bit. It had been an unsettling experience. Then Laura ran out of flyers, so, relieved, I went downstairs to photocopy more of the flyer. I was down there longer than expected because I couldn't find how to turn the photocopier on and had to have Stefan come down to help. But being downstairs, I felt I was able to relax my smiling, cheerful face I had been using because I wanted to show the people of that room that I was a happy, well-rounded, and stable Deaf person—an excellent outcome of using ASL!

"I spoke with the woman who was running the thing," Laura commented after I returned. "She was polite—not rude, but she did ask why we were here. And most parents accepted the flyer politely. One of them told me straight out that she didn't want the flyer at all." And that woman who appeared to be the leader of the group, she was tanned, tall and slender and in her late 30s or early 40s with a straight, patrician nose. Her shoulder-length straight hair was highlighted with blond streaks and swept upwards. She was not the usual matronly mother—she dressed smart and seemed upper-class. I felt that she and those of her ilk within VOICE looked down on us as if we were few rungs below them on the Darwin ladder—we were animalistic in using sign language when we should be trying our best to speak like everyone else. For them, there was only one kind of normal.

It was an interesting, eye-opening experience. We knew things like this went on, but it was one thing to talk and hear of it and quite another to see and feel it for ourselves. In my discussion about it later with Laura, I told her that we should just continue to show up and be ourselves. Just be there—we can continue to give out a message. We planned on going to the golf fundraiser which was the last VOICE event of the year before the summer, but we were talked out of it because the people there would probably be too busy playing golf rather than talk and the Deaf children probably wouldn't be there. Not all the supporters will necessarily be parents of Deaf children, anyways. And besides, on that Saturday of the golf fundraiser, it rained. Too bad for them.

This whole thing reminded me of another time, seven years earlier when Nadine Koehler, the exchange student from Germany, stayed with me as we were her first host family in Canada. I went along with her to a Rotary picnic one evening in Brighton in the fall so that Nadine could meet her sponsors. I was to go to keep Nadine company. When Nadine first arrived, she knew very few signs as she had been raised with the oral method in Germany. But at the time of the picnic, I was able to sign back and forth with Nadine in ASL. We both were seventeen, although I was nearly eighteen years old.

When we arrived with Nadine's Rotary supervisors—Robert and Rose Walker—I had my first taste of the controversy of to speak or not to speak. When I was sitting down with Nadine to eat supper, a loud, outspoken woman in her mid-30s with her father came over to speak rather heatedly with Robert and Rose. Nadine was called over to talk with them. I was wondering what they were talking about and Nadine turned around to tell me that the woman—also named Nadine and either Deaf or hard-of-hearing—told Robert and Rose that it was a big mistake to let her go to the school for the Deaf in Belleville and let her learn to sign. Did Nadine's parents back in Germany know about this?!? Nadine was called over and yes, she explained, her parents knew about it.

I remember staring down at my plate, feeling awful, as I could feel people's eyes on me as they listened to the discussion the Walkers were having with the Rotary members. I felt like crawling under the picnic table. I felt them comparing Nadine and me—Nadine who could talk with them despite her strong German accent and I who could not. I was mute, unable to stand up for myself and fight back because I could not talk. Nadine tried to assure Robert and Rose that it was perfectly all right, but while they believed her, they said they would felt better if they called her parents in Germany to check and make sure. They had no idea this was such a complicated and sensitive matter. Never before had I been painted as radical, a bad influence, and in the wrong—and as someone improper for Nadine to socialize with.

Nadine and I were both products of our own parents' choices. Who was right, who was wrong? The Deaf community and promoters of ASL? Or hospitals like CHEO and agencies like VOICE? Of course, I have my own opinion and bias but somehow, I feel this is something like the abortion controversy—both sides having strong arguments and the public opinion is constantly being swayed, like a pendulum, about what is best for Deaf children.

# TERESA BLANKMEYER BURKE

## Aristotle's Episiotomy

It had been more than a decade since I had communicated in sign language.

My best friend Laura and I first used the American Sign Language fingerspelling alphabet as a secret code in third grade after reading Helen Keller's *The Story of My Life*. Since I wore hearing aids, I claimed it as MY language.

As a college freshman attending a conference, I saw a group of people using sign language. I couldn't stop staring, even though I realized it was rude. A cute guy, sandy blond with twin dimples, smiled and waved me over.

When I reached the group, I fingerspelled my name, then pulled my long brown hair away from my ears and showed them my red hearing aids.

After four days at the conference, I had entered the Deaf-World.

I partied in American Sign Language, lunched with another hearing-aid-wearing chick from my home town, and dated a hearing guy who wanted to be an interpreter.

Our break-up was ugly.

The interpreter-wannabe convinced me that the people I thought were my friends were really his friends because he signed better than I did.

I left the Deaf-World just months after I entered it.

Ten years later I was sitting in a graduate school class on metaphysics with an oral interpreter who mouthed every word the professor and students said.

The interpreter was fidgety; his movements distracting as his head bobbed and his lips leapt from one location to another.

I asked him, "Why do you move so much?"

He replied, "Because I am also a sign language interpreter."

In a moment of chutzpah, I asked him to add his hands, figuring that I would have two chances to catch what was said—the words on his lips, plus the words on his hands.

That night I dreamt of people talking with their hands—words flying past too fast for me to comprehend.

Watching lips and hands simultaneously was harder the second time. Sleep-deprived from caring for a one-month-old infant, my ability to understand the interpreter's fingerspelling was severely compromised.

He spelled two words rapid-fire, A-R-I-S-T-O-T-L-E E-P something M something O something Y.

I caught Aristotle, but what was the second word?

I dove the fingertips of my right hand into the middle of my flat left palm.

"Again?" I asked.

He slowed down. E-P-I . . . Y.

Baffled, I shook my head. Right fingertips butted against my open left palm. "Again."

"Please," I asked, circling my open right palm in the spot where it rests for the pledge of allegiance.

The interpreter launched into gesture.

Arms encircled the space in front of his belly, followed by a cradling motion, as if holding a baby.

Aha, a pregnant woman!

The next sign puzzled me. Both hands cupped together to indicate a medium-sized hole, then the cradling baby gesture again, with one arm rising from the gesture, fist pushing through the hole and stopping midway.

I looked askance. He was signing baby head emerging through the birth canal, but what did this have to do with Aristotle's Metaphysics?

Had I overlooked Aristotle's discussion of the metaphysics of childbirth? As a new mother, surely THAT would be something I would remember.

The interpreter continued, gestured something sharp, nicking the opening, pushing the baby head completely through the circle.

Aha! That is an episiotomy.

My brain stuttered. Aristotle? Episiotomy? Huh?

Double A-HA! I laughed. Not E-P-I-S-I-O-T-O-M-Y, but E-P-I-S-T-E-M-O-L-O-G-Y.

That's it. Aristotle's epistemology. No midwife of ideas, this.

# AMBER CEFFALIO

## Interpreting Initiation

Finally! I was an ASL interpreter! I had my shiny new diploma to prove it!

I stepped off the plane, landing back in Alaska's capital city, and marched straight to Southeast Alaska Independent Living to register my services. They were expecting me, of course, as they watched me inch toward my dream.

"Tomorrow," the chair of SAIL said, "you can interpret the board meeting."

I signed the paperwork and shook her hand, excited to be part of the team.

Juneau boasted a handful of Deaf and hard of hearing people, and just as many interpreters. As with all small communities, boundaries were fiercely guarded. My arrival would over-saturate the market. I would be the only one with a four-year interpreting degree, but that marked me as over-compensating. The other interpreters—CODAs—had no reason to accept me and probably perceived my degree-getting as rank-pulling. Who gets a diploma in interpreting, anyway? This board meeting would be my opportunity to prove I was more than a piece of paper.

My last semester of college, during the Professional Readiness course, I built up an interpreter-appropriate wardrobe approved by my colleagues and professor: browns, blacks, and blues. I selected my outfit carefully. Yes, this was a professional board meeting. But the board consisted of at least one commercial fisherman who would be arriving off the boat in hip-waders and the chair was planning on a six-mile hike between work and the meeting. Being Alaska, "business casual" was heavy on the casual and light on the business. I wanted to look professional but not show up board members.

I ended up choosing a light blue shirt under a dark blue blazer—professional and color appropriate—with khaki pants and penny loafers. Casual, yet still appropriate. Business, but not snooty.

I sat, reviewing the agenda. I glanced up to see the entire community, interpreters and Deaf, file in. Did word get out I was back in town and they all showed up to asses my skills? What is a degree worth, anyhow? Or did Juneau have an unusually active community? I was expecting only the one hard of hearing board member and all of a sudden everyone was here to judge my sign choices, my syntax, my style, my clothes. As soon as I decided to say hello, the chairman sat down, gavel in hand, to call the meeting to order. I didn't even have an opportunity to say "Hi."

For a full minute I flailed. I kept wondering what they were thinking of me. But then I locked into my Deaf client, listened to the meeting, and let it all flow out my hands.

When I accepted this job, I didn't request a team interpreter. I knew it would be a two-hour gig, possibly longer. But I didn't want to be a pain—this was my first job and I wanted to be a team player. I also didn't know how to say I needed a team without prefacing it with "I learned in college . . ." The chair made it difficult to negotiate, too. "This isn't a difficult assignment," she said. "The client is hard of hearing," she added, as if the difficulty of my work was directly proportionate to my client's hearing level. An hour and a half into the job I was kicking myself for being a pushover. My interpreting was getting sloppy and my brain was mush.

The last item on the agenda was community discussion.

Unbeknownst to me there was a rift between the interpreters and the board. The reason everyone came to the board meeting wasn't to see what college did to me; it was because of a financial dispute and bruised egos. Names were called. Blame was thrown. Tempers flared. My hands, on autopilot, relayed it all . . . I think. My brain was too busy thinking, "WTF?!?"—

to consider the best sign choice for "You're a liar!"

A decade later, I found myself taking a workshop in Brooklyn, New York. The instructor asked us to share our worst interpreting moment. This assignment—a two-hour marathon followed by a bloodbath all while proving my validity—was my worst. Worse than the time a Deaf client asked me to sit down because they didn't understand me. Worse than when I was turned down for a job because I didn't act New York enough. Worse, even, than the time a client laughed at my sign name. (I no longer own up to a sign name because of that incident.) Back in Alaska, these were my people. These were the people whose approval I sought. These people, on both sides of the table, I needed them to like me.

I don't know how the meeting ended, but when the gavel went down, I sat there, shell-shocked. I wanted to shake hands with the chair and thank her for the job—yet I didn't want to take sides. I wanted to say hello to my fellow interpreters—yet I wanted more work. I wanted to curl up in bed and cry.

But I didn't. I stood up straight and gathered my things. I was hedging, trying to decide who I should shake hands with first, if anyone at all. Luckily, the decision was made for me. The head interpreter, if there is such a thing, came and gave me a hug. It was lucky for them, for everyone, I graduated. Because I was new to town and had no idea of the conflict, I was the only one who could interpret the board meeting and come out unscathed. She knew that. The chair knew that.

That was my first learning experience as an interpreter.

# JOHN LEE CLARK

## My Alma Mater

When people go blind, they are rarely in a hurry to pick up a white cane. They choose to train their eyes on the ground as they walk. Even after they begin to bump into poles and other people, they don't want to use the white cane, which would broadcast their blindness to the world. Some have been hit by cars multiple times before they finally unfold the metal feeler. By then, when their eyes are at last free to roam about again, they don't see much of anything.

Because I was born deaf in Minnesota, I avoided this fate. Not blindness, for I became legally blind when I was twelve and my vision continued to change until I was twenty-five. But I spent an unusually short season watching the ground before me. You see, it was my good fortune to be a student at the Minnesota State Academy for the Deaf, which happens to have some of the loveliest grounds I have ever laid my eyes on. It was this beauty that, in good measure, encouraged me to use a cane and retire my eyes to a life of leisure. This is not unlike how many deaf people enjoy music, reserving their residual hearing for pleasure instead of straining at speech. The rest of what I needed to embrace my deaf-blindness came from the culture of the school and from my family, both of which were, and still are, proud to be "different."

Like many schools for the deaf founded in the nineteenth century, my alma mater is on elevated ground so the poor unfortunates would be nearer Heaven. The campus rests atop a tree-filled bluff overlooking the Straight River and a winding road that soon intersects with the still-intact Main Street in Faribault, the seat of Rice County, about an hour's drive south of the Twin Cities. Sharing the same bluff but effectively separate is the private boarding school, Shattuck-St. Mary's, famous for its hockey teams and for expelling Marlon Brando.

Whether it was intended from the beginning and all along I do not know, but the layout of the buildings is in perfect tune with deaf culture. At the center is an open green, which has a baseball diamond and some maple and oak trees beyond the outfield. Olof Hanson Drive, a one-way road and the first state "highway" to be named after a deaf man (who was a one-time president of the National Association of the Deaf and a renowned architect and minister), circles this green. All of the main buildings except one more or less face this green and thus each other, giving the campus the feeling of an enclosed, almost secret garden. And it is a garden, with spacious lawns in front of the buildings, smooth white sidewalks, well-tended shrubbery, and green lamp-posts topped by white globes that shine orange-yellow at night.

The buildings are all of native limestone, smooth-cut where the stones meet one another but crag-hewn on the outside. Three of the newest were built during the Seventies, squat, saved from looking naked and bald by their dark wood-shingled tops. The rest, except two, were built in the early part of the twentieth century. Two of the older establishments are neo-classical masterpieces and are state landmarks. The limestone is still yellow on the newer buildings and it ranges from pink to brown on the older buildings.

The first building on the right of the curve that begins the circle is Tate Hall. It is a long, massive mansion featuring marching rows of tall windows with green shutters and white trim. At the end of either wing is an elevated porch with white columns and stone stairs on either side, going front or back. The main entrance has wide stairs leading up to tall columns supporting a wide Doric gable. If there were two marble lions, they wouldn't have been out of place. At the middle of the long slate roof is a white cupola. Tate Hall houses the girls' dormitory, the administrative offices, and the infirmary, as well as the old superintendent's apartments, now the school museum. James N. Tate himself dropped dead there in 1923—I can show you the very spot.

Past the playground near the south porch of Tate Hall, past a picnic pavilion, looms Lauritsen Gymnasium. Because of the way the two main entrances jut out a bit like the corners of a castle, with GIRLS carved in stone above one and BOYS the other, and above each at the top a gable, the structure has a somewhat gothic appearance. The fact that the large upper windows, where the basketball court is, are frosted adds to this appearance. They are like the heavy lids, half-closed, of a gargoyle.

When it opened in 1930, it wasn't called the Lauritsen Gymnasium, for Dr. Wesley Lauritsen had graduated from the school only thirteen years earlier and just in the beginning his long career, which included serving as athletic director and editor of the school's highly regarded and nationally distributed paper *The Companion*. He retired in 1962 in time to complete a history of the school for its centennial festivities in 1963. Until his death in 1991, he attended almost every home game, standing at the same spot where he stood as athletic director. It was only after his death that the then-current athletic director was able to stand at that ideal place, surveying the entire court, the bleachers, and the balcony above one of the hoops. When I enrolled, I quickly learned of Lauritsen's most famous saying, also the title of his editorial column, "Good Work Is Never Lost."

The gymnasium in its early days was such a jewel, with a court that could be divided into two still-full courts that colleges rented it for home games and tournaments. The University of Minnesota five played there, leading to some confusion in the local papers because both the university and deaf school teams were called the Gophers. The deaf school helped the situation by changing the name to the Hilltoppers. Because it proved difficult to design an attractive pictorial logo—they once used a hill with a spinning top at its apex, and at another time, inexplicably, a mosquito—the students voted in 1971 to change it to the Trojans. In time, the gymnasium ceased to be a coveted venue, but it remains a popular gathering place for the deaf community, especially when the opposing team is another deaf school. One wonderful part of the deaf school experience is traveling to other states to play their deaf school teams.

Across the lane that branches off Olof Hanson Drive and into Shattuck campus, with a Civil War-era cannon out in front, is Rodman Hall. It is where the students eat three meals every day and on the weekends the school is open to host home games against out-of-state deaf schools. It is a squarish building with trees close to its two main entrances, again one for girls and one for boys. Not that boys and girls have to enter at the one or the other like they were required to do in the old days, when all of the boys ate at one end of the dining hall and all the girls at the other, but the boys' entrance is closer to the boys' dormitory and Tate Hall is closer to the girls' door. The cafeteria is on the second floor, in a high-ceilinged room with huge windows. The first floor is a student community space, called the Friendship Room.

It is fitting that Rodman Hall and Lauritsen Gymnasium are next to each other, for the men they are named after entered the school together, although Roy Rodman never graduated. Instead, he was hired as a janitor. Over his long career, he accrued such respect and status that he was regarded as the personal owner of the entire campus. Dr. Frank R. Turk, an alumnus and the deaf youth leadership guru, loves to tell Rodman stories, which always illustrate the value of character and hard work. Legend has it that Rodman polished every single light bulb on campus, including the rows of high lights in Noyes Hall Auditorium, no small task. He protected the hardwood floor in the gymnasium with his body, not allowing a single outdoor shoe to tread upon it, not even if it belonged to a referee. During chapel on Sundays, in the days when most students stayed on campus for months at a time and the school still had such Bible talks, Rodman watched the chairs like a hawk, swooping down on anyone who caused a chair to get out of line.

About that cannon out in front: It was used to celebrate touchdowns in the days before football players wore helmets. Deaf people enjoyed hearing or feeling the booms. Our closest modern equivalent is the big marching-band bass drum, which some deaf football teams use for counting up to snaps and for cheers. My football coach, Mike Cashman, a history buff, once told me that the cannon was abandoned and wasn't found again for many years. It is now home to birds' nests, and from time to time students sit on it or lean against it or take team or group photographs with it. Down from the mouth of the cannon, about five feet underground, there lies buried a time capsule. During summer school 1990, before I enrolled in the fall, we were asked to make this time capsule and to return in the summer of 2000 to dig it up. That summer came and went without anyone doing such a thing, and I suspect I am the only one who remembers. I suppose I am waiting for it to be of a decent vintage before I go out there with a shovel.

Next to Rodman Hall is the boys' dormitory, Frechette Hall, one of the three Seventies buildings with the dark brown shingles all around the tops. It has three wings, each one a two-story building with narrow windows. Each is connected to the central area via a hallway that is all windows and a roof. At the very center of the common is a fireplace. Not just any fireplace, but one designed for big fires, with a large circular concrete bed and a huge iron chimney like an upside-down trumpet coming down from the pyramidal ceiling, its wide mouth not three feet above the bed. Students hang out there, in spite of other attractions in the common area: the row of booths, a large TV, a billiards table, vending machines, and other things. Perhaps it is the power of the circular that draws them here, or the fact that it is bright but with indirect light.

Out in the back are a playground, a tar-and-gravel basketball court, and a limestone cottage, the home of the school's Boy Scouts troop. This being the rear end of the campus, the backdrop is dominated by trees. This is the site of my earliest memories of the school, from the several summer-school sessions I attended before I transferred there as a full-time student for my sixth grade year. Both boys and girls slept in Frechette Hall, in separate wings of course, but we shared everything else—the T-shirts we painted in the kitchen, the barbecues we had outside, and the pillows and cushions we sprawled on to watch "Star Wars" flicker on the wall—the reels had come from the National Association of the Deaf, which captioned films before captioning became standard.

The next two buildings we students almost never entered. The power plant, a military-style block with Eisenhower written all over it, is where the school groundskeepers and maintenance men lurk. They all were hearing men in my time, and I think they all still are, many belonging to the same families, and I don't remember ever seeing any one of them sign. Their wives worked in the cafeteria and, because of their daily contact with students, more of them signed. The school during my time there had only one deaf janitor, a lady who was born in Taiwan. Because I had deaf parents, she knew them and always asked me to tell them hello for her. I remember grumbling about there not being more deaf people working in the cafeteria or in maintenance. But that they loved the campus was and is evident, everything there testifying to their care. The women cooked first-rate meals and one of them was a legendary baker of cakes. For them, the school must have been like, as it was for us but in a different way, a second home.

Tucked behind the power plant is the campus's oldest standing building. Erected in 1896, it used to be the school's laundry facility, where girls also learned dressmaking. Long boarded up and now beyond restoration, it will be razed sometime in the near future. Beyond the slowly-crumbling edifice is the same backdrop of trees, but with a faded sidewalk going all the way to the railroad tracks at the foot of the bluff, where the river glides by. If you pay attention, you will find an even fainter walk splitting off into the woods, ending at a fire pit. No doubt many sweethearts had their rendezvous here.

Back up the trail and back to Olof Hanson Drive, there is a pair of rectangular buildings opposite Tate Hall across the green. Mott Hall and Pollard Hall are on what used to be the original Mott Hall, the school's first large-scale building. Begun in 1868 and completed in 1879, the imposing structure was razed after it was declared a fire hazard. Many alumni thought and still think that this towering edifice should never have been destroyed. However, it had so many architectural flourishes that it made me dizzy when I first saw a sketch. I suspect that it would not have agreed with modern sensibilities anyway. The "new" Mott Hall houses a printing shop, a carpentry shop, and a metalworks and welding shop, all very important in the old days, when most deaf boys graduated fully trained for trade work, especially in printing. Pollard Hall houses the offices that offer various special services, such as the state information clearinghouse on deaf children.

Atop a gentle knoll is the campus's second state landmark after Tate Hall, an impressive domed building with two wings bent back so that it might look like, from above, a stubby boomerang with a ball at its elbow. Noyes Hall is named after the school's second superintendent, who served from 1866 to 1896. The nascent poet in me was often in awe of his full name, Jonathan Lovejoy Noyes. The main entrance leads into the auditorium, where there is a stage. At either side of the stage, in a recess in the wall, is a white bust, one of Tate and the other of Noyes. The central ceiling is the dome, where there used to be a skylight. Facing the stage and looking up, one cannot miss two massive paintings. A WPA artist during the Great Depression created these images. On the left wall, the painting is of a sunny day with a rainbow, some chubby clouds, and yellow-green grass—California grass, not Minnesota grass. In the middle of this idyllic landscape is a huge human hand, rising out of the ground like a mountain. The hand is dry and cracked. On the opposite wall the painting depicts a stormy night with bolts of lightning, but here the hand is smooth and luminous. I suppose the artist was telling deaf students that struggle is good.

There is a balcony, with fixed wooden theater seats, but the floor of the auditorium is bare except when chairs are set out. The school proms and dances usually take place there. There is a play put out by the students every spring. Commencement exercises. Visiting speakers. And weddings. By state law, the superintendent of the school is vested with the power to perform marriages. Alumni, teachers, and staff have gladly availed themselves of this service for over one hundred years. How nice it is to have a friend, not a stranger, officiate on your special day, and how nice it is, if you are deaf, to have your vows read to you in your own language instead of through an interpreter! Noyes himself—with his large Victorian belly straining against waistcoast, gold chains dangling, and whiskers on full display—loved to perform on such occasions. The new superintendent, Bradley Harper, the father of one of my classmates, had wanted to become the first American Pope. That didn't work out, but at least he'll be able to do weddings.

Behind the west wing of Noyes Hall is Quinn Hall, where the elementary classrooms are. It has another, smaller auditorium, one more suited to presentations and workshops because there are steps along the entire length of the stage. So it is a popular site for practical, as opposed to formal, presentations and meetings. The rest of the building is low and something of a maze. Outside, the same wood-shingled top of this Seventies building also roofs two open-air passages, one leading to the back of Noyes Hall, and the other to the last of the squat Seventies buildings, Smith Hall, where the high school is. It is named after my favorite alumnus, Dr. James L. Smith, who worked at the school for exactly fifty years, from 1885 to 1935, as a teacher and then principal, and a longtime editor of *The Companion*. Like Olof Hanson and another alumnus, the investment banker Jay Cooke Howard, Smith served as president of the National Association of the Deaf.

It being Minnesota, it is no surprise that there are underground tunnels. Tate Hall, Lauritsen Gymnasium, Rodman and Frechette Halls, the power plant, Mott, Pollard, and Noyes Halls are all connected. Because of asbestos, access to the tunnels is now restricted. But they once were used often enough for strips of wet green grass to fend off snow for weeks in the beginning of winter. I remember reading an issue of *The Companion* from the Twenties and the school's folksy science teacher, Victor Spence, reported observing a robin and her nest of pale blue eggs on one such green lane, not yet knowing, it seemed that it was winter. When I was a student, I entered a tunnel only once. It was football training camp before school started. A vicious wind descended, and we were told that a tornado was coming our way. We scurried into Tate Hall and down into its tunnel. We were soon joined by the freshly-showered volleyball players, and I remember thinking how we must have smelled, sweaty and mud-streaked as we were, in our long-unwashed practice jerseys. But the girls seemed not to mind, and we all picked up where we last left off in our never-ending conversation and laughter, our faces and hands glowing in the gloom.

That I was born in Minnesota and not another state is an important factor. Playing football and participating in academic competitions in the Great Plains Schools for the Deaf conference, and thanks to my parents' tradition of stopping by at deaf schools on vacations, I have visited many schools for the deaf and also some for the blind. No other campus compares in character and beauty to my alma mater. Call me biased, but I'm not alone in this opinion. In one old issue of *The Companion*, James L. Smith, reporting on the proceedings of a teachers' conference that took place on campus, wrote of entering an empty classroom and noticing a message chalked on the blackboard. It said, "I have never seen a grounds of a school for the deaf so beautiful as yours." In those days, the school surely had stiff competition in this department, as the deaf baby boom of the Sixties was still in the future. When that boom hit, many schools were forced to hastily erect new buildings. For some reason, my alma mater's enrollment numbers have kept between 150 and 250 students through most of its history, allowing the campus to retain its basic layout around the open green. It was beautiful then, but it must be even more outstanding now, in contrast to all of the schools marred by the boom and its aftermath—stuck with empty buildings.

One of the best things about going to a deaf school is acquiring roots. The first thing deaf people ask one another when meeting for the first time is "Where did you go to school?" Often there is only one degree of removal between any two deaf persons, so intricately and deeply connected is the deaf community. Before we even met, my wife, from North Carolina School for the Deaf, and I shared at least three points of connection: The fact my father graduated from her school, our having studied leadership under Frank R. Turk, and our having both served on superintendent selection committees that hired the same person, Dr. Katherine Jankowski, who first headed her school before moving to mine some years later.

And no graduate of a deaf school is a stranger to history. We are in awe of deaf luminaries after whom our buildings are named or who grace the walls of our school museums or Halls of Fame. Because we are there, too, walking the same paths they walked, sitting in the same classrooms they did, and even meeting them in the flesh, we grow comfortable with history, with the making of history. When I went to Gallaudet, University, the leading historically deaf college in Washington, D.C., it was already a familiar place with familiar names: The Elstad Auditorium, named after our sixth superintendent and later president of Gallaudet; the Hanson Plaza, named after Olof's wife, Agatha, the first deaf woman to graduate from Gallaudet and one-time teacher at our school; the Washburn Arts Building, named after a Minnesota alumnus, the impressively-named Cadwallader Lincoln Washburn, widely regarded as the best dry-point etch artist the world has ever seen; and all manner of other indications of Minnesotan presence. Some years ago, when I was invited to give a series of talks at the National Technical Institute for the Deaf in Rochester, N.Y., I stayed in Peterson Hall, named after an alumnus and longtime teacher at my school, Peter N. Peterson. I haven't been there, but when I do visit the Southwestern Collegiate Institute for the Deaf in Texas, I will smile because its founder, Douglas Burke, came from my school.

As historic my alma mater is, the years I spent there as a student, from fall 1990 until my graduation in 1997, were among the most exciting in its history. It was the peak of the Deaf Pride Movement. American Sign Language linguistics and Deaf Studies were taught for the first time. The students led a successful protest that brought in our first deaf superintendent. The 1992 football team won The Silent News national championship honors. The Academic Bowl team won five straight championships. And the girls' basketball team! Led by Nanette Virnig, the Johnson sisters, and the unforgettable Ronda Jo Miller, it won five straight national championships. Those girls went on to lead Gallaudet's women's team on an unprecedented run that garnered national attention, including two books. When Miller was lighting up Lauritsen Gymnasium, scholarship offers poured in from Division I schools, but she was only interested in Gallaudet, a Division III school. Hearing scouts, coaches, and reporters couldn't understand how she could sweep aside all those offers, but we understood. We all would have done the same. Miller finished her collegiate career as the all-time scoring leader in Division III.

I was there and I am still there. In 1993, a group of deaf teachers were fed up with hearing teachers and staff speaking in their presence without signing. They successfully passed a motion to declare the entire campus a "signing zone." Signs reminding everyone to sign would be put up everywhere. They held a contest, asking students to enter logo ideas. My drawing won. It shows a green slope with five figures on it, silhouetted against a yellow sun, and above this two blue cloud-like hands making the ASL word "signing." They ordered a pile of those signs, and my art teacher, Bonnie Gonzalez, asked me to add my John Hancock to every single one of them. But I wrote my name in print, "John Clark." She asked me why I didn't sign my name with a flourish. I said I wanted to make sure people could read my name.

So I have many fingerprints on the campus. On entering the campus, one sees a huge sign—my sign—with the words "Welcome" and "Please use sign language." On leaving the campus, the last things one sees are two of my signs, on either pillar of the entrance pillars, with the words "Thank You for Signing." The signs are also in every building (except, probably, the power plant). But this is not how I want to close this tour of my alma mater.

I have mentioned football but not where the football field is. It is behind Tate Hall and occupies part of a long level field that includes tennis courts and more flat green behind Lauritsen Gymnasium. Across the street that borders this field are old-fashioned houses and beyond them more houses and streets. I wonder if, during all those years, the residents of those houses, sitting on their front porches, have wondered about what it was like to be deaf and to go to that school across the street. All they can see, except for when we practiced or had games and the deaf community came out to root for us, is the back of Tate Hall and the back of Lauritsen Gymnasium. Did they have any idea what it was like to be inside the campus, to be like me or Maurice Potter, after whom the football field is named?

Whenever I saw the aged, stooped Maurice Potter, Class of 1928, star athlete and many years a professional baseball umpire, at our games, I made a point to say hello. He always had an interest in us students. Some years after I graduated, I ran into his son, Jim, who was my math teacher and who had retired at the same time my class graduated, giving us a moving commencement address. I asked after his father and learned that it was near the end. Maurice could no longer drive or attend the home games. But he would ask his son to drive him to the campus, just to take a slow turn around Olof Hanson Drive. And father and son would look out of the car windows and, as I have so often done in my mind, take it all in again.

# MARK DROLSBAUGH

## A Deaf Class Action Lawsuit Waiting to Happen—Or Not

Let me tell you the story of a deaf guy we'll call Dave. At 72 years of age, Dave is able to tell some remarkable stories about his educational experience back in the 1940s. His stories are both amusing and shocking. They inspire a sense of awe—and sometimes, anger.

Some younger-generation folks may be surprised to learn that the Pennsylvania School for the Deaf was not the only game in town. There was also a program known as the Wills & Elizabeth Martin School. It was known simply as "Martin School," signed "HH" (as in "hard of hearing"). I could be wrong, but I believe this is because the most successful students there were hard of hearing. They had to be, because the school was predominantly oral.

"Predominantly" is an understatement. As Dave explains it, anyone who dared sign on campus was physically punished. If a teacher caught any students signing, off to the principal's office they went. In some cases, students got their knuckles rapped with a ruler. In other cases the principal, Mrs. Davis, would haul students to the bathroom and prop the door open. It was in there where she'd give them a good old-fashioned butt-whipping. Students walking the halls would be wary when they passed the bathroom. A door wide open meant some poor soul's gluteus maximus was collecting splinters.

The ironic thing is, Mrs. Davis was actually a pretty decent lady. She was only doing what she'd been trained to do. After she retired, Dave's wife and some of her friends—all Martin School alumni—paid Mrs. Davis a friendly visit. Mrs. Davis not only welcomed them into her home, she *signed*. Go figure.

A significant number of Martin School students would transfer over to the Pennsylvania School for the Deaf. PSD was oral too, as were all schools for the deaf at that time. But at least there was a little more tolerance and flexibility from the staff. They even had some deaf teachers, mostly in the voc program, who signed. No one made a big deal about it because the majority number of hearing teachers continued to reinforce speech and lipreading skills.

PSD happened to be the popular choice because it had dorms, sports teams, and a much better social life. Sure, signing was still pretty much off limits in the classroom, save for the occasional deaf teacher. And of course, some of the teachers were, uh, unique.

One teacher was fondly known as "Mr. Nineteen." He earned his nickname due to his habit of picking his nose and rolling the boogers between his thumb and forefinger—a motion that happens to resemble the sign for "nineteen."

*I am not making this up. This is genuine deaf history, folks.*

Mr. Nineteen was also a strict fella. If you messed with him, he'd have you walk circles in the courtyard for an entire class period. There are also reports that Mr. Nineteen moonlighted as a dorm counselor. You'll find old-timers sharing stories about how he cured many a young dorm student of bedwetting (who needs *Depends* when you have Mr. Nineteen's School of Behavior Modification?). I'm not going into details for that one. Someone needs to document this and write a book, though. It's eye-opening stuff.

Bedwetting therapy notwithstanding, PSD apparently did a much better job of teaching than the Martin School did. Dave's wife and a former classmate confirmed that on many occasions, PSD staff would throw their hands up in resignation and mutter something along the lines of *Stupid Martin School.* It seemed that many of the transfers had arrived with little or no working knowledge of academics. How could they, if they couldn't understand their teachers?

Note: I'm not saying Martin School teachers didn't teach. I'm saying that many of their students simply couldn't understand them. The students who were adept at speaking and lipreading probably got a decent education. Everyone else was left in the dark.

The more horror stories Dave shared, the more I wanted to know why no one ever got in trouble for all of the abuse and neglect. Did anyone ever sue somebody for this?

Apparently the physical abuse is not grounds for a lawsuit. Face it, butt-whippings and other forms of corporal punishment were the norm back then. Not just in deaf schools but in schools *everywhere.* Hearing kids got their butts whooped, too. It's just the way things were back in those days. Just because everyone was doing it doesn't make it *right,* but it was the prevalent philosophy.

On the other hand, forced oralism . . . hmmm. Now *that* may be a lawsuit waiting to happen.

Let me explain. Or, even better, let Dave explain.

Dave comes from a deaf family. He grew up with access to language—sign language—straight out of the crib.

So great was Dave's early exposure to language that he had no difficulty absorbing either ASL or English. He was a bookworm. He attended a hearing public school and held his own as far as reading and writing was concerned, but he could not keep up with whatever his hearing teachers and classmates were saying.

And so his family moved to Philadelphia, where he attended both the

Martin School and PSD. Where once again, he could not understand his teachers . . . *because they didn't sign.*

In spite of having above-average reading and writing skills, in spite of being placed in classrooms with older students because of this (PSD was sensitive to his plight for the most part and tried to accomodate him accordingly) . . . Dave eventually dropped out. His two major complaints were inability to understand teachers and ridiculously easy homework assignments. He couldn't take it seriously. Boredom breeds trouble, and Dave got into a lot of it. Fed up, he left.

He was not alone in the era of oralism. Other students expressed similar complaints. Not just in Philadelphia. Not just in Pennsylvania. Everywhere. The Milan Manifesto of 1880 had sent deaf education plummeting into a hopeless abyss.

Deaf students who had language skills felt they weren't appropriately challenged because they could not communicate effectively with their teachers. Those who didn't have language skills faced insurmountable odds because they, too, could not communicate effectively with their teachers. All of this because they were not permitted to sign.

Now this, my friends, is definitely grounds for a class action lawsuit.

For hearing readers who are new to the deaf community, let me take a moment to give you a frame of reference. Imagine if, instead of attending the grade schools and high schools that you went to, you were sent to schools in another country where they spoke a different language. Given that sooner or later your hearing would allow you to pick up this different language, for good measure let's say you had NO language to begin with—and that in this foreign environment, you and your teachers were separated by a thick glass wall that prevented you from actually hearing them. How much do you think you would learn in this environment? Exactly.

This is the fun part where I get to pull the rug out from under everyone. Let me tell you that I can personally vouch that everything Dave said is true. That's because his real name is Don, and he is my father.

Don is—by far—much more well-read than I am. He always has, and still does, read the classics. Any classic writings involving fiction, non-fiction, history, or science, you can take my word for it: Don has already read it.

Me? I grew up reading *MAD Magazine* and *Archie* comics. Not too shabby, eh?

Regardless, I was granted sign language interpreters in high school and granted the opportunity to attend Gallaudet University where all of the teachers and students communicated in sign language. Don and his friends had no such opportunity. For many of them, high school was the end of the road. A road they could have continued traveling on if they were allowed to sign.

Once more, I have to ask: Is this grounds for a class action lawsuit? Yes. Opportunities were denied due to oppression of deaf students' most accessible language, ASL. Generations of deaf students wound up working menial jobs or unemployed altogether because they were denied a fair education.

But then again . . . who are they going to sue?

Mrs. Davis? Long dead.

The higher-ups who trained her? Duh, they're dead too. What is this, an audition for the sequel to Michael Jackson's *Thriller*? I said, we're not digging anyone up.

The Martin School? There's no such deaf program anymore. I did an Internet search and found a Bache-Martin School at the same location. There's probably a connection somehow but it's irrelevant. I'm pretty sure the people there now had nothing to do with the Wills & Elizabeth Martin School that my parents attended.

PSD? Or any other deaf school that was oral way back when? What for?

Several of the old deaf schools have already closed. Most of the ones that are still open, including PSD, are very aware of the needs of today's Deaf culture. You'll find bi-lingual/bi-cultural education, ASL specialists, deaf studies classes, interpreters, smart boards, e-mail, videophones, and all sorts of accessibility that didn't exist way back when. Many of these schools are practically on the cutting edge of Deaf culture. What good would suing them do? The administrators and teachers who dished out those butt whoopings have long since retired or died. They've been replaced by more appropriately qualified staff.

The government? Heh. Some wise guy I talked to said we've already got a form of reparations from the government. It's called SSI.

Well, I honestly don't know. But I do know that generations of deaf students have passed through the halls of numerous deaf educational programs and came out of them with nothing to show for it.

I think the least we can do is to talk to these former students and document their stories. Today we live in a world of much-improved accessibility which is great, but easily taken for granted. There are still people out there in politics and education who oppose a deaf-friendly approach. That's as good a reason as any to appreciate the stories that Don and many others have shared . . . and to never, ever, forget.

# DONALD GRUSHKIN

## I Am a Success!

I am an Oral success.
At around two and a half years old, I started talking.
I started to learn to read at four.
Today I can (if I so choose) order a hamburger at McDonald's without
   having to repeat myself.
I can speak to family, friends, and strangers, and they can understand me
   without problems.
I can call my children to dinner from another room, or sing them a good-
   night song.
I can lipread with fairly good accuracy, and in a one-to-one situation, I can
   usually handle myself well.
I came to think of myself as a "Hearing person who cannot hear."
This you call a success.


Despite my speech, I still cannot hear.
In a group situation of two or more, I usually find myself lost in the
   conversation before five minutes are up.
I'd rather be alone with a book than with nonsigning people at dinner or
   at a big family gathering.
This you call a success?


I am a mainstreaming success.
Without the help of an interpreter, notetaker, or any support services, I
   attended public schools and got good grades.
I progressed at grade level, and learned to read well beyond my age and
   grade level.
I eventually got a Ph.D. from a major Hearing university.
This you call a success.


In the "mainstream" I always felt alone.
For thirteen years, I could count the number of my "friends" on one hand,
   and still have fingers left over.

These friends were themselves the "misfits" and "outcasts" who could not
gain friendships with the "in group."
I was bullied, shunned, and ignored by the "cool kids" and the "not so
cool" kids.
I was pushed to the brink of a mental breakdown. One day, I stabbed one
of my "friends" with a pencil—not because he'd done something bad
to me, but because it was what I really wanted to do to those other
kids.
I got labeled "emotionally disturbed."
This you call a success?


I am an ASL success.
I went to a school for the Deaf.
I learned to sign.
I was in school plays, on sports teams, and involved in student
government.
Today, I teach Hearing students at a major Hearing university.
I own my own house and two cars.
I am married and have two children.
I cannot count the number of my friends on my fingers and toes, because
I don't have enough fingers and toes.
Some of my friends are Hearing; most are Deaf.
I no longer dread sitting at a table, because I am surrounded by people
who sign.
No longer do I feel alone.
You call this a failure.
This you call a failure?

# SUSAN HAJIANI

## Connections

I can't recall now exactly when it happened—perhaps in 1953 when I was in third grade at Lincoln Elementary School. It was one of those normal, exciting days, learning to read, doing numbers, wondering if the boy sitting in front of me would fold up my assignment and slip it in his pocket because he had a crush on me. The bell rang and we all rushed outside, boys on one side, girls on the other. What to do with 20 exciting minutes of recess? Six or seven of us who were best friends had to quickly think of a fun game. How about playing telephone? A great idea. We sat down in a circle right on the playground and my friend Barbara started the game . . . whispering into the ear of the girl on her left, my friend Ruthie.

Then it was my turn but I wasn't quite sure what Ruthie said. I made something up and whispered it into the next ear in the circle. I waited for the message to get back to Barbara. She listened to the last person and looked dismayed. "That's not what I said, that is completely wrong." She seemed quite upset. The message was not supposed to be so far off the track. Barbara decided to back up and see what had happened. One by one, counterclockwise, each 8-year-old repeated what she heard and then it was my turn. I said my line and everyone pointed at me, "What? It's her fault; it's totally stupid. Now we know where the telephone message went haywire. Right here, with Sue!"

The game was over, but for me it was the start of something new—a feeling of shame that descended, making my face hot and tying my stomach in a knot. This playground moment took up residence in my head and made me wary. I was going to make sure this never would happen again. From now on, no one would catch me being stupid at the game of telephone. What seems so odd is that I had no name for what was wrong with me. No one had ever called me deaf or hard of hearing. My friends complained, "Why do you say 'what?' all the time?"

I could not hear very well. No, I wasn't actually deaf. People would have noticed that and labeled it if I did not respond at all. Still, there were a lot of times I seemed to be doing the wrong thing, a little off beat. So began another game, spawned by the telephone game, and I was the one who made it up, decided on the rules, and did not invite any other players to join me. The object of the game was to appear normal, not lose my friends, and especially not to appear to them as stupid. Of course, I had to constantly revise the rules to fit all kinds of seemingly ordinary situations to keep them appearing just that.

Taking a spelling test posed one of the most difficult challenges. Even from the front of the room, it was impossible to tell whether the teacher was saying "sunny" or "funny." If I was lucky, she might create a sentence that would clue me in to the word I needed. But I could allow myself to count on this. Suppose there was no sentence? No repetition of the puzzling word. The thought of failing the spelling test was not a pleasant one and I devised a way to prevent it. I memorized the spelling list forward and I also memorized it backward just in case my teacher decided to be clever and reverse the order. Since she never thought to be really creative by giving the list at random, I won my game. If I scored 100 percent, a feeling of relief hooked me on playing it again.

I was desperate to fill in the blanks, to make the connections that would restore everything to its proper order. The high and dangerous stakes of my game never occurred to me. I was setting myself on a long and lonely path where there were no safe havens to ask for help. It was all up to me to look perfect. In normal games, you win and you lose and everyone expects that as the outcome. But in my game, there was nothing in the rules about losing or going directly to jail. I had to win.

Of course, my strategy did not work all the time. On more occasions than I care to remember, I was exposed despite my efforts. Like when Mrs. McKinney gave the instructions as she turned to the other side of the class. Lip-reading, a skill I had developed unconsciously, was no help in this situation. Memory was also not an option. Certainly raising my hand and asking for help was out of the question. What else might work? I took a quick peek at the paper of the boy sitting next to me. Mrs. McKinney saw me. She said nothing but her beautiful face was no longer beautiful. She knitted her strong black eyebrows into a scowl, pursed her lips tightly, and shook her head slowly from side to side for an eternity. Lucky for me, the other students did not seem to notice my shame.

I felt sick to my stomach and my face was hot. What a horrible thing I had done. I still didn't know I was deaf. Mrs. McKinney obviously was disappointed in me as a cheat. I wanted to explain to her, "I was not looking for the answer, I was only looking for the page number." But how could I do that in front of 27 fourth graders? No, definitely not possible. I was clever but not brave. My stomach took another turn. I wanted to run away and hide. I felt tense and different from my classmates. They seemed so carefree and easygoing while I struggled with my pretense of being a person who could hear.

Now it wasn't just the game of telephone that I avoided. Nearly every game had some moment that could cause panic. The instructions, what was that . . . what did you do first? What are the rules? When it was time to play a game, I pretended that I was not interested or had other important things to do. It was a good time to disappear to the rest room, get a drink at the water fountain, or climb on the playground slides. At slumber parties, I feigned exhaustion and slept early while my friends chattered into the night. They were upset that I was not participating in their fun and decided to do something about it. They filled a bucket with water and dumped it on me to wake me up. They succeeded but I did not view my dousing as fun. I was deeply humiliated and stopped attending slumber parties.

Class was becoming more awkward too. At times I was not sure if the teacher was calling on me or on someone else. How many times I raised my hand to share a thought only to learn that another student had beaten me to it. Or I would answer when someone else in the back of the room was still talking. In-class films became another source of anxiety. As the images fluttered across the screen, I struggled to make sense of the distorted words of the narrator whose voice I could not make sense of and whose lips were nowhere visible on the screen. My heart and stomach fluttered along in rhythm at the thought of the pop quiz at the end of the film. In spite of my poor grades on these quizzes, I managed to increase my scores in other areas, keeping up the fiction that all was well.

Somewhere along the line, one of my teachers finally discovered what I thought was my secret. I believe I was writing at the blackboard and did not respond to her prompts. My first hearing test did not occur until I was ten years old in the basement of Lincoln School while my classmates played ball outside the window. I cannot recall who administered the test, but it was apparent to me that I was not doing well. The tester seemed quite perturbed by my lack of appropriate answers, and I was equally tense waiting for the beeps of the testing machine amid the screams of the ball game outside.

But all that came of the tests were some comments that I should sit in the front of the class and pay more attention. Unfortunately, my new education plan made it very obvious to the class that I could not hear well. In those days, the class was most often seated alphabetically, starting with the Andersons and ending with the Zanders. My name started with H, propelling me into prominence as out of order again. The day seats were assigned in each class became an additional burden, but I had no idea how to deal with this problem. I simply hoped my new classmates would forget my seating embarrassment.

When I got to junior high school, the telephone itself became a terror to replace my game. I later learned that Alexander Graham Bell had invented the telephone as a result of his quest to help his deaf wife. The irony of his well-meaning efforts, which only caused me agony, was all too apparent.

Not only was I missing out on a lot during class, I was also missing out on all the long telephone discussions which teenagers have after getting home from school and into the night, making sense of what happened in biology class or in the halls. My phone did ring but it was hard to giggle and be relaxed when I had so much trouble deciphering exactly what was being said. I marveled that some girls talked on the phone for a whole hour. A couple minutes were more than enough for me.

I showed up at the wrong house to baby-sit several times and, of course, my would-be employers decided that I was undependable. On the few jobs I landed, I worried that I would not be able to identify suspicious sounds. There was a popular horror story about that time of someone entering a home and harassing the babysitter from the upstairs extension.

Once I misunderstood the name of a boy who was asking me out. I told him no, when really I would have been thrilled to go out with him. He was disappointed and mentioned it to my girlfriend. He did not call me again. I didn't hear the phone ring when I was home alone and my friends started to say how hard it was to get hold of me when they changed their minds about the place or the time. My best friend even decided that I wasn't much fun, never got the joke, and should not be invited at all.

It made me feel so sad and angry; didn't they know how hard I was trying? Of course, they never noticed I had memorized nearly everything that happened in class or that I was lip-reading or smiling constantly? How could they notice when I was so adept at keeping my efforts a secret?

My family still had not acknowledged or accepted my hearing loss. They were all preoccupied with their own concerns and often found my blunders amusing, which only added to my shame. "What a strange answer," they would say. "Sue seems a little aloof; sometimes she is unpleasant and tense, even has a bad disposition." I took it all to heart. It certainly seemed much more serious than not being able to hear— something I was not about to admit. Besides, it seemed more reasonable to have a bad disposition than a hearing "problem." You could work at changing the first but not the second. And I did desperately want to blend in. I added new techniques to camouflage my bad disposition. I smiled and smiled. I volunteered to erase the blackboard. In discussions, I agreed to the majority because I wasn't sure what the choices were.

Thus started another variation of the game. Subterfuge had not served me well, so I would try self-improvement. I found a lip-reading instructor who mouthed to me short passages from the "Life in These United States" section of the Readers' Digest. He was amazed to see that I had already learned this skill in my survival game. However, he failed to mention that only around 30 to 40 percent of speech is visible through lip movements, leaving the lip-reader to figure out the remaining 60 to 70 percent. And most real life situations are much more complicated than the simple vignettes in *Readers' Digest*. Even with my efforts to gaze relentlessly on the moving mouth (or mouths) in front of me, I continued to lose the connection. People, especially men, sometimes asked why I was staring at them so intently. "Just interested in what you are saying," I would lie. It was easier to lie than to explain I was deaf and that a walrus style mustache or dangling cigarette made my game harder to play. Not only did I want to avoid discussions of my failure to lip-read; I hated the pity and shock that sprang up if I had to admit to being deaf. Well-meaning people would recoil and say, "What a shame. Oh, I am so sorry." Then they would inquire either "Can you lip-read?" or "Why not get a hearing aid?"

By the time I was thirty, I decided to try hearing aids. My hearing had been tested many times before, always with disappointing results. The doctor or audiologist would sigh gravely: "Your hearing is worse; you are very deaf." I never asked for an explanation and indeed they never offered any. Nor did they explain the tests to me in any sensible way or suggest hearing aids or sign language. I was very focused on getting out of the office as quickly as possible. I had developed a certain toughness or resignation in my struggles which did not include looking for answers or cures.

The audiologist would start with the faintest sounds in his search to assess how much I could hear. Beep. "Can you hear that?" I was supposed to raise my finger at the sound so he could mark his graph of frequencies and decibels. But I heard nothing for a long time and sat there wondering if it was time to raise my finger or not. My tester progressed up the sound scale to 90 decibels. Roar. "Can you hear that?" He seemed relieved to finally get an entry on the graph that would complete the audiogram and give him an idea of which powerful hearing aid might make me hear.

But the hearing aids only slightly improved my wild guesses at what was going on. I was still left with my struggle to pass as normal and appear to understand the myriad daily events that engulfed me. Plus, the amplified noise and the constant stress had caused a new problem: migraine headaches.

The migraines appeared at odd and unpredictable times, only occasionally when stress was most evident. I would be out shopping, looking through a rack of dresses when my head would unexpectedly begin to throb and little stars and dots would appear in my vision, swim around and leave a black hole. Or one side of my tongue or my right arm would go numb. It was very frightening and the first time it happened, I rushed to the emergency room where they checked me for a stroke. The doctor prescribed a powerful drug that decreased the symptoms but did nothing, of course, to alter the underlying reason for my headaches, my ongoing, stress-filled game of normality. The migraines alternated with something even more ominous: panic attacks in which my heart raced and I felt absolutely trapped. It seemed I would die if I could not escape before anyone noticed my flushed and sweaty face. The panic attacks were very specific to communication situations when all my coping strategies had led to a point blank misunderstanding, leaving me stranded on the beach of my deafness. And I did not know how to be deaf.

Parallel to my struggles with my deafness, I proceeded with other areas of my life. It seemed as if I was leading two lives. I went to college and graduated with honors with the help of my powerful memory that had been developed throughout grade and high school. My major was technical communications. I wanted to be a newspaper reporter, but by the time graduation arrived, I was starting to realize the impact of my deafness and knew it would never work out. I decided to pursue a master's degree in political science with the thought that I could be involved in editing. Since I was not in the habit of exploring my very personal deafness with others, I did not think to seek advice on how to deal with my career conundrum. Among the 10,000 or more students at the university, I now know that I could not have been the only one struggling with this issue.

Then I married, had children, and worked at a variety of jobs in editing and publications but when the telephone rang, I quickly left my desk so my seatmate could answer the phone. Nothing much had changed over all the years except that my terror was increasing along with my expertise. By this time I was in my forties and I knew I would soon become totally, profoundly deaf. In spite of considering myself an intelligent person, I still did not have a clue about what to do with my knotted stomach, my migraine headaches, my panic attacks, or my deep sense of shame as my body continued its rebellion at my psychological fraud.

I wasn't really any different than the eight-year-old on the playground in spite of my efforts all through the years. I take that back. I was different. In spite of my game, I was not making the connections that would make sense to my life and make me feel good. My life, the real me, was as far off the mark as the message I had delivered so long ago on the playground of Lincoln School. There were only a couple parts that were right. I had a devoted husband and two beautiful sons. The rest was gibberish, carefully crafted by many years of my determined but misguided efforts. In spite of this recognition that I was a fraud, being deaf was still not what I had in mind. But I did have a creeping suspicion that I needed to stop playing my game and try something else.

The first "something else" I tried was volunteering for a disability council at work. By this time, I was no longer looking for acceptance of my pretend self but acknowledgement of my reality. My colleagues had, not surprisingly, already realized I was not hearing them. My boss, however, was not happy when I took my old nemesis of telephone communications by the horn. I asked for a special telephone for the deaf, which has a keyboard (a TTY) at my desk so I could make and receive calls to my husband instead of asking a peer to call for me. The monthly cost of the device would certainly add up, my boss cautioned me. I was very insensitive to his concerns.

I toyed with the TTY for a while but could only connect to others who had one also. Since I didn't know many deaf people, my life did not change radically. But the machine was right there on my desk in public view... my badge of deafness. I had stopped hiding in the shadows of the not perfect me.

Little did I know that I was about to become the recipient of the spoils of a hard-fought battle when the Americans with Disabilities Act was passed in 1992. Activists in Berkeley, California, had started this effort of accessibility for wheelchairs and spent much time demonstrating and lobbying to turn their dreams into law. They wanted equality of access in housing, education, employment, and, last but not least, telecommunications for the deaf. When the law finally passed, deaf people were assured statewide relay services. It was a laborious system with the deaf person typing in a message to an operator. The operator then voiced it to the hearing caller and back again through the conversation. Tedious, yes, but very liberating also.

I started making calls here and there. First, I called a few friends. Then I called the bank to check my account. It seemed amazing to be making these calls on my own instead of guiltily working up the nerve to ask someone else to do me this favor. A few people hung up on me because the relay operation took a lot of time, or they thought I was soliciting money for a "handicapped" organization. However, it seemed more irritating than shameful. I was shedding some of my humiliation and liked the feeling.

How nice it would be to say my life was immediately made whole by the technological and legal revolution that restored the telephone to my life after years of torment by that jangling instrument. I enjoyed the irony of the situation, but first I had to work on undoing all the damage of my efforts to avoid the telephone whether in play or reality. I had the habits of many years to conquer and even though I had begun to realize they no longer served a purpose useful to my life, my reactions seemed to be a matter of instinct, deeply ingrained. I was always on edge, waiting to bluff or escape.

I was still having migraines and panic attacks when communication broke down. It was slow going and I was alone at the beginning of my awareness, especially since I had not learned how to connect and ask for help. But the possibility of connecting was there; it snaked off my desk TTY, outside across the wire to wherever I could think of going. I started talking to other people with various disabilities. I went for counseling. I called to register for sign language classes. Through enormous effort, this time positive, I learned sign language and became reasonably fluent, though I could never match the skills of a born deaf signer. By doing this, I was able to pursue a master's degree in social work and a new career working with people with whom I could communicate. Along with this came a new sense of acceptance and the pleasure of life without migraines and panic attacks. I was on my way to leaving behind the haywire Sue who had lived in my chest and head for such a large part of my life.

A few loose wires remain. The message still goes awry sometimes and when it does there's that old, familiar feeling that I'm not connected and the sudden urge to escape, to hide, to fix it up. And I fight it down and sign, "Say that again please," with the relief of knowing it is a real, imperfect, human request and not a game.

# CHRISTOPHER JON HEUER

## Billy Joel: The Reason I Won't Get a Cochlear Implant

About four years ago my older brother Warren got a cochlear implant. He had the surgery done in the spring and the processor was all hooked up by the time my wife and I came home to visit that summer. Mom called and told me the news. While she didn't come right out and say it in so many words, I could tell she was hoping I'd follow his lead and get one next. For her sake I tried to appear neutral and open-minded.

To be clear: I'm not the type of person who really cares all that much whether a deaf adult gets an implant or not. As far as I'm concerned, once you're eighteen you call your own shots. I'm also fully aware that parents are having their kids implanted at earlier ages in order to counter language acquisition barriers. But as an educator, what I see is all too often the end result of a parental fantasy. Too many of them are hoping—in some cases desperately—that an implant is going to make everything okay. When it inevitably doesn't, the disappointment shuts them down all the more. What kid deserves that?

But that wasn't the case here. Though Warren and I both share the common bond of deafness, our lives didn't develop around it in the same way. He was mainstreamed his whole life and never learned how to sign. I was mainstreamed until high school, and then went to the Wisconsin School for the Deaf. I've since worked mostly in signing environments, and while half of my friends are hearing, most are signers. He, on the other hand, worked in hearing environments his whole life. His friends are hearing, and so is his daughter. In fact he never really showed much of an interest in getting an implant until she was born.

That's why I decided to keep my opinions about CIs to myself around him. He was getting one because of *her*. His decision wasn't about identity issues or making a political statement. We'd never really talked about ASL or Deaf culture. I always got the sense that he didn't want me to. At the time I thought I understood. If his mainstream experience was anything like mine, he got through it by blending in as much as possible. Keep living your life that way, and sooner or later your entire personality becomes a survival skill. And while ASL can offer you many things, invisibility isn't one of them. So . . . live and let live. From that perspective, ASL isn't an option.

But I was curious. Did the implant work or didn't it? When he was a teenager, his hearing aids (like mine) ended up in a box stuffed in the back of his desk drawer. It wasn't just because of the "don't stand out" thing. They honestly didn't do much for me. A couple of years back I picked up some Widexes, just to see if the Age of Digital Technology really had anything on the older models. I knew it would take a bit of time to get used to wearing them again, but nothing could have prepared me for the raw amount of *racket* that hammered my skull while riding on the metro. Blaring announcements in foreign gibberish, deafening squeals (yes, deafening all over again) every time the subway braked to a halt . . . I had a throbbing ache in my neck by the time I got home. Even my eyeballs hurt.

Don't get me wrong, this wasn't a Widex problem. It's an expectation problem. "Racket" isn't all we used to hear; either me or Warren. We weren't born deaf. We *went* deaf—gradually—and the onset followed pretty much the same time frame: mild losses and hearing aids by the second grade; profoundly deaf by age twenty-five.

But there's a lot of space in twenty-five years for listening to things that sound like harmonic masterpieces. My hearing faded out with the popularity of Guns N' Roses. His faded soon after *Billy Joel's Greatest Hits* came out. And while I won't go so far as to say Guns N' Roses ever produced what you could call a harmonic masterpiece (though they did rock), Billy Joel is right up there with the angels.

Warren loved the whole album, and so did I. *Allentown, Piano Man, The Longest Time* . . . all are pitch-perfect. Our hearing sister never even had to write out the lyrics to his stuff (the way she did for other songs) so we could follow along. We could pick out the words easily; his voice is a musical instrument in and of itself. Remember that scene in *Children of a Lesser God* where William Hurt gets stuck trying to explain Bach to Marlee Matlin? As a person who can appreciate the complexities of the task from both perspectives—his *and* hers—let me tell you something: If he'd been a Billy Joel fan instead, it wouldn't have been such a problem.

In fact there was a Billy Joel CD sitting on Warren's television that day when the two of us stopped by his house to pick up an air conditioner for Mom. Warren walked through the door ahead of me. I called out his name to see if he'd turn around. Call it a test, a propaganda buster. Is the technology really getting better all the time? Put your money where your ears are.

To my surprise he *did* turn around, though I had to repeat his name a few times.

"What?" he asked.

I tapped the side of my head and pointed at his implant. "Level with me. Does that thing really work?"

"Sure."

"Better than hearing aids?"

He nodded. *"I think so."* I glanced over at the Billy Joel CD, and he caught this. "You thinking about getting one?"

I shrugged, suddenly uncomfortable again.

"What's the problem?"

In retrospect, I think that was the day I realized there was a lot more to my resistance to implants than just the theory that hearing parents who get them for their deaf children are living in denial. Want to know what new conclusion I came up with? Through a Widex, Billy Joel doesn't sound like Billy Joel. He sounds like a Mack truck crashing into a church. But take it off, and he sounds like Billy Joel again. Like I said, it's a question of expectation. No hearing aid or implant is ever going to beat that mental radio in your skull. If you already know what things *should* sound like, it's very tough to settle for what they *don't* sound like.

"How about music?" I asked.

"It's not the same, no."

"The implant screws it up?"

"Yeah."

His answer pretty much told me all I wanted to know. And in the years since, I've never really explored the question further. After all, what place is better than that for giving up? Still, whenever I go home, there he'll be, talking with his daughter and listening to her tell him how her day went, what she did in school. I've taught her a couple of signs, and in our own fashion we do the same thing. But you can tell that she's starting to notice: he has an implant, and I don't. I sign, and he doesn't. Actually most of our family doesn't. Why is this? My sister's hearing children have already asked me these questions, and when they did I explained to them as best as I could. There's no reason to expect that Warren's daughter won't ask me, as well.

I wonder what I'm going to say to this time around.

# KAREN LLOYD

## Different Enough to Be Normal

As a girl growing up in rural far-north Queensland in the 1960s I was fascinated by people who were different from us. Aunty Clare was a dressmaker and was always working on something beautiful at her kitchen table; she dyed her hair black and painted her long fingernails red, and she put margarine instead of butter on her bread. My friend Linda's parents were from Yugoslavia; I loved staying over at their house and the food they ate was deliciously different. The children of an Indian family came to school every day with their hair neatly plaited and oiled. A classmate had two cousins living with her family because their mother had run off and left them. To me different was exotic, endlessly interesting.

When I was eight I became very ill and almost died and was suddenly profoundly deaf and more different than anyone else in my small world. Different wasn't so exotic anymore. For a long time my life became a lot about a struggle to not be different. Now, more than forty years later, I look back and it seems to me that "different" has been a defining word in my life. People who are different still fascinate me, and I've known a wonderfully diverse range of people who have enriched my life with their difference. Of course, "different," once you start to think about it in any depth, is one of those relative and ultimately meaningless words, like "normal". "Different," for me, has been both a joyful and a painful word, but I think that I've emerged from it all to be quite "normal."

Becoming deaf was a shock and I had quite a strong reaction to it, tantrums so spectacular and depression so severe that I mostly don't remember, I guess as a protective measure my mind has closed it off. A little I remember, but mostly what I know of it is what my family told me in later years when I asked. If the saying *What doesn't kill you makes you stronger* is true, then that period of my life has made me immensely strong.

Growing up in a community where I was unique, the only deaf person I knew, I stood out from the crowd just because I was deaf and different. I was shy and didn't want to stand out or be different. I was mortified when people did things that drew attention to me and the fact that I was deaf, like the year eight science teacher who insisted that while my classmates worked on some set task I sit with her at the front of the room and learn to correctly pronounce the names of the species. But sometimes I enjoyed the admiration that being deaf brought, like dancing the Highland Fling and the Strathspey solo in concerts and doing it well and in time to the music, assisted by a loyal friend who sat beside the pianist "to turn the page for her" and silently mouthed the counts for me, afterwards denying to anyone who asked that she had helped me keep in time.

Deafness seemed so often to be something that could be used against me, often in conflicting ways. When kids wouldn't let me play with them, they'd say I couldn't do it because I was deaf. "Of course she can," my older sister often said, "You've got to let her play with you!" But when I did well in class they'd say it was only because I was deaf. "Don't be so mean and nasty," one teacher said to a classmate who claimed I'd only done well on an exam because the teacher felt sorry for me. It was something I used sometimes too when it suited me. I loathed athletics and took to using my deafness as an excuse. I couldn't be in a running race I'd say because I couldn't hear the starter. That worked for a while, until we got a new headmaster who looked at me pitilessly, pulled out an enormous white hanky and said, "When I drop my hanky, start running!"

When I was ten I went to the school for the deaf at Dutton Park in Brisbane for one year as a boarder and spent most of the year feeling bewildered and homesick. People there were very different and with one or two exceptions I thought the adults were cruel. But I made some friends and I began to learn some sign language from the other kids in the playground and the dorm. The school at that time was an oral school; we had to speak and lipread and use hearing aids. Signing was banned. So we signed in secret. The first sign I learned was the thumbs up sign for "good." We were on a bus going somewhere and some boys sitting behind me tapped me on the shoulder and stuck their thumbs up at me when I turned around to look at them. At home, sticking your thumb up at someone was an insulting gesture. I couldn't understand what I had done to deserve it and turned away, hurt. Another tap on the shoulder and I turned around again. "No, no," they said, grinning at me and signing. Thumbs up. "Means good." Little finger up. "Means bad. You not bad." Thumbs up. "You good. We like you." Ah! All smiles now, I stuck my thumb up at them and grinned. I was delighted. I was being initiated into the secret tribal lore.

But all through that year it was drummed into me that I must not sign: I could speak, I was learning to lipread, I was doing well, I must not sign, signing was bad, I didn't need it and if I used it I would forget how to talk. And I retained the lesson, unquestioning, believing it to be true, for many years afterwards.

One of the things I found most striking about life at the deaf school was that there was no privacy. I came from a family of five children and all through my formative years I shared a room with my three sisters in our small house, but in our family everyone had space and everyone had privacy. At the deaf school no one seemed to understand the concept of privacy, at least not for us kids. I had been there a week when I wrote my first letter home, a letter of agony, I was so unhappy and so homesick. The next day a teacher took me aside and said I had to write another letter home, a happy letter. It was then that I also began to notice how people kept telling me what to say, what to think, and what to feel, and this was a theme that coloured my life for a very long time afterwards.

After a year I left the deaf school. I returned to my old school and I stayed in the mainstream for the remainder of my formal education. Except for a visit a few years later from one of the kids I had been friendly with, I had no further contact with any of my deaf school friends for almost thirty years and that year was like a lost year. I couldn't talk about it with anyone at home; they were not there, they didn't understand what it was like and I could not explain it, it was too different. When I finally did meet up again, when I was almost forty, with some people who had been in my class, I felt I was reclaiming a part of myself.

For a long time after I left the deaf school I tried to be "normal" and live like the hearing people around me. It was expected of me. I went to mainstream schools, I joined the Brownies for a while, learned Scottish dancing, played basketball quite badly and went to parties and family events like other people. I had good friends and a family that in its way was supportive and in many ways my life was very full and happy.

In my last two years of high school I went to boarding school again, this time by choice. My sister had been there and loved it. It was a church school and I too loved it and did well. However, in my final year I had an experience that turned me away from the church and it was twenty years before I chose to go to church again.

A faith-healing mission that our headmistress more or less commanded me to attend failed to restore my hearing, as I had predicted it would. Of course it was declared my fault; I did not believe. It unleashed an extraordinary outpouring of disappointment and confusion among those around me.

People cried. People accused. Classmates sat in the dark long after lights out and talked, trying to make sense of it all. Friends and classmates begged me to try again, to believe. A teacher, an atheist, took me aside and asked, genuinely concerned, if I was all right. Through it all I walked steadfast and unbowed. I wouldn't go through that again, they could expel me if they liked, but I wasn't doing it.

Early one morning a friend walked with me across the oval and cajoled, "Don't you want to hear the birds sing? The wind in the trees?"

I looked at her and said, "Yes, I'd like to hear the birds and the wind in the trees. But it's not going to happen. I'm deaf. The little hairs in my ears are dead, and when something's dead, you can't make it come alive again."

"God can!"

"God can't. Not this time. And even if it were possible, I don't want it. When I became deaf I had to adapt to being a different person. It was hard. If I could hear again I'd have to go through it all again and get used to being a different person all over again. I don't want to have to do that. I'm happy to be the person I am now."

And as I said the words, I knew that it was true. At some fundamental level I had made peace with my deafness. I was happy to be who I was. For me, being different was normal.

A few years later I got involved with a school for the deaf as a volunteer. It was an oral school and it didn't take me long to start thinking about the usefulness of sign language. It seemed ridiculous to me that these kids who had quite minimal communication skills were being forced to use a language, spoken English, that they clearly couldn't access. At the same time I met a man who challenged me to think for myself and I began to dig myself out from under all the things I had for years been told to think and feel and say.

I started reading whatever I could find about deafness and deaf people. According to almost everything I read, deaf people who used sign language were failures and lived in a ghetto and I was incredibly fortunate to be able to speak and lipread and not need to use sign language. But still, I wanted to meet other deaf people and make up my own mind. I also thought that my life wasn't that fabulous; there were a lot of barriers and too many people telling me what I could and couldn't do and saying stupid things like, "Will it help if we shout?" And I noticed that all these people who knew what was best for me were hearing people. How could they know if they weren't deaf? Where were the deaf people? What did they have to say about it all?

It was time to meet other deaf people. But doing that wasn't a simple thing. I knew nothing about other deaf people except those I'd met at the deaf school and what I'd read about them. So I went to the Deaf Society, there is one in every Australian state. A hearing man who worked there interviewed me and passed judgement. "You're one of the 'elite' deaf," he said. "Deaf people won't accept you. What do you want here? Are you having problems coping in the hearing world, so now you're looking to the deaf world?" I was devastated. He wasn't any different, I thought, from all those cruel adults at the deaf school in Brisbane. Defeated, I left and went back to my "lovely elite life."

A couple of years later I tried a different tack. I enrolled in a sign language class—at the Deaf Society, and when I turned up on the first night who should be teaching it but the same judgemental man who knew everything about deaf people? I cringed, and prayed he wouldn't remember me, and he gave no indication that he did.

And so over time as I learned to sign I started going to some social events at the Deaf Society. Very early on I was lucky enough to meet Dorothy Shaw, a deaf person, a legend in the Australian deaf community, one of the kindest and most nurturing people I have ever met, and she took me under her wing. Dorothy was an activist and she encouraged me to get involved with her advocacy organisations and because I had good English skills I soon took on secretarial roles and became quite "political." I loved it, and I figured that if I worked with groups like this to try and make life better for all deaf people then my life would be better too. I had found my passion. I had also found a way to develop skills I'd not been able to develop as someone who "lived in a hearing world" because in the "hearing world" I could not participate in group events as I was unable to follow discussions.

At school and university I'd spent a lot of time pretending to understand what was going on and studying late into the night to try and keep up with what I missed in class, and at university where I had even less support than at school, having a social life was possible but difficult. Trying to be "normal" and fit in was often traumatic, frustrating and exhausting and I cried often, quietly and alone. Now, getting into the deaf community and learning Auslan (Australian Sign Language) was a revelation. Far from being the ghetto I had for years been told it was and limiting my life as I'd been told sign language would, the deaf community and Auslan opened up my life and expanded my opportunities and my social life. I'll never forget the day when I sat in a meeting and watched a guest speaker make a presentation in Auslan, having by then learned enough Auslan to understand her presentation. After all the years of sitting in classrooms and lecture theatres and meetings and church, not understanding anything much of what was said and trying to look as if I did in order to fit in and be "normal," it was incredibly liberating. And I met a lot of people and went to a lot of parties where having a good time was easy just because communicating was easy.

But it wasn't all simple, plain sailing. The deaf community, like any community, is complex and people can be cruel. There is a level of easy acceptance and communication, to be sure, but there is also suspicion, rivalry, and hostility. Being Dorothy Shaw's protégé in the beginning helped smooth my passage and acceptance into the community but I encountered suspicion and hostility too. Interestingly, most of this suspicion and hostility was from hearing people, CODAs and workers, who questioned why I was there and from deaf people who themselves were relatively late comers trying to find their place in the community. Some of the most welcoming and encouraging people of all were deaf people who, like Dorothy Shaw, came from deaf families and formed the nucleus of the deaf community.

Now, some thirty years after I made my first forays into the deaf community, I have met a lot of people, learned a lot about them and from them, seen wildly varying levels of education, knowledge, skill and ability, confidence and self assurance and the lack of it, and observed a lot of different points of view. And I have a lot of thoughts about it, but that would need to be the subject of separate essays. If any generalisation can be made it is that the deaf community is like any other community. In fact, in many ways it is a lot like the small rural community where I grew up. It has its characters, controversies, and conflicts. It enfolds, nurtures, and protects, and it rejects. Its biggest problem is that it continues to be demonised by people who know little if anything about it and who indulge in that age-old response of assuming they know best, rejecting and criticising what they don't understand.

As for me, I have found my place in the world and it's a pretty good place to be. I have hearing family, colleagues, and friends, and I have deaf colleagues and friends and I love, respect, and cherish them all. There are hearing people I dislike and there are deaf people I dislike, just as there are hearing people and deaf people who evidently feel the same way about me. I spend some of my life in "the hearing world" and some of it in "the deaf world." I speak and write in English and I sign in Auslan. I feel very fortunate, I like my life and I like who I am. And if that's not "normal," then "normal" is something I don't want to be.

# DOMINIC McGREAL

## My Father

In September 1976, I was at St. Joseph's School for Deaf Boys in Cabra, Dublin. It was a lovely afternoon when my aunt came to our nursery, unexpectly. She did not have any words for me; instead, she ran right past me and on toward the kitchen, where two nurses were.

They closed the kitchen door. I was bemused and looked at the group of boys in the room. I had no idea why my aunt had come. One of nurses came into the room and told me that I needed to pack my clothes right away.

So I went upstairs to pack. Within in few minutes I was down again and met my aunt at the hall. I said goodbye to my friends and the two nurses and I got in my uncle's car.

I asked my aunt, "Why am I going home?"

She replied, "Yes, you are going home today."

My aunt had not said a thing to me. I was so happy and excited to be going home to Mayo to see my family. I arrived at my aunt's house in Cellbridge, County Kildare, where she and her husband worked a big farm.

I greeted my two cousins and we began to play. I stayed at my aunt's house for a few hours. She packed her bag. She had organised with one of her neighbours to drive us both to Mayo. My aunt's husband stayed home to look after the farm and the two girls.

About halfway to Mayo we stopped in a small town, where we got something to eat before continuing on our journey. It was almost evening when we arrived at my home in Thallabawn, County Mayo, in the west of Ireland. I noticed that there were a few cars around the place. I got out of the car and ran toward the house.

Suddenly, I was overcome with confusion. I saw a great many people in the hall and the sitting room. It was very strange to see them all looking very sad and talking sombrely to each other. These people were smiling at me in a strange and somewhat false way; it was all very unusual and odd.

I wandered around looking for my mother. I finally found her in the small kitchen, she was standing there, clearly upset. One of my aunts forced me out of the room. They didn't want me to see my mother crying. My aunt told me to go outside and I obeyed her.

Naturally, I ran over to the farm yard, calling my father: "Daddy, where are you?"

I continued to yell and shout for my father, but he did not answer. I began to feel more confused as to why Daddy wasn't there and everything felt so odd, with all the people and my mother upset. I remembered all the times I would call my father in that very place, and how he would always appear calling me over to him.

I began to feel very sad and walked toward the house. I went upstairs to the bedroom and began to cry. I was very upset. I fell asleep in the bed and later awoke with a fright in the darkness. I jumped out of the bed and ran into the hall. I screamed with terror. My mother was there suddenly, hugging me. She persuaded me to go back to bed, and comforted me till I fell back asleep.

I woke up early and looked through the window. The day was rainy and miserable. After breakfast I dressed up in nice clothes to get ready for mass at our church. I looked at my mother, she wore a black dress and a black scarf around her head. I had never seen my mother wear a black dress. It made me creepy to look at her sad face. I went into the church and my mother stood beside me. She gestured to the cross where Jesus lay above the altar. She said to me, "Your Daddy is up there."

I looked at my mother's lips, reading them with confusion. I pointed at the cross and asked, "Up there?"

My mother pushed my finger down and spoke gently,

"Yes, Daddy is up there."

I could hardly understand what she was saying and I had no clue what she meant by these words. I was only seven years old.

I grew lonely without my father. I had not seen my second oldest sister at home, because she stayed at my grandmother's house in Curradavitt. There were just my youngest brother who was only one and my youngest sister who was still a small baby. They had stayed home, where my uncle was looking after them.

After the mass was over, we went home for the dinner. My mother told me that I must go back to school. I got very angry and threw a tantrum. I felt like she was rejecting me, I just wanted to stay at home, but she would not allow it. So my aunt came to see me and encouraged me to stay with her in Kildare for a few days. My mother agreed. I began to feel a little happier, my aunt was saving me.

At that time I still did not know where my father was. I went to my aunt's place in County Kildare for a few days and I returned to school.

A few months later, I was in class and my teacher was telling us about God and the Heavens. It made a big impact on me, because I began to understand what these things meant. Suddenly, I began to cry, realizing for the first time that my father was in Heaven. I never knew until that time that my father had died. I was very upset because my family had never told me the news of my father's death. It was the worst thing that happened to me in my life.

I felt much better as I began to understand what the teacher was explaining to me. I was glad to finally know these words that I had never known before. I felt a bit angry with my mother for not explaining to me about my father. I knew my mother couldn't communicate with me and she was too upset over my father's death. She never talked about my father dying, because she had such a terrible experience when she saw my father die in the tractor accident on my grandfather's farm in Curradavitt, County Mayo. My mother is very stubborn. I knew this and had to accept that I would never speak to her about my father's death again.

I had not attended my father's funeral. My mother would not allow me to see it in case it gave me terrible nightmares.

I could scream all over the place and throw more tantrums at my mother because she was not able to use sign language and she would only speak to me. I know I wish I had been there to attend my father's funeral. It was hard for me to accept it.

# LAUREN RIDLOFF

## Waiting for the Super

You are locked out. There you are standing, scattering items around in your purse when it slowly dawns on you. The image of your keys sitting on the bookcase next to the door materializes in your mind, accompanied by a sinking feeling in your stomach. You take your hands out of your purse and hold them up in embarrassed surrender. "My keys are inside the apartment," you tell your friend. He is someone you like very much, and you two are kinda sorta friends. You already kissed, already fucked but that's it. This being locked out brings you up to a new level, and you hope he doesn't think it is some clingy damsel-in-distress scheme. You just have a bad habit of misplacing your keys, and he has not yet learned that.

You and your friend are standing outside the super's apartment, waiting for an answer. He is the man who can let you in. But no one comes to the door. "I think I have his number," you say, checking your pager. You do. You text him. The super tells you he will be there in two hours.

Now you have two hours to kill, and it's a warm late Sunday afternoon in the fall. Your friend and you had spent the night together, and he drove you home, ready to let you go again for another couple weeks of email tag and date-making. He was ready to let you go. You were ready to come home. But now you have two homeless hours. Your friend offers to keep you company. You wonder if it is an act of kindness and he does not expect you to accept the offer. You are not sure if you want the company because you were set on spending your dwindling weekend day in solitude. He does not see your hesitation because you are putting your pager away in your purse.

It is a lovely October day and to spend it in solitude is a shame, so you decide to go to the Mediterranean café with the oilcloth tables a few blocks away. You also decide that your friend's offer is a genuine display of friendship. You walk three blocks up the main street to the café. Your old roommate had told you that their pita sandwiches were legendary. The arms of your shadows on the sidewalk are touching.

In the back of the café is a room. Paneled, beveled mirrors on the wall sparkle and replicate you and your friend. Every move you make, every gesture he makes is repeated an infinity in the background. You are reminded of a mirror maze in a haunted house you once paid to go in with your aunt and your cousin. You had giggled your way through with your cousin, wanting to be scared, pretending to be scared and finally being scared.

You are waiting for the food to come, and you are relishing this moment with your friend. He is talking. He is drinking Turkish coffee and talking about his ex-girlfriend. LaRue. Her last name sounds irresistible, nothing like your last name. You play her name in your head again and again, just because you like the way it sounds.

He tells you about the black and white photograph he took of her, how he entered it in a photography contest and won. Pixel by pixel, the image of his ex-girlfriend appears in your mind. You can see her just like he did, lying fetal in a hammock, staring sullenly at something off to the side, one hand curled protectively under her chin, forever unavailable. He won $500 and lost her.

The food has not arrived yet. Your Turkish coffee leaves a gritty residue on your tongue. Your friend tells you about the night he woke up and found LaRue shivering in the bathroom, embedded in between the sink and a cloud of delusion. You sense his fear and exasperation as he remembers coaxing her out, cajoling her back into bed.

He tells you LaRue is mentally ill. You notice how gentle and quiet his eyes are. His usual bravura has a patina to it, you realize. He recounts the moment when she begged him to come back, dull knife on her wrist. You can see the back of his head weaving in the mirror behind him as he talks. You wonder what he notices behind you. Whether he notices.

The gaudy mirrors multiply and triple your friend's every move, repeating this moment in the café. The oilcloth is pink and stained with coffee rings. The table is infinitely stained in the mirrors.

As you take this in, you realize you want to remember everything. You want to replace the pixilated image of LaRue. You want to kiss the beveled pieces of his heart and smooth them into a smooth curve. You want to become the loved subject he talks about in some café with stained tables in the distant future. You feel this moment mirrored again and again, stored infinitely.

The legendary pita sandwiches arrive. Sitting there in the café, the two of you eating crispy falafel, he learns that you are bad with your keys and you learn that you were locked out, and you are being let in.

And then the super calls.

# DEAN SHERIDAN

## IFYOUCANREADMYHANDYOUARETOODEAF

"WHATISYOURLASTNAME?" A Deaf speaker's hand was suddenly in my view, an inch away from my face. The question was rapidly fingerspelled, it was almost a blur to read. There are other polite ways of asking one's name, of course.

I answered. The Deaf speaker was a bit surprised.

"HOWTALLAREYOU?"

Geez. My Deaf parents warned me about "Good/Bad Deaf people" but this was becoming ridiculous.

I answered again, in normal signed expression. I was hoping that the speaker would back down if I was polite. Silly me!

Undeterred, the speaker quickly said, "CANYOUUNDERSTANDMYHAND?"

I've had enough. I slowly raised my signing hand, perfectly centered into the speaker's face, an inch away from the speaker's eyes:

"NOJUSTYOURDIRTYFINGERS."

Smile. That moment was the first and last time I've ever encountered such an aggressive greeting. It was a precious gift for me, though: That particular moment revealed a rare insight into Deaf-to-Deaf Fencer interaction.

The speaker was shocked that I could handle such a challenge ("You're not supposed to be THAT Deaf" was the speaker's reasoning.)

Was the speaker being a jerk? Sure. Was this a one-time incident? Of course not. This incident only highlighted what we humans do on an everyday basis: We tend to categorize people ("label").

I remember attending a wonderful seminar hosted by a well-known Deaf lecturer. On a whiteboard, he drew wonderful overlapping circles (in a flower pattern) in an attempt to illustrate "The Deaf Community." Each circle was labeled: The Interpreters, The Teachers, The Schools, The Parents/Guardians, Deaf/HOH students & adults, and The Social Clubs. It was a logical presentation.

And then the lecturer's comment: "Everyone is well-accepted and respected within the Deaf Community."

I slightly cringed at that comment. There's no Utopia, folks. "Martha's Vineyard" and those idyllic settings were ancient history.

There's theory and then there's reality. Guess which one wins?

In the back rows of the audience, one person slowly stood up with a hand in the air. The person was an interpreter and flatly disagreed with the "everyone's well-accepted" statement. "What about the Us vs.Them mentality? There's still animosity with Deaf vs. Hearing. Teachers see this all the time. What about the 'newbie ASL' attitude? Generally, there's no patience in welcoming newcomers into the ASL world."

I cringed at that comment, too. Reality was becoming rather harsh; can we go back to theory again?

I stress that categorizing people is nothing new: Tiger Woods (a well-known hearing professional golfer) had experienced this phenomenon constantly. Very often, the public would focus on his African-American roots while minimizing his Asian roots. Tiger has always been proud of both of his heritages—actually, there's a few more heritages. Unfortunately, the media tends to focus only one aspect of his life.

AHHH! You might argue: "But we're talking about Deaf Culture. This is not a racial issue!" You're missing the point: We always try to "label" people. It's a human trait that is both potentially good (we quickly size up a person, for safety) and bad (prejudice—or pre-judge, as in "You're not supposed to be THAT Deaf").

In cultural terms, there's a Deaf Community and a Hearing Community. Two different groups, nice and simple.

It's the Hard of Hearing Community, however, that challenged these "labels" because of its inherent range-of-variety found in individuals. In *Deaf Life* magazine's "For Hearing People Only" article (October 1997, page 8):

"'Hard-of-hearing' can denote a person with a mild-to-moderate hearing loss. Or it can denote a deaf person who doesn't have/want any cultural affiliation with the Deaf community. Or both. The HOH dilemma: in some ways hearing, in some ways deaf, in others, neither."

In this very same article, you'll find an early attempt in describing a "Fencer":

"Can one be hard-of-hearing and ASL-Deaf? That's possible, too. Can one be hard-of-hearing and function as hearing? Of course. What about being hard-of-hearing and functioning as a member of both the hearing and Deaf communities? That's a delicate tightrope-balancing act, but it too is possible.

"As for the political dimension: HOH people can be allies of the Deaf community. They can choose to join or to ignore it. They can participate in the social, cultural, political, and legal life of the community along with culturally-Deaf or live their lives completely within the parameters of the 'Hearing world.' But they may have a more difficult time establishing a satisfying cultural/social identity."

Yes, there are choices to be made by any person: Comfort level, Mode of communication, and acceptance of hearing loss. The problem occurs when a Fencer is still conducting a tightrope-balancing act, all the while observing all sorts of rules and expectations.

Is the Fencer "on the fence" by choice or by society pressures (Deaf and Hearing Communities)? Or is it both?

Before you answer that question, consider this one well-known ASL Deaf person's greeting:

"Hi. I just got my cochlear implant. Do you hate me now?"

What's your response? (Maybe we all need an aggressive greeting from time to time.)

# MICHELE WESTFALL

## Dear AGB

Dear AGB:

You will note that I think of you by your initials, rather than your name. "Alex" sounds too chummy, and "Alexander" implies a civil, friendly status, which I do not feel. "Bell" is worse, given your obsession with trying to get Deaf people to relate to the world of sound. Somewhere in your warped thinking, I know you sincerely thought that your telephone would somehow help Deaf people. Unfortunately, you were wrong about that. I wonder how you would feel if you knew that your invention has often been used as an instrument of discrimination.

But let's move on. AGB, let me tell you about myself. I am an educated, signing Deaf woman married to another educated, signing Deaf man. We have two Deaf children. Yes, we know we are your worst nightmare come true. You did what you could to prevent this scenario from happening. However, my husband and I would not have been born Deaf if our hearing parents had not married each other. Yes, you heard right: our parents are hearing. Statistics show that 90% of Deaf children are born to hearing parents. Guess you should have focused on preventing hearing people from marrying each other. They're far more dangerous than Deaf people, believe me.

During your lifetime, a man named Gregor Mendel did studies on pea plants and drafted Mendel's Laws of Heredity, which was published in 1866. It was largely overlooked, and in 1900, several people rediscovered Mendel's publication and ran with it. Mendel's Laws became widely accepted by 1925, three years after your death. I tell you all of this, AGB, because what I have to say has a direct bearing on your views of genetics, which were totally, completely, absolutely wrong. Now, listen to me carefully. My husband and I participated in a genetic study done by Gallaudet University. We had our blood taken and analyzed. What Gallaudet told us threw us for a loop, and I am confident that it will also do the same to you. We are carriers of a recessive Deaf gene called connexion-26. Under Mendel's Laws, a recessive gene needs two parents for it to appear in their children. Additionally, people with connexion-26 are products of white European background, and get this: one in every 30 white, European hearing people carry this gene. Yup, you really should have worked your magic on hearing people. They're dangerous, I tell you!

But I can be generous. You didn't know about Mendel and his Laws, and you probably didn't want to read boring scientific journals to keep up with advances in the emerging, new field of genetics, which began after 1900 and ballooned after 1925. However, there is one big sin you committed, which I'm still angry about. Your sin is the sin of rigidity in your thinking. When you were a young man, you discovered there was a Deaf community on Martha's Vineyard and you went there to see for yourself. What you saw there blew your mind: everyone on that island signed, both deaf and hearing. They lived together, worked together, and treated each other as equals. What you saw on that island proved conclusively that you were wrong about Deaf people's ability to function in hearing society.

Yet you turned your back on what you saw and learned on that island. You returned to the mainland, determined to cling to your thinking and your theories, no matter what. You told everyone in America and the rest of the world that sign language could not be used to help mix deaf and hearing people, and that only deaf people could use it amongst themselves. That, coupled with your blasted telephone, all but guaranteed that Deaf people would endure years and years of continued negative attitudes against Deaf people and sign language. Thank you, AGB, for that. We just love having to spend our entire lives repeatedly, endlessly educating hearing people about the benefits of ASL and about our capabilities. Thank you . . . so very much!

Michele Westfall

# MORGAN GRAYCE WILLOW

## Double Language

An eclectic mix of writers, folk singers, political activists, and family members are gathered in Minneapolis to honor the cultural legacy of Meridel LeSueur. I stand at the front of the chapel as the crowd re-gathers after a long intermission. They wander in from the atrium where an array of booths display books, art prints, jewelry, political pamphlets, event flyers. Bright primary colors of hand woven rugs from Guatamala and paperback book covers mingle with the embroidery of peasant blouses, the crisp designs and slogans on t-shirts, the beads and buttons worn by the browsers themselves.

The first half of the program included an assortment of poets, fiction writers, political speakers, and singers, each performing a tribute to Meridel. The guest of honor looked on, smiling, from her wheelchair situated in the aisle at the front. Now, as the second half of the day is to begin, Meridel's daughter and a few friends maneuver her—chair, papers and microphone—into a workable arrangement in front of the altar, which today serves as a stage. There is no ramp to provide access to the raised dais itself. Meridel, recently released from the hospital, has just written a new poem and has decided, at this last minute, to read it for us. With the other writers in this room, I am moved by Meridel's presence, by her determination and generosity, but most of all, by her remarkable ability to generate new work whatever her circumstance.

Today, however, I'm not here as a writer. I'm here as an American Sign Language interpreter. For weeks I've been carrying around a folder full of manuscripts and lyrics. In every spare moment on my job as ASL interpreter in a suburban high school, I've poured over these pages, marking them with ASL gloss, preparing and practicing translations of poems and songs for today's event. I've not had the benefit of audio tapes to hear the poets reading their work, no opportunity to sample their pacing or vocal inflection. In some cases I've not even heard the songs I will interpret. My colleagues, two other interpreters who have agreed to work this event with me, have also been prepping for weeks, doing as much textual analysis and translation work in advance as we've had the resources and time to do. Since I am a poet, and the lead on this team who recruited the others to join me, all the poems have been assigned to me. The theater sketches, political speeches and prose have been divided between Mary and Kim. Our job is to render the message from spoken, sung and performed English into ASL as faithfully as possible, and as beautifully as we can. Each of us has done everything we know to do to prepare for the performance we've been told to expect.

This moment is, however, not expected. Because of Meridel's illness, neither the planners of the event nor even Meridel's daughter had expected that she would read. As the person most familiar with Meridel's work, we agree that I will interpret her reading. Kim sits facing me in the support role, ready to toss language my way if I miss something since, as with most sound systems, the sound travels more effectively her way than mine. I am poised, ready to begin, running quickly through my mind some of the themes and imagery Meridel tends to use in her poetry. Then suddenly the dispassionate working interpreter in me gives way to the writer who has just realized that this may very well be the last public reading Meridel LeSueur ever gives. A poet who has become an icon among writers in Minnesota, a standard bearer for social justice, a woman who was blacklisted as a communist by the House Committee on Unamerican Activity, a phoenix who lifted herself out of obscurity and decades of wage labor to reclaim her role as a leader through the power of her writing—a woman who will soon be lost to us will read perhaps the last poem she will ever write.

My eyes fill up. Kim leans forward. She signs to me—eyebrows raised, one hand passing over the other—asking whether I want her to take over. I consider this, but there is a place in me where poet and interpreter converge. That part of me is unwilling to give up the moment when one language enters and another leaves. I give myself an emotional shake, sign to Kim that I'm ok. Meridel begins. I listen to the first few lines. I let them settle far enough into me to have visual sense, then lift my hands and begin. My hands move in the space before my body. My face takes up her syntax.

As I write this several years later, I have no memory of the poem, either its English or the ASL translation. I remember only the sensation of convergence, of being in that meta-linguistic state when the language of Meridel's poem passes through me, changing form on its way. My sojourn there engaged my total awareness, all of my faculties at once. It's a brief sojourn, though it feels long, and involves only short-term memory. The interpreting mind holds only what it needs of the English to squeeze out meaning, and then lets it go. Nothing to spare. The poem didn't make its way into my long-term memory. I hoped, however, that the emotional charge my poet self brought to the process carried the energy and spirit of the poem through and into the end result, the poem in ASL. Later, Kim tells me this was so.

●

I'd never meant to become a sign language interpreter. Like most hearing people, I knew nothing about deaf people, deaf culture, or ASL. My only experiences of interpreters had been in California during the late 1970's at women's music concerts. Performers like Holly Near and Sweet Honey In the Rock always included interpreters—I called them signers—on stage with them. Like most in the audience, the beauty of the signing captivated me. I saw poetry in their movement, but in a metaphorical sense only, for I knew nothing then of ASL poetry. What language I was able to ferret out of the movement of the language was more like the vocabulary of dance. I did attempt to match up specific hand movements with English words, an uneducated nod toward what I suspected to be purely linguistic about this particular kind of movement. With some iconographic signs, this worked, I later learned. The word "love," for example, seemed to match the crossed arms held to the chest in what looked like a mimed hug. There were many love songs. So the word —and the sign—came up often enough for me to make a conjecture about a word-sign match, then test my guess the next time the chorus came round. Sooner or later, however, I wearied of the close concentration this required, and my eyes began to ache from looking in that different way. Then I'd turn from the "signer" and simply listen. I occasionally even felt mildly annoyed that the presence of the interpreter forced me to divide my attention in that way. In theory, I appreciated the commitment these performers were making to accessibility, but I'd come for the music.

Neither these concerts nor other early encounters with ASL prepared me for the doubleness of interpreting. Around the same time I was attending those concerts, I worked at a California state hospital for developmentally disabled persons. My specific assignment was to a small unit known as the deaf-blind program. The children in the program were housed on the hospital grounds, assigned to various cottages by virtue of space availability and their particular combination of disabilities. Every morning, we drove round the grounds in a little bus, gathering up our charges, and transporting them to a small, blue house that was outfitted as a school.

We were glad to spend our days in this more intimate setting where the living room was a classroom and the dining room doubled as both lunch and art rooms. On any given day, our census included maybe a dozen kids. In addition to congenital cognitive delays, each student had varying degrees of vision and hearing loss. No one on our staff or in the cottages really knew exactly how much of either. These children, each distinctly different from the other in physical capabilities, were notoriously difficult to test and measure. Some could detect light, enough to take advantage of it as a source of self-stimulation. They'd flutter their fingers at the edges of their vision, apparently mesmerized by movement. Others seemed to hear enough to distinguish one staff person's voice from another's, especially if their hearing aids were properly fitted and the batteries were charged. Most gathered information about their world through touch. All delighted in taste and smell. Our job as staff was to teach them basic life and language skills. For this, I learned signs that we shaped in their hands or close to their faces within their narrow fields of vision. During in-service workshops, a hearing trainer taught us the signs we needed: EAT, MILK, COOKIE, MORE, WALK, SCHOOL, HOME, BOOK, CLEAN. I learned, for example, to knock my right closed hand against the outside of my left elbow to make the sign for CRACKER, our most commonly used sign since crackers were used as treats and rewards in the school. I learned individual signs, but I did not learn ASL.

I had another close encounter with Deaf culture during this period, though I didn't know it at the time. I'd been writing poems and had joined the Feminist Writers' Guild. Their newsletter announced an opening in a writers' group that met monthly in Napa, one valley over from where I lived in Sonoma. After an interview, they accepted me into the group.

At the first meeting after joining, I was particularly struck by the work of one writer who wrote highly concrete poems using an odd syntax that I took to be fresh innovation. Her poems were never clogged with the abstractions and Latinate diction common to beginning poets, myself included. I envied her that she seemed to avoid those pitfalls so naturally while I stumbled into the same pitfall time and again. I might, for example use the word "exist" in a draft. A poem of hers would turn on a phrase like "bare bones live." I would read this as a turn on the English idiom "bare-bones life," then discover from the discussion that she'd meant to use the idiom but had mistakenly substituted the verb for the noun. Sometimes the syntax in her poems appeared inverted, a verb showing up almost without a subject, or with its subject distant enough from the verb to feel lost. Again, I tried reading this difference as technical innovation. Sometimes it succeeded, sometimes not.

At one meeting after she'd been coming to the group for a while, she mentioned that her parents were deaf, and that she'd grown up using sign language. She presented this information to us as an admission. She seemed shy about revealing her parents' deafness, even a little ashamed, and went on to tell us that her English was "bad." I suddenly realized that what I'd often found fresh and artless in her work, she'd considered a lack. While she longed to have a facility with the English language that matched ours, we envied the distinctive concreteness in her use of it.

She didn't call the language she used at home to communicate with her parents American Sign Language, nor even use the common abbreviation ASL. In the seventies, formal research on ASL had only recently begun. It was not commonly recognized as a language, even among deaf people.

People called it, simply, sign language, and most considered it a form of broken English. Now, ASL is recognized as a fully intact language, replete with its own distinctive morphological structure and syntax. It's the language that lies at the very heart of a minority Deaf culture. To honor this culture, "Deaf" has become a proper noun and is capitalized when used to refer to members of the culture. When used to designate the audiological condition of deafness, it's a common, uncapitalized noun. Hearing children born to Deaf families are embraced by Deaf culture and bear the appellation "Deaf." Like their parents, their native language is ASL. English is for them a second language.

The young poet in our group was one of these, a child of a deaf adult or CODA, as the culture fondly designates them. The strengths I read in her poems, she read as evidence of "poor" English. Unfortunately, she stopped coming to the group not long after making her disclosure. All of us were too uninformed to take advantage of a rare opportunity to explore identity, language, and culture in her poems. And none of us who remained in the group could communicate in her native language.


In 1989 my relationship with ASL began to change. I was working for the Minnesota chapter of Very Special Arts, an organization founded by Jean Kennedy Smith in the seventies to create arts opportunities for people with disabilities. As the organization's first program director, I managed programs such as arts festivals, concerts and residencies for developmentally and physically disabled children and adults. Encouraged by the board to bring my writing background to bear on the position, I initiated a writing program for Vietnam vets in a post-traumatic stress disorder recovery program at the V.A. hospital. We had programs in schools, group homes, hospitals, neighborhood parks. The range of programs, participants, and artists was broad; yet, we had none who were deaf.

One day, I was alone in the office. The phone rang. I answered it with our usual greeting, announcing the organization's name followed by my own. There was a brief silence at the other end of the line. "Hello?" I spoke into the phone. After another second or two, a series of beeps pierced my ear. I pulled the receiver away from my ear and stared into it for a moment, declaring to it, "This isn't a fax number!" Then I hung up.

Moments later the phone rang again. Almost the exact same sequence of events occurred. Again I hung up. The third or fourth time it finally occurred to me that the call might be coming from a TTY, a telecommunications device for the deaf. On yet another attempt, I stared in exasperation into the receiver's mouthpiece and shouted, "We don't have a TTY."

Eventually, deaf actress Marian Lucas succeeded in contacting our office. She called through the Minnesota Relay Service (MRS), a state funded system of computers and hearing operators designed to make telecommunications accessible for deaf and hard-of-hearing people. This time, when I answered the phone, an MRS operator explained the service to me, then voiced what Marian was typing from her end on a TTY. When I spoke, the operator typed my responses into her computer, which were then transmitted to Marian's TTY display. Marian, who worked in the deaf and hard-of-hearing program at a local high school, was fundraising to bring the National Theater of the Deaf (NTD) to her school for a performance. Deaf kids from all over the state would be bussed in for the show. They needed sponsors. Could we help?

Marian and I met to discuss her request. This was my first experience communicating with a deaf person through an interpreter. Unlike the interpreted public performances I'd seen in the past, this interpreter was close, very close. She sat to my left, Marian directly in front of me. Somehow I had the good sense to resist the temptation to watch the interpreter, however distracting and engaging her movement, and direct my eye gaze at Marian with whom I was communicating. And in spite of the indirectness of that communication, Marian and I took an immediate liking to each other. I was able to commit a small amount of funding to her project from our organization, and our friendship began.

The day of the performance at Marian's school, a typical Minnesota snowstorm hit. Snow accumulated at roughly two inches an hour. Wind pressed it into a blur against windshields, wiper blades doing their best to clear a trapezoid of clear view for bus drivers. Busses pulled into the lot from as far away as Rochester, Duluth, and Mankato. Deaf students from the Minnesota State Academy for the Deaf came up from Faribault, an hour away from the Twin Cities. Some kids arrived in groups with classmates from mainstream deaf/hard-of-hearing (D/HOH) programs where kids are clustered for part of a school day in self-contained classrooms with teachers who sign. The rest of the day they disperse into regular classes, accompanied by interpreters, the kind of program where, a few years later, I would work. Other kids came from isolated, rural school districts where they were the only deaf kid in a school full of hearing students, the only student for whom all communication was mediated by an interpreter. For some of these students, the event was their first experience with deaf peers.

I stood in a corner watching them tramp snow off their boots as they came into the vestibule, then file into the auditorium. Once inside, some waved and immediately began signing to kids on the opposite side of the room. Others mingled hesitantly, gradually becoming more and more animated as they realized that everyone was signing.

When the show began, I stationed myself at the side where I could see their faces. I realized as I did so that many, perhaps most, of these students had never seen a live theater production before. I guessed that few had seen any such production in ASL, fully accessible to them without the intermediary of an interpreter. The performance was a gateway opening language to them. While the arts administrator in me counted nearly two hundred and fifty kids, the poet in me quietly wept.

During the same tour to the Twin Cities, NTD performed a mainstage play, *King of Hearts*. On Marian's recommendation—and, frankly, out of curiosity—I went to see it. I had loved the movie starring Alan Bates about a soldier sent to disarm explosives in a French village near the end of the German occupation. He accidentally releases the inmates from an insane asylum, the only inhabitants remaining in the village. As they each act out their appointed roles in the community—barber, bishop, Madame, duchess, tightrope walker—the soldier falls in love and, almost inadvertently, saves the village from destruction. I couldn't imagine an adaptation of this whimsical film for the stage, much less a production in ASL. The show bill claim—"You'll Hear *and See* Every Word!"—had me wrinkling my brow.

I arrived at the World Theater with a co-worker who, like me, knew no sign. Marian had explained that the company included hearing actors who would voice what the deaf actors were signing. Having seen the show, she also assured me that I would understand much of what was going on from mime, movement, and other theatrical elements incorporated into the play. Nevertheless, I'd been apprehensive about going. As soon as we stepped into the lobby, I felt utterly displaced.

Everyone in the crowded vestibule was signing. I heard gentle slapping sounds as hand connected with hand or torso. It had never occurred to me that making language in sign would generate noise. Laughter erupted in varying levels of volume at what seemed completely odd moments, since I understood none of the context that prompted it. Some voices, high pitched and lispy, rose above the muffled din. Out of courtesy, I tried not to stare. Yet, I couldn't help but notice the animated faces, most of which wore smiles.

Inside the theater the hubbub continued. People in the boxes at house left signed to people across the theater or up in the balconies. Communication seemed to be going on in every dimension. Hearing people, like me and my colleague, chatted in hushed tones, our voices seeming unusually loud. Some hearing people signed and voiced at the same time. Others switched in and out of signing or voicing as they turned from one person to the next. Ultimately, I fell completely silent in the face of this blizzard of communication. Then the lights went down and cut off the visual cacophony. All eyes turned to the stage.

The production was a masterpiece of theater. After a few moments of disorientation, I gave up trying to sort out which bodies the voices came from. I was so drawn into the visual experience, an amalgam of choreography, mime, and signing, that I let go trying to figure out which actors signed and which spoke. The characters emerged as clearly themselves. The action unfolded at a measured clip. And tying it all together were the set changes, created ingeniously by a character in the play, an asylum inmate who'd adopted the persona of a painter. Into the midst of the movement and action, characters by turns brought long rolls of white paper onto the stage. On these, the painter applied sketches using several brushes, all attached to a rack with one handle. He dipped his rack of brushes into several pots of paint—alternately black or red as each scene required—then swept them over the white surface in movements smoothly choreographed into the play. As his brushes stroked the canvas, outlines of soldiers marched in rank formation into the village, or asylum inmates leapt onto the stage. I watched the show in delight, my sense of the possibilities for theater expanded beyond anything I had known.

I began attending performances by Northern Sign Theater (NST), a local deaf company. Marian performed in several of their shows. She always greeted me with enthusiasm. If there were an interpreter available, as was sometimes the case after the show, we'd exchange commonplaces with their assistance. If not, we'd smile to each other, nod and gesticulate. She was always trying to tell me more than I could understand. I felt both awkward and inadequate. Exchanging even the most surface pleasantries was such a challenge, yet the more I got to know Marian, the more I wanted to really converse with her. Knowing that she would not suddenly become able to do so in my language, I began to study hers.

My first ASL classes were those offered by the theater. Classes met in a small rehearsal space in the basement of a building at Lake and Bloomington, opposite end of a block from In the Heart of the Beast Puppet and Mask Theater, where much later I would interpret poetry and plays. Instructors for NST classes were always deaf people. My feelings of awkwardness and inadequacy deepened and intensified with each class as I began to understand at every stage how much more I had to learn. In these classes, unlike the in-service training I'd received in California, my instructors were not voicing, "The sign for 'walk' looks like this . . . ," then showing us. Explanations, instruction, everything was in ASL. The more skilled teachers in these beginning classes were able to mime and act out much of the message. Most refused to give in to writing the English word on the board then showing us a comparable sign, forcing us to work in a visual, non-English mode. It helped that we had a text to work from, *ABC: A Basic Course in American Sign Language*, but the real key to the language —and its challenge—was the shift from a cerebral, linear language to a physical, three dimensional one.

There was the alphabet to contend with—and numbers. I struggled to remember which handshape matched which letter. In some instances, as with the numbers seven and eight, even developing the muscular coordination to make the shapes was difficult. I practiced obsessively, fingerspelling license plates of cars in front of me, billboards, exit signs, sometimes even missing my turn-off because I'd been trying to fingerspell a street name, searching, for example, for the difference between "f" and "d."

Little by little, I learned more. I could talk about weather, how I was feeling (mostly FINE, since I could easily sign that), arrange to meet somewhere at a specific time. Yet, Marian and I continued to have paper and pen handy for the moment when the conversation would go further than my language capability. Then, reading her written responses, I struggled to disentangle an English meaning from her more ASL-like written syntax. We laughed, often, about our misunderstandings and mistakes, as once in a restaurant when I used the sign for LESBIAN when I meant LUNCH. (Both are made with an L handshape at the chin, but for LUNCH, thumb touches chin and palm orientation is toward the left. For LESBIAN, the index finger touches the chin and palm orientation is toward the upper torso.) Add to this the complication that when I was with Marian in public places, wait persons and others often expected me to interpret for them Marian's intended meaning.

Meanwhile, I had been working with a hearing friend, a sculptor named Jill Waterhouse, on a collaborative show for the Intermedia Arts Gallery in Minneapolis. Jill had created a series of plaster cast female torsos, elaborately ornamented with found objects such as nails and satin fabric; bones, sand, and driftwood; miniature dolls and accouterments. One piece featured a tiny refrigerator in the torso's heart, inside it a three-layer cake. Images such as these seemed lifted from lines of the poems I'd selected to read. Our shared theme was women's body image. We invited Marian to join us and make it a three-woman show. Marian would perform ASL translations of the poems. We called the show *Body/Language*.

We had no idea, any of us, what we were asking of her. To do her translations, Marian pursued a process involving several steps. I gave her print copies of the poems. At her request, I also made an audiotape of them. She took the tape to an interpreter who'd agreed to videotape transliterations of each poem. This interpreter spent five hours in a room before a camera, signing literal English versions of poem after poem. Much later, when I knew enough ASL to understand what she was signing, I looked at the video. I was stunned by how frequently the interpreter, one of the most highly skilled interpreters in the state, interrupted herself, rewound the audiotape, referred to the printed page, then looked into the camera and shrugged. She often signed, "MEAN WHAT? I DON'T KNOW.

POETRY THAT. I DON'T UNDERSTAND POETRY." This was the first of many times I would hear that refrain among interpreters. The complexity of the language, progression and layering of images was outside the ordinary working experience of this interpreter, as, I discovered, is the case with most interpreters. Her goal, which she achieved admirably despite her disclaimers, was to make visible for Marian the essential meanings of the poems. If she became thoroughly stuck, she simply "froze" the English, which means she signed an exact rendition of the line or phrase, down to fingerspelling each article, conjunction, and adverb—words that, in a pure ASL translation drop away or are expressed by facial grammar. From this videotape, Marian worked the poems into ASL, going back over them, revising and shaping. When she'd arrived at a version she liked, she memorized it and worked up its performance elements which would be accompanied by my voiced English originals.

We worked together as much as we could during the translation work. Marian had many questions for me about specific passages in the poems. My ASL, however, was still very minimal. Occasionally, interpreters— friends of Marian's who would become role models for me—volunteered their time to facilitate our communication during rehearsals. Most of the time we were on our own. I, who have always been too shy to even attempt theater skills, was forced to act out the simplest meanings in the poems. In a narrative sequence of one poem, for example, two little girls—sisters —are playing, jumping on the bed in their room. As their enthusiasm builds, they begin jumping from the dresser to the bed. Soon their mother bounds angrily up the stairs and punishes them for not being in bed per instructions. I was not able to set up this scene using the spatial elements natural to ASL, so I clumsily pantomimed the action. From the inside, it stretched me to take unprecedented risks for the sake of communication. From the outside, it must have been a comic sight.

The show was a success. Despite the fact that we were playing against the first Minnesota Twins 1991 World Series game at one edge of town and the Barnum and Bailey Circus just down the street, we packed the house both nights. After it was over, I wanted to do more artistic collaboration with Marian and/or other deaf artists. For that, I'd need to really know ASL, so I began to study in earnest. I transferred to St. Paul Technical College (SPTC), which had a strong reputation for ASL instruction, a good-sized staff of deaf instructors, as well as an interpreter training program. I started over with level one, and worked my way through all the ASL classes they had to offer.

Had I been studying a spoken language—German, say, which I had taken in high school and college—I might at this point have traveled to immerse myself in the place and culture of the people speaking that language. But there is no "Deaf Country" to travel to. In the absence of place, perhaps language becomes place. I wanted to learn more. Marian had returned to Gallaudet University in Washington, D.C. to complete her degree. I wanted more of the language, but I didn't yet know other deaf people who might teach me. And, to be honest, I also hoped for a trade, a career more lucrative than poetry alone had been. I applied to the Interpreter Training Program (ITP) at Saint Paul Tech, and was accepted.

The program was like graduate school in intensity and pressure, entirely unlike it in structure. I'd entered graduate school with a set of poets and fiction writers and had finished with essentially the same group. However, beyond workshop and required critical courses, our specific schedules varied. Our choices about electives were directed by our specialty areas and one major writer whose entire body of work we had to know for comprehensive exams. The ITP was a lockstep program, nine months with the same students in the same rotation of classes, Monday through Friday, eight a.m. to two thirty. Monday, Wednesday and Friday: ASL language and lab, beginning, intermediate, advanced interpreting classes. Tuesday and Thursday: Deaf Culture, history of the interpreting profession, professional ethics. It felt like high school. In fact, many of the students were not long out of high school. I was a good deal older than most and impatient with the structure. But I grit my teeth and dug in.

In ASL classes we were required to leave our voices at the door. The goal was total immersion in ASL. We were to rely on it for all communication, and if our language skills failed—which they often did since we were still learning—we were forced to improvise, just as we would if we really were in Deaf Country. Frankly, we often cheated. English was so much a habit, so embedded in our behavior and cosmology, that we often lapsed into our comfort zone. As the year progressed and our language skills improved, however, we complied more readily with the rules.

It was a physiological transformation. From kindergarten when I'd first been permitted to go to school, I had always been a good student. I was good at paying attention, sitting mostly still, reading, taking notes, passing tests, writing papers—all the stuff I associated with being in school. For lecture classes on Deaf culture or the history of the profession, these familiar skills were all I needed. For ASL language classes and lab classes in the actual processes of interpreting, none of what I'd known before was enough. I discovered that I needed to take in this visual, visceral language the way I'd learned dance. I learned to stop taking notes. Instead, I stood at the back of the classroom copying the signs, movements, and expressions of ASL, drawing them into and through my body. I needed to allow the cells of my brain to relax, in order for the cells of my muscles and fascia to embrace the language of ASL.

In one way, however, my dance experience turned out to be detrimental. Dance instructors mirror their students' movements. If the teacher intends for the student to make a grapevine step to the right, the instructor makes a grapevine step to the left, thus moving her body with the group of students across the floor in the same direction. In ASL, instructors never mirror. They simply make the sign with their dominant hand. If a right-handed instructor signs LEAVE, for example, both hands, palms outward, move toward the right side of the signer's body, closing as they approach the right side of the signing space. From my vantage point as student, I see the movement going toward the left. To copy, as a right-handed student, I need to make the same movement toward the right side of my signing space. The viewer, in this case student, makes the transposition. For deaf people this transposition process is internalized and automatic. For hearing people, it's not. It can lead to a great deal of bewilderment. Then, as soon as we've half figured it out, we meet our first left-handed deaf person and the confusion erupts anew.

This was retraining of brain, eyes, and ears. By the end of a day of only sign communication, my ears, used to a steady onslaught of sound, would be ringing from lack of stimulation. Sensitive to noise by nature, I had for years listened only to classical or instrumental jazz on my car radio. After a few weeks into the program, I began tuning my car radio to rock and roll and cranking up the volume the instant I pulled out of the college parking lot. And my eyes! All of us complained of eye fatigue. Our eyes, used to being passive sensors, were rapidly learning to pick up very subtle movements, and to re-perceive those movements as significant linguistic information. Our ears already knew how to do this with the slightest variation in vocal intonation. Now, we had to train our eyes to detect the boundaries between signs, the beginnings and endings of sentences, the difference between a declarative sentence and a question. Raised eyebrows might indicate the kind of question that anticipates an answer of yes or no, or it might signal a shift in topic, roughly comparable to the beginning of a new paragraph. A twitch at the side of the nose, which we might previously have believed to be a nervous tick, now communicated agreement, or simply indicated active listening. From this new kind of looking, our eyes became dry and felt like they were bulging from our overfull heads. We had headaches. Sometimes our brains just shut down from fatigue.

Being an interpreter is not entirely unlike being a writer. As a writer, I feel like a professional watcher. As an interpreter, I am a professional listener. It's the interpreter's job to hear everything, and then to convey as much of that everything to the deaf person as possible. That includes the obvious—all the language in the spoken environment. I worked in public schools for a fair amount of my interpreting career, so I'll use an example from an imaginary high school English class. In a classroom, what constitutes the obvious is what the teacher says and what the students say—to the teacher and, as much as possible, to each other. What's less obvious is the ambient noise in that environment. An ambulance screaming past the school. A kid running in the hall outside the classroom. An airplane temporarily blocking out the teacher's voice. A kid in the back row listening to gangsta rap on a headset, against the rules of the building. A loud bang, such as a gunshot. All of this the interpreter must relay to the deaf student, or at least as much as she is able, being only one channel for the transmission of sound. She will need to be selective, weigh priorities. It may be the deaf student, sitting usually in the front, needs to be informed about the kid with the headset in the back, for the teacher may suddenly interrupt the lecture and send the kid out of class. And certainly, if the fire alarm goes off and there are no visible alarm systems—as was the case in several of the schools where I worked—she must interpret that sound.

As hearing people, we listen selectively, unconsciously choosing moment by moment which among myriad sounds to attend to. A trained interpreter makes this process conscious. It helps that the deaf student in the classroom, as a visual "listener," is doing the same thing with his or her visual acuity. Eventually, an interpreter develops a sense for how much and what kind of visual information is sufficient in a given communication transaction, specific to those deaf and hearing people, specific to that environment. This helps to narrow the field of responsibility. Nevertheless, the responsibility for conveying so much information—and to convey it accurately, with as little contamination of judgment or alteration from personal worldview as possible—is fatiguing. Add to this my own acute sensitivity to noise. By the end of some days of paying close attention and sorting out so many sounds, I was reduced to nervous exhaustion. In this state, I reacted to sounds as if I were allergic to them.

As an interpreter there is plenty of opportunity for voyeurism. The writer in me enjoys that. Interpreters sit at the front of the classroom, facing the students, never turning our backs, as teachers do to write on the board. When the teacher leaves the room with disruptive students to talk to them in the hall, we stay behind, ready to lift our hands and interpret whatever might happen in the language environment. Actually, unless it is test day, interpreter's hands in a classroom rarely get a break. But even as we interpret, we observe. We see everything: one student passing a note to another, girls in the corner passing lipstick back and forth, a student nodding off in the back, deaf students signing to each other behind propped up books, a face a kid—either hearing or deaf—makes at the teacher after a reprimand. Sometimes we are also handed teachers' observations and confidences to hold. In one instance, a gym teacher, concerned that a student might be pregnant, mentioned it to me on the sidelines while the students played soccer. During the next class meeting, the teacher said that school nurses had confirmed the student's pregnancy and found that in fact, she was already dilating. The student was completely unaware of her condition. Interpreters, like writers, are witnesses. Unlike writers, interpreters may not tell.

Interpreters are bound by a strict code of ethics. Probably the most important of the eight tenets of this code is the one pledging interpreters to silence. "Interpreter/transliterator shall keep all assignment-related information strictly confidential." Reasons for this are obvious. In a medical setting, for example, involving a hearing doctor and a deaf patient, very private information is exchanged through the agency of the interpreter. She learns intimate details about the deaf person that a hearing person would voice directly to the doctor in an examining room. Even the doctor's nurse might not be privy to what passes between hearing doctor and patient. That same information—say positive results on an HIV test —must go through the interpreter. Rules respecting confidentiality among hearing people are violated by the nature of the interpreting process. So the interpreter carries the burden of confidentiality, a witness sworn to secrecy. For this reason, the examples I use in this essay are fictional, of public interpreting occasions for which confidentiality rules are less rigorous, or instances about which I have been granted permission to speak, though still without citing names.

There is one exception—the student in gym class. The interpreter and the writer in me quarreled over this. The writer demanded a specific example to make vivid for the reader what the burden of this secrecy can sometimes mean. The interpreter in me charged that any mention, even in the broadest terms, is a violation of trust. The writer insisted that these are the kinds of things that happen in our schools. It's true, and therefore, not only can be told, but must be told. The interpreter claimed that someone might read this and be able to identify from the details the name of this unfortunate student. Our compromise is a concrete example lacking in specific detail. Neither school, student, nor teacher is identified. There is no indication of geographic location or year. No clue given about the student's grade level, race, socioeconomic or deaf/hearing status. This struggle, though more exaggerated for me as a writer, is one that interpreters live with every day, carrying information like static at the end of a work day, checking oneself constantly so as not to inadvertently give any of it away.

When it's working, the interpreting process can be a meta-linguistic high, as writing is—use of language and self-awareness about use of language functioning at the same time. Let's return to the classroom setting and make it an English class. The teacher is lecturing on Elizabethan England. Her everyday American English comes into my ears. I listen to it, divest it of form, letting syntax go, aiming as near the core meaning of what's been said as I can get. At the other end of the process, I compose in another language, wrapping meaning in the grammar and syntax of ASL. This involves movement from an auditory, linear language to visual, gestural language. Plus, the syntactic structure of an ASL sentence is opposite that of an English one. I need to hear the entire English sentence all the way through the direct object in order to get the topic which comes first in the ASL sentence. This transformation moves from vocal apparatus to ear drum and brain, then from brain to hands, arms, torso, face, eyebrows, mouth, eyes, and fingers.

Now suppose that the teacher launches into Mercutio's Queen Mab speech. I kick into overdrive. The source language is no longer the American English I am used to hearing every day, even in the more formal register of a lecture. Now I hear Elizabethan English, and via the delivery of a teacher, not an actor. Shakespeare describes the tiny fairy queen's chariot, an empty hazelnut:

> Her waggon-spokes made of long spinners' legs;
> The cover, of the wings of grasshoppers;
> Her traces, of the smallest spider's web;
> Her collars, of the moonshine's watery beams;
> Her whip, of cricket's bone; the lash, of film;
> Her waggoner, a small grey-coated gnat,

All these descriptors occur, by the way, before Shakespeare names Queen Mab's vehicle as a chariot.

I sizzle inside my meta-linguistic state, minimizing my signing as much as possible to represent visually the scale in the metaphor. I make major translation decisions in an instant, having had no time for textual analysis in advance. Do I go direct to meaning, adding cultural information —what is called expansion—showing the deaf students concretely in the translation that the scene is basically one dude teasing his buddy about going off the deep end in love? Does my expansion include the explanation that Shakespeare uses an elaborate metaphor of fairy intervention to do this, a use of metaphor that is neither common nor often needed in ASL? Or do I transliterate instead, attempting to make visual the quality of Shakespeare's language so deaf students have an experience of Elizabethan English comparable to the hearing students'? Of course, I do not know an older form of ASL in which to make such an interpretation really match Elizabethan English. Plus, I am skimming along as quickly as I can in the process without the benefit of time to translate this delightful passage in advance. I can't do more than work line by line, setting up the tiny chariot in the left side of my signing space and the images from the analogy—spiders, grasshopper wings, moonshine, cricket bones, a gnat in a grey coat—on the right. I knit the two together as best I can with a sign for metaphor, such as THINK-SAME or LOOK-SAME.

Meanwhile, half the hearing kids have completely tuned the teacher out, to say nothing of William Shakespeare. They're more interested in weather out the window, the back of the head in front of them, a buddy's sarcastic jeer, or perhaps even the interpreter's curious facial expressions. Do I portray for the deaf students through my interpretation a poet's love for this speech, giving them an advantage the hearing students don't get? Or do I simply accept the fact that the deaf students are really no more interested in Shakespeare than their hearing counterparts and leave them to their own daydreaming? If I choose to do the latter, I can relax, not fret so much over translation decisions as I fling them off my hands.

When you're on, though, you're really on. The process can feel like writing a new poem when it comes almost whole the first time out of the pen. You've found the right form for the subject. The images ring true. The lines fit like geometric precision in the corners of a spider's web. The rhythm comes right out of the body unmediated by the brain. When it's happening while interpreting, the message comes in clear and seems to drop directly into meaning, without struggle. ASL comes off the hands with a fluency you didn't know you had. The deaf audience closes the loop. Fully engaged, they watch, nodding their heads, faces reflecting a visceral response to what they're getting—occasionally that linguistic twitch at the side of the nose. Then you know you've nailed it. Interpreting, when it works this well, is like being a crystalline channel, wide open and totally clear. One's sense of identity disappears into that crevice between two languages, just as it does when words come well to the page.

I have experienced this synergy while interpreting. On one such occasion, I'd been engaged by a small community theater company for an event that included a reading by poet Elaine Shelly. Theater staff arranged for me to have copies of the poems well in advance as well as access to Elaine for questions I might have while working through the poems. I spent a good deal of time with these poems, at first just reading them through again and again. My objective was to fully embrace the images and rhythms in her work, to draw them deeply into myself, to know them almost as well as if I had written them myself. I couldn't have written them, of course. Elaine and I have vastly different cultural backgrounds. I am European American; she is African American. Her lines ". . . the call of cotton/waiting for sweat to cover skin . . ." and "journey south to my people" cannot be the same for me as for her. Yet it was my responsibility to convey the fullness of her message from as far inside her heart and language as my human and poetic empathy enable me to travel. With each poem, I worked out its main goal or primary message around which all the language and images were hung. Each page was marked up with notes, ASL glosses, sometimes sketches to capture the visual relation of one element of the poem with another.

I'd not heard Elaine read before. Nor did I have an audio tape to practice with. I didn't know what to expect from her delivery: pacing, vocal inflection, volume. We worked out some details in the minutes before the show: where I would stand (she wanted to be able to see me in her peripheral vision, while I needed to be clearly visible to the deaf audience), the order of the poems, last minute questions about lines or images. Till almost the last possible moment, I returned to the page. I wanted to burn each poem's energy and integrity into place inside the language and memory centers of my brain, there to await the moment when the lines wrapped in her voice would ignite the confluence of two languages.

When Elaine began to read, her voice was rich and steady. "While the Oklahoma wind blows sharp/enough to consume your soul and breath. . . ." I continued listening for the line I knew was coming, the words I needed to begin the ASL sentence: "my people are inside resting praying working a bit." Her pacing was perfect, giving me plenty of time to set up her grandmother's house in space. In English, it doesn't appear until the second stanza: "Only in dreams my grandmother's house/still exists." In ASL, I needed it first. I placed it in the lower left quadrant of my signing space. Now the sharpness and threat of the Oklahoma winds would make sense. From that beginning, I could show people in the poem taking shelter together against danger, resting, praying, working. My body merged with Elaine's poems. I trusted it, let it revel in its instinct for both English and ASL. The deaf audience was deeply moved by Elaine's work. My work succeeded.

On another occasion my body at once betrayed and rescued me. I was working in a college education setting and had been assigned to interpret a beginning poetry class. The conflict of my identities had emerged on the very first day of class when my interpreting partner and I introduced ourselves to the instructor. He looked directly at me and asked, "Aren't you a writer?" I knew him, a poet of some renown, from the writing community, so I was pleased that he remembered me from those contexts. All the more pleasing was the dialogue about the issues and difficulties of interpreting in class that this introduction opened among the four of us: instructor/ poet, interpreters, and deaf student. Though, as it turned out, there was not enough time to pursue this conversation as much as we wished, the presence of it throughout the course added a level of awareness about the interpreting process I rarely experienced in interpreting situations. This added a measure of ease to the whole dynamic.

The course text was *Contemporary American Poetry* edited by A. Poulin, Jr., whose translations of Rilke's *Duino Elegies* I'd particularly liked. Among the students' assignments was the requirement that they read around in this anthology and select one poem to memorize and recite for the class. One student selected "The Jacob's Ladder" by Denise Levertov. I'd been reading Levertov's work for years. Her influence in line break and rhythm shows in my own poems. I am thrilled by the student's choice. I am "up," my interpreting colleague having just completed her twenty-minute stint. I feel fresh, ready to engage the process, excited to do this poem, one of my favorites by Levertov. Before the student begins, in a pause while other students shuffle to find the page in the book, I mentally review the images I remember from the poem. Then, just as the student is about to begin, the instructor mentions, as an aside among introductory remarks about Levertov, that she is in advanced stages of cancer, not expected to live much longer.

My breathing halts. My eyes fill up. My brain performs a kind of hiccup. I've fallen completely out of the interpreting process. But before my colleague even has time to notice, the student begins: "The stairway is not/a thing of gleaming strands. . ." I am beyond choice. My body takes up the translation from its own memory, in its own way scrambling and scraping up the stone steps in the poem, shoving aside till later the full impact of the news I've just heard. The student continues. My hands show angels descending, a lone human climbing the staircase in my signing space. From the imprint of language in my body, Levertov's ". . . poem ascends."

In professional jargon, the borderland interpreters inhabit is sometimes called the Third Culture, a peculiar blending of hearing and deaf worlds. Perhaps it's not so much a territory that we occupy as a language that occupies us. When deaf people join our private lives, we facilitate communication during our own social events. At the very least, we develop a habit of signing and talking at the same time in the presence of mixed company. The contact language resulting from this bastardizes English as well as ASL. However, it does get the message across to both hearing and deaf so no one is left out of a conversation. Sometimes we forget who's present, our bodies and the dual languages propelling their own syntax. Once, after a party at my house—the guests a mixture of hearing writers, deaf friends, and interpreter colleagues—one of the writers commented, "It's odd being at a party with so many deaf people and signers. It's like a net of double language."

# PAMELA WRIGHT

## Meeting Clayton Valli

I stood outside in the sweltering Florida heat with the conventioneers walking around me. I was parked outside a bathroom door, staring. "Should I go in? Should I not? This is the men's bathroom. Go in. No, no. Go. No. GO. NO." My fifteen-year-old mind could not get past the figure on the door declaring that the territory behind the door was for "Men" only. The faceless figure stared back at me, its legs and arms splayed to indicate that no dresses were allowed inside. I knew it would not kill anyone, or me, to just walk in and find out what the precocious little three-year-old I had sent in there alone was doing. It had been fifteen minutes.

Carey needed to go to the bathroom, and I, as his babysitter, and a naïve one at that, sent him into that bathroom alone. That's exactly how I found myself in this predicament. What the heck could a three-year-old find to do in a men's bathroom for fifteen minutes? I just had to find a man to go in and check for me, or muster up the courage to completely embarrass myself. My fifteen-year-old face was not up for embarrassment, so I started looking for eligible male passersby.

A man walked by. He didn't look friendly. No. Not that one. Maybe that one. I began to speak, but my deaf voice was intelligible. "Never mind," I said. That I could say clearly. The man walked away. OK, this one. I started to speak, but this one looked at me and shook his head. Oh, what a relief! This one's Deaf, too! I signed in a flurry, "I babysit. I sent kid agethree bathroom. Stay-stay-stay, fifteen minutes. Me worry. Help me. Check inside. Please?"

He looked at me with a puzzled expression. "Oh, great. He's going to think I'm a rotten babysitter," I thought. "Please?" I signed again.

His surprise disappeared with a start, and he signed, "Oh, fine-fine. OK," and disappeared into the dim bathroom.

"Okay, great. In any second, this guy's going to come out, and tell me what Carey found to do in there." I began to conjure up images of his little body falling in the toilet and getting stuck, or him playing in the water and flooding the whole bathroom. Or maybe he had some kind of toilet paper sculpture in the works. Maybe he slipped, fell, and is comatose? My imagination began to hyperventilate, because seconds were ticking away, and had become minutes. The guy had not come out. My mind went haywire, "Maybe I sent in a freak? Maybe the guy was an escaped convict from the state prison 300 miles away? Maybe he's a murderer!" I reassured myself, "He's deaf. He's a conventioneer. He is not a freak. He's okay. He looks nice." Over and over, I told myself, "He's okay."

After a cliché sort of eternity, the door whisked open, and the guy and Carey came out. Actually, Carey trotted out, and the guy, with his head hung down, looked up at me with a wan smile.

"Everything OK?" I asked.

"Yes. Fine-fine. Boy just busy toilet. Help him, he fine."

Later, I was gleefully enjoying my "time off," meaning Carey was with his mother until she needed me again. That enabled me to wander around the conventioneers without having to pay the fee, and buoyantly converse with anyone I could get a few words out of. It was during one of those times I saw the guy from the bathroom sitting at a table, reading a book. He smiled warmly when I asked to join him and within a few minutes I learned he was one of the presenters. He was there to talk about American Sign Language and invited me to watch his presentation.

American Sign Language. Yeah. ASL. Sign Language. So what? Within a few hours my mind underwent an explosion. An explosion of information, of empowerment, of passion, of familiarity, of knowledge, of richness and incredulity. No longer was I just another signer, I had become enamored, an advocate, and a crusader. I fell in love with my hands and what my simple fingers could do! I had discovered a deity, and his name was Clayton Valli.

Three years later when I went to Gallaudet, Valli welcomed me once again. This time, he welcomed me on a weekly basis in his office at Dawes Hall. Inside those office walls, which were covered with colorful posters about ASL and linguistics, my mentor taught, and I learned. We shared ideas, frustrations, and laughter. Especially laughter.

And oh, what really happened with Carey? My mother ratted me out to Carey's mother. Fortunately, Carey's mother was upset, but, with chuckles, she explained what must have happened. Carey had been trained, when he did a number two, to sit and wait for someone to come wipe him.

# CONTRIBUTORS

**ANDRIA ALEFHI** has lived and worked in the Deaf community for fifteen years. She is the editor and creator of the creative nonfiction journal *We'll Never Have Paris*. Raymond Luczak and Lauren Ridloff, who also appear in this book, have both been published in *We'll Never Have Paris*. Andria is also the creator of the Pete's Mini Zine Fest in Brooklyn. [neverhaveparis.blogspot.com]

**ALISON L. AUBRECHT** is a child of the world, though she has often felt more comfortable experiencing it through books. A licensed clinical counselor, she is currently on haitus from the counseling field, working full-time as a social activist with Facundo Element. She has been published in several places, including *Deaf American Poetry*, *The HeART of Deaf Culture*, *Clerc Scar*, and *Kiss-Fist*. Alison currently resides in Minnesota with her two cats. [faccundoelement.com]

**VERONICA BICKLE** is from a half-Deaf, half-hearing family and attended Sir James Whitney School for the Deaf. A graduate of Carleton University, she now works as a counselor at The Canadian Hearing Society. She has been involved in social activism for many years, most recently serving as president of the Toronto Association of the Deaf. She is working on a historical novel about the signing community on Martha's Vineyard.

**TERESA BLANKMEYER BURKE** is a philosopher and bioethicist at Gallaudet University. An emerging poet whose work has been featured at the National Hispanic Culture Center, Teresa is an award-winning blogger at Duke City Fix, and currently blogs at Deaf Echo. She earned her Ph.D. in Philosophy from the University of New Mexico and is writing a book based on her dissertation, *Creating a Deaf Child: Ethics and Genetics*.

**AMBER CEFFALIO** has worked as an interpreter since 1998 when she graduated from Western Oregon University with a B.A. in interpreting. In 2010 she created the blog Ethical Dilemmas for ASL Interpreters as a place for interpreters to discuss decisions made while interpreting. Amber currently lives in Brooklyn with her husband and three sons. [terpethics.blogspot.com]

**KAREN CHRISTIE** ("KC") grew up in California and is professor of Deaf Cultural Studies and English at the National Technical Institute for the Deaf. Along with Patti Durr, she produced and edited a multimedia DVD set, *The HeART of Deaf Culture: Literary and Artistic Expressions of Deafhood*. Most of her writings have appeared/disappeared in her trash, although some have made it into *The Tactile Mind Quarterly* and *Clerc Scar*.

**JOHN LEE CLARK** was born deaf to an all-deaf family. He later became blind during his years at the Minnesota State Academy for the Deaf. From 2001 to 2006, he and his wife, Adrean, ran a small press dedicated to signing community literature called The Tactile Mind Press. A chapbook of his poems, *Suddenly Slow*, came out in 2008 from Handtype Press. He also edited the anthology *Deaf American Poetry* (Gallaudet University Press, 2009). [johnleeclark.com]

**WILLY CONLEY**'s writings have appeared in *American Theatre, The Washington Post, The Baltimore Sun, Deaf American Prose, Deaf American Poetry, Teaching from the Heart and Soul, The Deaf Way II Anthology, Deaf World, Stages of Transformation, No Walls of Stone, Signing the Body Poetic, Theatre for Young Audiences Today, The Tactile Mind, Daring to Repair,* and *The HeART of Deaf Culture.* He is the author of two books, *Broken Spokes* and *Vignettes of the Deaf Character and Other Plays.* Conley is a professor of Theatre Arts at Gallaudet University. [willyconley.com]

**T. K. DALTON** is a writer, teacher, and ASL-English interpreter. His short fiction and nonfiction appear in *Red Rock Review, Radical Teacher, Rain Taxi,* and elsewhere. Drafts of his novel *More Signal, More Noise,* from which "Explode-a-Moment" is excerpted, have earned him residencies at the Montana Artists Refuge and the Vermont Studio Center. He currently teaches composition and creative writing to hearing and Deaf students. He lives in New York City. [tkdalton.com]

**MARK DROLSBAUGH** graduated from Gallaudet University with a B.A. in Psychology (1992) and an M.A. in School Counseling and Guidance (1994). He works as a school counselor at the Pennsylvania School for the Deaf. He is the author of three books: *Deaf Again* (1997), *Anything But Silent* (2004), and *Madness in the Mainstream* (2013). He also co-edited the anthology *On the Fence: The Hidden World of the Hard of Hearing* (2007). Mark lives in North Wales, Pennsylvania, with his wife Melanie and their three children.

**FRANK GALLIMORE** earned his M.F.A. at Johns Hopkins University and works as a sign language interpreter in Seattle. A child of deaf parents, he is the creator of the "CODA, That" comic strip and is the editor of *Kiss-Fist Magazine*. His poems have been featured twice on *Verse Daily*, and have appeared in journals such as *Smartish Pace*, *Measure*, *The Cortland Review*, and *Slate*. [frankgallimore.com]

**DONALD GRUSHKIN** was born Deaf to an all-Hearing family. Raised orally, he attended public schools until the age of thirteen, when he attended a school for the Deaf and began to learn ASL. He is a professor of Deaf Studies at California State University-Sacramento and lives with his wife, two children, and a dog.

**SUSAN HAJIANI**, a Minnesota native, lives in Los Angeles where she is a therapist and director of a community mental health program for Deaf and hard of hearing persons. She is currently exploring the interplay of Deaf and hearing experiences that have resulted from receiving bilateral cochlear implants after 30 years of profound deafness and 15 years of using ASL. Susan enjoys travel, biking, theater, and writing.

**KRISTEN HARMON** is a professor of English at Gallaudet University. She has published short stories, personal essays, and creative nonfiction along with her academic publications. She and colleague Jennifer Nelson recently published *Deaf American Prose* with Gallaudet University Press, which features creative writing by Deaf Americans in the years between 1980 and 2010.

**CHRISTOPHER JON HEUER** is the author of *All Your Parts Intact: Poems* and *Bug: Deaf Identity and Internal Revolution*. His work has appeared in several anthologies and magazines. He is a professor of English at Gallaudet University and lives in Alexandria, Virginia, with his wife Amy and their son Jack.

**PAUL HOSTOVSKY** is the author of four books of poetry, most recently *Hurt Into Beauty* (FutureCycle Press, 2012). His poems have won a Pushcart Prize and two Best of the Net Awards. His work has appeared on *Poetry Daily*, *Verse Daily*, and *The Writer's Almanac*. He was recently chosen as a featured poet for the 2012-2013 Georgia Poetry Circuit. Paul works as a sign language interpreter in Boston. [paulhostovsky.com]

**KAREN LLOYD** grew up on a Far North Queensland sugar farm and after stints living in Townsville, Sydney, and London, she now lives in Brisbane. A qualified librarian, she worked in libraries for twelve years before moving into community information and advocacy for deaf people. She currently works as Executive Officer of Deaf Australia. Karen has had a couple of short stories published and for a short while in the early 1990s she and a group of friends produced a magazine of deaf writing, *Sound Off*.

**RAYMOND LUCZAK** is the author and editor of 15 books, including *How to Kill Poetry, Assembly Required: Notes from a Deaf Gay Life*, and *Silence Is a Four-Letter Word: On Art & Deafness*. His novel *Men with Their Hands* won first place in the Project: QueerLit Contest 2006. He is the editor of *Jonathan*, a fiction journal featuring gay, bisexual, and transgender male writers. A playwright and filmmaker, he lives in Minneapolis, Minnesota. [raymondluczak.com]

**DOMINIC MCGREAL** was born in County Mayo, Ireland. From 1975 to 1989, he attended St. Joseph's School for Deaf Boys in Dublin, and continued his education at Roslyn Park. He joined the Dublin Theatre of the Deaf in 1994 as an actor. He directed his first play in 2001, and soon afterwards received a Fulbright scholarship to study theater arts at Gallaudet University in Washington, D.C. Dominic has long been active in many Irish Deaf organizations, including the Irish Deaf Youth Association, Greenbow Deaf LGBT Society of Ireland, and *Irish Deaf News*. His work has appeared in the anthologies *The Most Important Thing* and *Eyes of Desire 2: A Deaf LGBT Reader* (Handtype Press, 2007).

**LAUREN RIDLOFF** started out in Chicago, Illinois. She graduated from Model Secondary School for the Deaf in Washington, D.C., and completed her studies at California State University at Northridge. She relocated to New York City to receive her M.S. in Education. Today Lauren is a teacher turned stay-at-home mama and blogger. She loves John Updike, traveling, and pumpkin pie. Lauren lives in Brooklyn with her husband and their son.

**KRISTEN RINGMAN** is currently living in New Hampshire and working on a young adult urban fantasy saga. Her first novel, *Makara*, was published by Handtype Press in 2012; it was a finalist for the Lambda Literary Award in LGBT Debut Fiction. She received her M.F.A. from Goddard College in 2008. [kristenringman.com]

**CURTIS ROBBINS** is a retired professor of computer science at Gallaudet University. He earned his bachelor's degree there in 1967 and went on to obtain master's degrees at New York University and the University of

Maryland, where he also got his doctorate. His poems have appeared in many publications, including the anthologies *Beyond Lament: From the World Wars to the Holocaust*, *No Walls of Stone*, *The Deaf Way II Anthology*, *Blood to Remember*, and *Deaf American Poetry*. [curtdeafpoet.com]

**SARAH SEGAL** is an M.F.A. candidate in American University's Poetry Writing program in Washington, D.C. She lives in Fairfax, Virginia, and works in Montgomery County Public Schools as a paraeducator in a deaf and hard of hearing program. She is currently at work on her first collection of poetry.

**DEAN SHERIDAN** is a graduate of Gallaudet University and attended graduate school at the University of California at Los Angeles and the University of Southern California. He has worked as a teacher, a manufacturing biochemist, an electronics technician, a lab technician, and an actor. He is currently a mechanic building Boeing's 787 planes. He was a contributing writer for the books *Rules of Thumb* and *Never Trust a Calm Dog*.

**ROBERT SIEBERT** is a graduate of the Minnesota State Academy for the Deaf and earned his B.S. in Business Administration from Gallaudet University in 2012. He currently resides in Washington, D.C., and is an assistant coach of the Gallaudet men's basketball team. [Twitter: @bobbysiebert]

**EDDIE SWAYZE** studied art at the National Technical Institute of the Deaf, where ASL poetry was being revolutionized by the likes of Peter Cook, Debbie Rennie, Clayton Valli, and Patrick Graybill. He earned a B.F.A. in 1989 and a M.F.A. in 1995, both from the Rochester Institute of Technology. He currently works at the Center for Disability Rights. Eddie's poetry appears widely, and he has performed his ASL poetry extensively. [wildpoetperformanceartsandpoetry.blogspot.com]

**PIA TAAVILA-BORSHEIM** grew up in Walled Lake, Michigan, and now lives in Fredericksburg, Virginia. She earned her B.A. and M.A. in American Literature from Eastern Michigan University (1977, 1979) and her interdisciplinary Ph.D. (1985) from Michigan State University. she is a professor of literature and creative writing at Gallaudet University. Her collected poems (1977-2007), *Moon on the Meadow*, was published in 2008 by Gallaudet University Press and *Two Winters*, a chapbook, was published in 2011 by Finishing Line Press.

**STEPHEN TENDRICH** is a 32-year-old hard of hearing former disc jockey from Miami, Florida. He attended mainstream schools and received a B.A. in Communications from Flagler College and a Master's degree in Teaching American Sign Language as a Foreign Language from Teacher's College, Columbia University. Tendrich currently teaches ASL at Montclair State University and provides ASL tutoring; he has recently become an actor. He plans to educate students on ASL worldwide, especially in Africa, and provide ASL baking classes in his future bakery. [kookiemonsterbites.com]

**MICHAEL UNIACKE** writes extensively on themes relating to disability, deafness and hearing loss. More recent work includes comedy writing and historical fiction around deafness. His work has appeared in numerous publications, in print and online, and he has written and presented comedy material to camera. In 2014 he will launch *Deafness Down*, the first of a two-part memoir, on his web site. He lives in Castlemaine, an old gold-mining town in Victoria, Australia, and blogs about deafness and hearing loss. [theunguardedquarter.com]

**CLAYTON VALLI** *(1951–2003)* was a prominent deaf linguist and ASL poet whose work helped further to legitimize American Sign Language and introduce people to the richness of American Sign Language literature. As a poet, Valli created original works in ASL that he performed to appreciative audiences around the country. His poems make sophisticated use of handshape, movement, use of space, repetition, and facial expression. Valli often chose nature imagery to convey subtle insights into the Deaf experience.

**MICHELE WESTFALL** is a Deaf freelance writer currently living in Austin, Texas, with her two young Deaf sons and two gerbils. Her life pre-children included working several years as Youth Programs Coordinator at the National Association of the Deaf, writing for *Deaf Life* magazine for several years, getting a bachelor's degree in English from State University of New York at Albany and graduating from Model Secondary School for the Deaf.

**DONNA WILLIAMS** is a British Sign Language poet based in Bristol. She recently graduated from the University of Cardiff with an M.A. in Ethics and Social Philosophy. Her short plays have been performed by Deafinitely Theatre, and she keeps a blog, which is occasionally featured on Limping Chicken. Donna also enjoys writing English poetry; this is the second time she has been published in this form. [deaffirefly.wordpress.com]

**MORGAN GRAYCE WILLOW**'s poetry collections include the recently released *Dodge & Scramble*, as well as *Between, Silk,* and *The Maps are Words*. An award-winner in prose as well as poetry, Morgan's essay "Signs of the Time" received honorable mention in the Judith Kitchen Prize in *Water~Stone Review*. "Double Language" first appeared in *Third Coast*. Both of these essays, which were inspired by her experience as a sign language interpreter, are included in her manuscript entitled *A Matter of Translation*. [morgangraycewillow.com]

**PAMELA WRIGHT** has worked as an English teacher, ASL teacher, actor, and translator. She received B.A. degrees in Theater Arts and English Literature from Gallaudet University and a M.S. in Deaf Education from University of Minnesota. She currently enjoys being a student in Linguistics at the University of Colorado and working on many side projects that keep her plate full. Pamela has been featured in *The Deaf Way II Anthology, Deaf American Poetry, Deaf American Prose*, and *Introduction to American Deaf Culture*.

# ABOUT THE PUBLISHER

Handtype Press is a company that showcases the finest literature created by signers, Deaf and hearing alike, or about the Deaf or signing experience the world over. Our titles include John Lee Clark's *Suddenly Slow*, Kristen Ringman's Lambda Literary Award finalist *Makara: A Novel*, and Raymond Luczak's anthology *Eyes of Desire 2: A Deaf GLBT Reader*. [handtype.com]

CPSIA information can be obtained at www.ICGtesting.com
Printed in the USA
BVOW02s0652230915

419295BV00012B/133/P